INFORMED TRANSITIONS

INFORMED TRANSITIONS

Libraries Supporting the High School to College Transition

Kenneth J. Burhanna, Editor

LIBRARIES UNLIMITED

AN IMPRINT OF ABC-CLIO, LLC
Santa Barbara, California • Denver, Colorado • Oxford, England

Library of Congress Cataloging-in-Publication Data

Informed transitions : libraries supporting the high school to college transition / Kenneth J. Burhanna, Editor.
  pages cm.
  Includes bibliographical references and index.
  ISBN 978–1–61069–128–4 (hard copy) — ISBN 978–1–61069–129–1 (ebook)
1. Library orientation for college students—United States. 2. Information literacy—Study and teaching (Higher)—United States. 3. Academic libraries—United States—Case studies. 4. Academic achievement—United States—Case studies. 5. College freshmen—United States. 6. High school libraries—Vocational guidance—United States. 7. Library outreach programs—United States. 8. Libraries and students—United States. 9. Libraries and teachers—United States. I. Burhanna, Kenneth J., editor of compilation.
  Z711.25.C65I54   2013
  025.5′677—dc23   2012040519

ISBN: 978–1–61069–128–4
EISBN: 978–1–61069–129–1

17 16 15 14 13   1 2 3 4 5

This book is also available on the World Wide Web as an eBook.
Visit www.abc-clio.com for details.

Libraries Unlimited
An Imprint of ABC-CLIO, LLC

ABC-CLIO, LLC
130 Cremona Drive, P.O. Box 1911
Santa Barbara, California 93116-1911

This book is printed on acid-free paper ∞

Manufactured in the United States of America

Contents

Acknowledgments

This book represents a collaboration of countless librarians, educators, and researchers, which is fitting in that this book is a collaboration about collaborations. I would like to acknowledge all of these individuals who have directly or indirectly contributed to this work. Without their dedication to the role of information literacy in student success, this book would not have been possible. I send special thanks to my contributing authors. I feel privileged to have worked with such esteemed colleagues.

I would also like to thank a few key individuals who have supported this work over the past few years. I am grateful to Barbara Schloman, former Associate Dean at Kent State University Libraries, not only for her unfaltering commitment to student transitions, but also for her priceless mentorship. I am also grateful to Terri Fredericka, Executive Director of INFOhio, for her relentless drive to collaborate across the educational continuum. I also want to thank several colleagues, former and current, who have supported my work on this book, either through their contributions or their support and patience. Thanks go to Mark Weber, Carolyn Radcliff, Mary Lee Jensen, Tammy J. Eschedor Voelker, Julie A. Gedeon, Jamie Seeholzer Salem, Vanessa Earp, and Edith Scarletto.

Finally, I would like to express thanks to my family. I am grateful for their love and support and patience.

Introduction

Kenneth J. Burhanna

This book arrives at a seemingly paradoxical moment in time for librarians in North America. On one hand, we find auspicious the impressive record of collaboration, engagement, and outreach demonstrated by librarians working to transition students successfully across the educational continuum. On the other hand, budgetary deficits, librarian job cuts (especially within K-12), and unrelenting criticism of our educational system present a more ominous outlook. Whatever the future may hold for librarians and their fellow educators, we surely can agree that now, more than ever, is a time for educators to work together in common ways for a common cause: the success of our students. The good news for librarians is that working together is what they do best (or at least among the best things that they do), and they are well positioned to potentially play leading roles in helping to create seamless educational systems within their local states and provinces.

With this in mind, it would seem well-timed to present the first title devoted exclusively to libraries' role in supporting high school to college transitions. Named after the high school outreach program at Kent State University Libraries, *Informed Transitions* has two major objectives. First, this title will provide a comprehensive overview of the role of libraries and information literacy education in preparing high school students for college success. Second, it will share model collaborations and programs, best practices, and important, low-cost resources focused on the high school to college transition. Focusing on the work of librarians in the United States and Canada, it will cover collaborations and programming within and across multiple educational contexts, including high schools, community colleges, and universities. It will also discuss multiple approaches to this work, including on-the-ground programs and virtual, technology-based approaches. As such, this book may also appeal to those who work and collaborate with or supervise librarians. Readers are encouraged to share this work with teachers, professors, program coordinators, and appropriate administrators.

This title is necessarily limited in a number of ways. While students encounter many transition points throughout their educational careers and lives, this title, as already indicated, will focus on transitions from secondary to postsecondary educational systems. This then is not a book about library programming for first-year college students. It certainly can inform such efforts, and first-year students are certainly discussed throughout this work, but largely within the context of how to prepare them before they reach their first year. This work also does not specifically address career readiness. While it is an educational outcome important to all librarians, it does not fit within the scope of this work. Certainly all types of librarians and libraries play an important role in student transitions, but this book will focus mainly on the work of school and academic librarians within the educational system.

Also, a brief note on terminology. The terms "school librarian," "school library media specialist," and "teacher-librarian" are used interchangeably throughout this work. The term "academic librarian" is used to refer to librarians working within higher education, but sometimes they may be called college librarians. Also, the reader may encounter multiple terms referring to the educational continuum, such as K-16, P-16, and K-20. They have not been normalized, as they are characteristic of the educational contexts described throughout this book.

ORGANIZATION

Authored by a mix of librarians and educators from K-12 and higher education, *Informed Transitions* is comprised of 22 chapters organized into three sections.

Section I: Background, Expectations, and Skills

The first section provides a foundation for the book. It explores the history and context of the high school to college transition movement. Oakleaf and Owen discuss ways high school and college librarians can create evidence-based partnerships. Sigalet, Barton, and Savage study the expectations of college professors for incoming student skills. Transitions issues of students with disabilities are also covered.

Section II: Conversations and Collaborations

The second section highlights several collaborative efforts, many of which began with conversations. Several state- and citywide collaborations are discussed, including those in Ohio, Louisiana, New York City, Kansas City, and Harrisburg, Pennsylvania. Also, the issue of grant funding is discussed by Huisman and Orr as they share their experiences in trying to find support for their collaborative efforts.

Section III: Programs and Resources

This final section reports on several programs and resources focused on libraries' role in supporting high school to college transitions. Many of these began like the collaborations discussed in section II but have matured to the point where they can serve as models to others, or as direct resources, like the K-12 information literacy assessment tool TRAILS. Zoellner surveys and discusses the many low-cost resources available to librarians and educators planning transition programming. Smalley and Suchy describe an innovative teacher training program in the Minneapolis–St. Paul metropolitan area. Walk and colleagues explore transition efforts underway at early college schools in New York City. Pritchard and colleagues highlight the work of librarians and educators at the University of Guelph in Ontario to develop a web-based toolbox of resources for high school science teachers and students. Other chapters focus on pre-service teacher education, postsecondary enrollment students, high school class visits to colleges, and online information literacy tutorials designed for high school students. The final chapter presents a selective, annotated bibliography of the most important publications related to libraries' role in the high school to college transition.

Section I: Background, Expectations, and Skills

1

The Transition Movement: From Blueprint to Construction Zone

Kenneth J. Burhanna

If you are reading this book, you may be part of a movement. While you might not have been aware of a movement in any formal sense, for several years now librarians across the educational continuum have been organizing themselves and collaborating with each other and other educators for one of the most timely and important causes of our day—helping our students succeed. The movement we speak of is the library profession's role in supporting the high school to college transition. For our purposes, let us call it the transition movement. While all libraries surely contribute to the transition movement, including public and special, this work focuses on libraries working within the educational system. We will talk mainly of school and academic libraries, and more specifically of their collaborative efforts that have driven and distinguished this work. This chapter will seek to define this movement—its origins, context, chief characteristics, and most common methods and activities. It will also turn a critical eye to the transition movement, questioning its success and looking to its future.

But is this really a movement? Have libraries not always strived to prepare students for college success? Indeed, academic libraries have a long history of reaching out to high school students (Cosgrove 2001), and certainly preparing students for college has been given significant attention by school librarians and they have sought out experiences with academic libraries (Ameika 2008). Beginning in the early 1960s and progressing through the 1970s and 1980s, the library literature shows a persistent yet sporadic consideration of the topic (Craver 1987). This trend continued until the late 1990s, when right around the turn of the century, the discussion suddenly changed, it became more serious, more educators showed interest, more librarians took action, and since then, the topic has remained an important interest of librarians across the educational continuum. But what happened toward the end of the twentieth century? Had years of consideration, no matter how sporadic, finally given birth to our aforementioned movement?

Not really. What happened was that the debate about the need to increase educational attainment, to improve student preparation for college, needs that had been of pressing public and political concern at least since the publication of the 1983 report *A Nation at Risk* (National Commission on Excellence in Education), reached a crescendo, and librarians found themselves buoyed and brought forward under the surge of two different but related educational movements: information literacy and P-16.

INFORMATION LITERACY

It is no surprise that information literacy is a large (maybe even the central) influence on the transition movement from the library's point of view, as it is nearly synonymous with the educational role of librarianship. Information literacy is a complex set of abilities requiring individuals to "recognize when information is needed and have the ability to locate, evaluate, and use effectively the needed information" (ALA 1989, 1). Two main forces can be identified behind the rise of information literacy. The first is the hand-in-hand explosion of information and technology witnessed throughout the later part of the 20th century (and to this day). Technologies, increasingly powerful and inexpensive, have made information increasingly easy to create and disseminate, thereby making the ability to navigate and effectively use information and technology an essential requirement of our times. Second, the general educational reform movements in the United States and worldwide, which we shall discuss in more detail later, have placed information literacy among the important attributes of a successful learner, and as such, information literacy has been articulated in several sets of standards. For these reasons, information literacy has come to be recognized as a crucial component of critical thinking, independent learning, democracy, and lifelong learning (AASL 2007; ACRL 2000; Partnership for 21st Century Skills 2011; Lupton 2008). And for many of the same reasons, the story of information literacy is also, for librarians in K-12 and higher education, the story of their professional transformation from passive stewards of resources to active participants in the learning process (Eisenberg, Lowe and Spitzer 2004).

The American Association of School Librarians' (AASL's) publication of *Information Power: Guidelines for School Library Media Programs* made it clear that school librarians and their programs were essential to ensuring "that students and staff are effective users of ideas and information" (1988, 1). *Information Power*, which was developed cooperatively with the Association for Educational Communications and Technology (AECT), called for school librarians to provide instruction and work with educators to design learning strategies (1). When the final report of the American Library Association (ALA) Presidential Committee on Information Literacy came out in 1989, it noted that schools and colleges would need to "appreciate and integrate the concept of information literacy into their learning programs" (1). Almost without hesitation, librarians, especially those in K-12 education, began to behave like their colleagues in other subject areas and set about developing standards and learning outcomes for information literacy. By 1998, the AASL, again working in collaboration with the AECT, published *Information Literacy Standards for Student Learning* as a section of the revised *Information Power: Building Partnerships for Learning*. The Association of College & Research Libraries (ACRL) followed with its *Information Literacy Competency Standards for Higher Education* in 2000. ACRL also established the Institute for Information Literacy, which has helped support librarians and their role in teaching information literacy in higher education, sponsoring professional development such as immersion programs and consulting with other ACRL sections on the development of subject-specific information literacy standards (e.g., *Information Literacy Standards for Anthropology and Sociology Students*) (ACRL 2008).

This brings us back to that time just before the beginning of the 21st century. Librarians, armed with their information literacy mission, had begun to address educational reform issues with a broader sense of purpose. In 1998, the joint AASL/ACRL Task Force on the Educational Role of Libraries was charged with "recommending ways of initiating and fostering, through the organizational structures of ACRL and AASL, ways and means of affecting closer collaboration between librarians in K-12 and post-secondary education to the benefit of the constituencies they serve" (2000, paragraph 1). The task force published its report called the *ACRL/AASL Blueprint for Collaboration* in 2000, and with it the transition movement within libraries began in earnest. But before taking a closer look at the *Blueprint* as well as the pieces and parts of the transition movement, let us examine how this all fit into the context of educational reform leading up to the 21st century.

P-16 REFORM

Since the publication of *A Nation at Risk* in 1983, educational reform has been a constant focus of debate, first centered around K-12, then higher education, and finally the need to align the two into a seamless system (Davis and Hoffman 2008). Clearly the reality in our educational system indicates a problem. Only about 21 percent of students in the United States transition successfully through high school straight to college and graduate within six years for a baccalaureate degree or within three years for an associate degree (NCHEMS 2012). One in four students attending a four-year institution will take a remedial course (Walsh 2009), and graduation rates are significantly lower for students who require remediation (DOE 2004). Low graduation and high remediation rates would seem to indicate a lack of alignment between K-12 and higher education (Walsh 2009), and the research has concurred with this conclusion. Kirst and Venezia (2001) found that high school graduation and college admissions standards do not match, that curriculums are not aligned, that school and college budgets are separate, and that student data is not tracked across educational systems. Further studies of alignment found a system in which students aspire to college but receive confusing signals about how to prepare (Kirst and Venezia 2004).

The P-16 reform movement has responded to these systematic deficiencies. P-16, meaning preschool through the conference of a baccalaureate degree (sometimes called K-16, K-20 or even P-20) began in the mid-1990s and developed into the movement we have today, focused on creating a seamless educational network. Currently, at least 41 states have some form of P-16 initiative (Davis and Hoffman 2008). The America Creating Opportunities to Meaningfully Promote Excellence in Technology, Education, and Science (COMPETES) Act (signed in 2007 and reauthorized in 2011) marked a major step forward for the P-16 movement because it authorized federal grants to states to better align secondary and higher education. The act also formally recognized the P-16 concept and provided support for the establishment of statewide P-16 education data systems (America COMPETES 2011).

Librarians, particularly those focused on information literacy education, were acutely aware of the issues that inspired the P-16 movement (Cosgrove 2001) and as

early as 1993 began calling for "good articulation programs between educational institutions" (Jesudason 1993, 30). Librarians, through observation and research, knew (and
continue to know) that many of their students were poorly prepared for college-level
research and had unrealistic expectations of their abilities (Fitzgerald 2004; Katz
2007; Salisbury and Karasmanis 2011). In the "Background" section of the *Blueprint
for Collaboration*, it is no surprise that the report's authors note that their joint work
is "timely and appropriate" (2000). While sharing a commitment to lifelong learning
and ensuring student success across educational levels, the task force's report under-
scores the value of information literacy in the 21st century and indeed how vital these
skills are within the context of current educational reforms. As if ready-made for the
P-16 movement, the task force's report represents not only a blueprint for collaboration,
but also a blueprint for the transition movement within libraries.

THE BLUEPRINT: A MOVEMENT DEFINED

As Cosgrove noted, with the joint AASL and ACRL initiative behind the *Blueprint
for Collaboration*: "Thus, three issues that have garnered much attention over the past
three decades dovetail in the mission of the Task Force: a call for cooperative initiatives
between librarians at K-12 and college levels, a belief in the importance of information
literacy skills, and the role that librarians have in helping students develop those skills"
(2001, 18). Librarians and information literacy found opportunity in the cooperative
imperative of the P-16 reform movement, and the *Blueprint* began to give meaning
and structure to the transition movement. The report presents a comprehensive list of
recommendations clustered into four areas: collaboration, joint association activities,
continuing education, and outreach. One can find all the major elements of the transition movement in the joint task force's report and recommendations: shared responsibility for information literacy and its standards, the call to collaborate across the
educational continuum, and the ultimate goal of preparing students for lifelong learning
and college success.

With the *Blueprint* in mind, one can offer a definition of the transition movement:
libraries and librarians collaborating across the educational continuum to prepare students for academic success, lifelong learning, and educational attainment by imparting
information literacy and 21st-century skills and abilities. These efforts are character-
ized by shared responsibility, a standards-based approach to learning, and a variety of
outreach models. And now with this definition in mind, let us look more closely at
the major elements of the transition movement.

STUDENT SUCCESS, INFORMATION LITERACY,
AND SHARED RESPONSIBILITY

As we have already seen, student success and information literacy are very much
tied together for librarians. The joint task force notes that the AASL and ACRL "share
goals for fostering lifelong learning and ensuring that students at all educational levels
are prepared to meet the challenges of the 21st century" (paragraph 2). And it more
boldly asserts that "Information literacy skills are necessary for student success" (paragraph 2). What is new in their report is the formal recognition "that there is a shared
responsibility among academic and school librarians for information literacy" (paragraph 3). While prior to this recognition many librarians likely believed that they

shared in this responsibility, it had never been articulated formally from such a position of influence. This shared responsibility is what has driven and continues to drive the transition movement (Carr and Rockman 2003). The library profession, perhaps better than many others working within the educational continuum, has understood that we are all in this together and that *what we are in* is the act of helping students to succeed.

INFORMATION LITERACY STANDARDS

The *Blueprint* acknowledges information literacy standards in several ways. First, the joint task force recognized that previous collaborative efforts surrounding the development of information literacy standards taught librarians "the benefits of collaborating" (paragraph 3). Second and more importantly, the report recommends the promotion, advocacy, and dissemination of the AASL and the ACRL standards and calls for "a seamless continuation" of these standards across the K-16 educational continuum (recommendation I.C). Last, the report advocates for several joint and collaborative initiatives focused on promoting information literacy standards, such as recommendation I.D, which calls for dissemination of the AASL and ACRL standards to foster dialogue.

When we examine the transition movement since the *Blueprint's* publication in 2000, we find a standards environment where K-12 is progressing while higher education plods slowly behind. Several authors have pointed out the similarities between the AASL's and the ACRL's information literacy standards (Cahoy 2002; Carr and Rockman 2003; Burhanna and Jensen 2006), but when the AASL replaced their old standards in 2007 with their new *Standards for the 21st Century Learner*, they created separation from the ACRL standards. The *Standards for the 21st Century Learner* actually "travel beyond information literacy to address multiple literacies" (Johns 2008), including digital, visual, textual, and technological. They present a holistic view of learning that spans from the academic to the personal. They stress critical thinking, the social context of learning, personal responsibility, and the role of technology, and as Marcoux notes, in many ways they summarize much of the research and thinking surrounding information literacy (2008).

The development of the *Standards for the 21st Century Learner* can be seen as a response to the standards movement within K-12 (Carr 2012) and exemplary of librarians taking a leadership role in educational reform. Also indicative of the standards movement and underscoring the perceived importance of information literacy–based abilities, two other national standards for K-12 learning debuted shortly after the new AASL standards, and they reflected a similar focus on student-centered learning, technology, and the need for a broad range of skills and abilities. The International Society for Technology in Education (ISTE) released its National Educational Technology Standards for Students (NETS-S), and the Partnership for 21st Century Skills (P21) published its 21st Century Student Outcomes (21CSO). As in the case of the AASL's *Standards for the 21st Century Learner*, both the NETS-S and the 21CSO include information literacy not as the central focus of learning, but as a critical ability among a broader set of skills and literacies required to perform important behaviors.

The Common Core Standards, a state-led effort coordinated by the National Governors Association Center for Best Practices (NGA Center) and the Council of Chief State School Officers (CCSSO) is the most recent development in K-12 and represents a major step forward, as it provides standards on a national level that can be commonly applied by all states (currently 45 states and the District of Columbia have signed on to the Common Core). The Common Core Standards purport to "define the knowledge and skills students should have within their K-12 education careers so that they will graduate high school able to succeed in entry-level, credit-bearing academic college courses and in workforce training programs" (Common Core State Standards Initiative 2012, About the Standards). What is major forward movement for P-16 can be a major opportunity for librarians and their role in transitioning students. Quite appropriately, the AASL has created the *Crosswalk of the Common Core Standards and the Standards for the 21st Century Learner* to help school librarians and educators understand how the two sets of standards align (2011).

While information literacy within the K-12 environment has been evolving, the movement within higher education has been less progressive. The ACRL standards have not been updated since their publication in 2000. University, college, and community college librarians have been active and diligent in advocating and teaching information literacy on their campuses. They are often leaders in outcomes-based assessment and have embraced other national standards such as the Association of American Colleges & Universities (AAC&U) LEAP Campaign's Essential Learning Outcomes (of which information literacy is an essential intellectual and practical skill), but they have not formally articulated at the national level a new vision for how information literacy fits into current learning models. Yet this may soon change, as the ACRL's Information Literacy Competency Standards Review Task Force recommended in June 2012 that the current standards should be " ... extensively revised in the near future" (ACRL 2012, 1). The task force points to a broader set of revised information literacy standards that are student-centered, recognize complementary literacies (e.g., visual literacy, digital literacy) and are simple and easy to use. Most importantly, the task force recommends that revised standards must provide continuity with the *Standards for the 21st Century Learner.*

Some subject-specific information literacy standards have been developed within ACRL, for example, the aforementioned *Information Literacy Standards for Anthropology and Sociology Students.* Most noteworthy of these examples is the *Information Literacy Standards for Teacher Education* authored by the Education and Behavioral Sciences Section of ACRL. These standards, in recognizing the role teachers play in K-12 information literacy education, provide both for the building of information literacy competencies and awareness in preservice teacher candidates, as these individuals must not only be proficient information users, but value and build these skills into the educational experiences of their future students (ACRL 2011).

Information literacy has also emerged as a concern of higher education accreditation. A 2007 study found that all six regional accreditation organizations for higher education mention information literacy within their standards (Saunders, 306), an increase of three from a 2002 study (Gratch-Lindauer). Yet as stated earlier, despite exciting changes from ACRL in the offing, the advances of information literacy within higher education have been incremental and not progressive, as they have been within K-12.

MODELS OF COLLABORATION AND OUTREACH

The *Blueprint for Collaboration* says that collaboration was an imperative if educators are to fulfill their mission of "helping students acquire information literacy skills effectively" (Background). Indeed, collaboration is the single most prominent theme of the report and of the transition movement in general. While "Collaboration" is one of four named sections of recommendations found in the report, suggestions for collaboration are found throughout the other three sections. In the report's "Appendix I: Models of Collaboration," several known examples of collaborative high school to college information literacy partnerships are identified. These examples anticipate many of the models of collaboration and outreach found in the literature since the *Blueprint*'s publication. These include collaborative dialogues, professional development, preservice teacher education, instructional experiences, and the development of transition tools and resources. Through a review of the recent literature, we can examine updated examples of each model and gain some sense of the activity seen within the transition movement.

Collaborative Dialogues

Dialogues have been at the heart of the transition movement, for as Burrell and Neyer note, an informative dialogue can start "with a casual conversation between two people who just met" (2010, 8). And it can be argued that all of the collaboration, instructional outreach, professional development, and resources surrounding libraries' role in the high school to college transition have been made possible by engaged and sustained conversations. After all, the *Blueprint for Collaboration* came into being through intensive dialogue. The task force, comprised of academic and school librarians, engaged in an in-depth exploration of the existing literature and activity related to collaboration between K-12 and higher education. It opened its understanding to a dialogue through an open forum at the ALA 2000 Midwinter Meeting and in its final report, it incorporated feedback gained through the forum.

The literature itself has served as a primary platform for dialogues surrounding the transition movement, including Carr and Rockman's 2003 article "Information-Literacy Collaboration: A Shared Responsibility." Their article served as a clarion call to librarians in the wake of the *Blueprint*'s publication. It acknowledged a shared responsibility for information literacy collaboration and outlined common goals for school and academic librarians. It also shared several ongoing model collaborations. Professional publications began to focus on transition issues. The AASL devoted almost an entire issue of the journal *Knowledge Quest* to information literacy and collaboration across the educational continuum (Abilock 2004). The library literature had begun to create a sustained dialogue on the transition movement.

But when we think of collaborative dialogues, we traditionally think of people getting together and talking, and indeed, many examples of collaborative meetings and conferences can be found in the literature, and they often have been the genesis for instructional programs and resources. *Library Conversations@Belmont* serves a good recent example of academic and school librarians building a sustained conversation. Beginning in 2006, librarians at Belmont University in Nashville began to invite local school librarians for dinner conversations about "preparing high school students for academic research" and related topics (Fuson and Rushing 2009, 567). Both school and academic librarians proved eager to share, and these conversations have continued annually. Librarians in Colorado provide another model of collaborative dialogue (Schein et al. 2011). Theirs evolved into a travelling dialogue. It began when librarians from Colorado College, the University of Colorado (Colorado Springs), and 20 high schools jointly sponsored a panel discussion about how "to bridge the gap between college expectations and reality" (2011, 1). The conversation continued at the Colorado Academic Librarians Conference in the spring of 2010 and at the Colorado Association of Libraries annual conference in October 2011. Topics discussed included developing information literacy courses, professional development for teachers and librarians, the formation of an interest group, and academic library visits.

In some cases, these collaborative dialogues have taken on formal organizational structures and have begun to produce resources and programs. In Ohio, a 12-13 transition task force comprised of librarians representing INFOhio and OhioLINK (school and higher education library consortia) has been at work for almost six years now (INFOhio and OhioLINK Special Task Force 2008). Renamed the College and Career Readiness Task Force, the group continues to work to articulate the major goals they outlined in their 2008 report *Preparing 21st Century Ohio Learners for Success: the Role of Information Literacy and Libraries* (INFOhio and OhioLINK Special Task Force 2008). In Bakersfield, California, college and school librarians have been collaborating since 2002 (Dobie, Guidry, and Hartsell 2010). Over the years, these librarians, working at meetings and in small groups, have identified common information literacy skills and developed common assignments to support them. They have created a library of 30 generic library activities and shared guidelines for web evaluation (Kern High School and Bakersfield College 2012). Most recently, they developed a College Library Survival Skills Project, a professional development presentation aimed at arming school librarians with the knowledge and skills they need to advocate for research experiences within the high school curriculum (Guidry and Dobie 2010).

Professional Development

Like collaboration, professional (continuing) education is a theme that runs throughout the *Blueprint for Collaboration*, and certainly many of the collaborative dialogues mentioned earlier in this chapter represent professional development experiences for participants. Over the past decade, several librarians have contributed to the transition movement by way of formal professional development programming targeted at both librarians and high school teachers. As we shall see, most of the professional development outreach originates with colleagues in higher education, who seem to who have more autonomy and resources to sponsor such opportunities. In California, Martorana and colleagues developed a workshop series on information literacy targeted at high school teachers (2001). The Institute for Library & Information Literacy Education, a grant-funded initiative at Kent State University (Kent, Ohio), made professional development one of its main goals and has offered multiple workshops and continuing education opportunities for school librarians throughout the past decade (ILILE 2012). Nichols, Spang, and Padron write of in-service information literacy workshops for high school teachers and librarians delivered in Michigan as a collaboration with Wayne State University (Detroit, Michigan) librarians (2005). More recently, librarians at Arizona State University (ASU) used a small Library Services and Technology Act (LSTA) grant to offer Saturday workshops for local high school teachers and librarians (Ewbank et al. 2011). They collaborated with ASU Writing and Academic Success Programs to create conference-like experiences focused on college-level assignments and shared statewide information resources.

Preservice Teacher Education

The *Blueprint for Collaboration* quite rightly identified preservice teacher education as a strategic area of focus, and librarians have made significant progress in this area. Prior to the *Blueprint*, librarians were already calling for better integration of information literacy into teacher education (Carr and Zeichner 1988). The Instruction for Educators Committee of the ACRL's Educational and Behavioral Sciences Section (EBBS) established *Information Literacy Standards for Teacher Education* in 2006 and then updated them in 2011. These standards seek not only to impart strong information literacy skills in future teachers, but to also advocate for their value as an educational outcome in the learning experiences they will design and deliver to their future students. In 2003, the journal *Behavioral & Social Sciences Librarian* devoted an issue to information literacy instruction for educators, with preservice education as a focus (Stover 2003). The articles in his special issue were published simultaneously as the book *Information Literacy Instruction for Educators: Professional Knowledge for an Information Age* (Shinew and Walter 2003). One article from these publications (Witt and Dickinson 2003) describes a program at Illinois Wesleyan University focused on fostering librarian-teacher instructional collaboration built around the *Information Literacy Standards for Teacher Education*. The authors applied a mixed-method approach to this work, including pretests, self-paced tutorials, face-to-face library instruction, research consultations, and collaborative course design. At the University of New Mexico, education faculty and librarians collaborated to integrate information literacy throughout the preservice curriculum (Emmons et al. 2009). Their assessment of student learning demonstrated measureable gains in information literacy competency among teacher candidates. Bushong and Boff (2008) shared their experiences in developing a masters-level standalone information literacy course for graduate students in education. A 2010 study attempted to gauge the role of information literacy in the preservice teacher curriculum and found that while awareness of information literacy is high among education faculty, fewer than half formally include information literacy standards in their lesson plans, and only about 40 percent had a tool in place for the assessment of information literacy (Kovalik et al.).

Instructional Experiences

Because information literacy is at the heart of the librarian's transition work, student instructional experiences are at the heart of collaborative programming efforts designed by librarians. The point of collaborative discussions, professional development, and preservice teacher education reforms is to better educate librarians and teachers to prepare students for college success. In general, the literature reflects instructional outreach to three categories of precollege high school student. The first is outreach to current high school students engaged with their high school curriculum. Typically, this involves class field trips to a local college or university. Several authors have outlined the development, operation, and curriculum of high school visits (Burhanna 2007; Pearson and McNeil 2002). These visits usually include library tours, information literacy instruction, workshop time, and optional borrowing privileges for students. While demanding on staff and resources, these programs provide authentic, immersive experiences for students, though little research has attempted to measure their impacts. These collaborations have typically occurred with reference and instruction librarians at universities, but recently outreach collaborations with university special collections and archives units have begun to appear in the literature (Fernekes and Rosenberg 2008; Manual 2005). Academic librarian visits is another approach to reaching high school students. Ameika (2008) describes a program initiated at West Ashley High School in Charleston, South Carolina, that invited several college librarians and professors to present to senior English classes. Speakers addressed a number of topics, including expectations for college research, online databases, evaluating and citing sources, and academic integrity and plagiarism (408). As a result, the author observed not only increased library usage by students, but also increased research requirements by teachers.

The second category of high school students are those who are participating in pre-college programs conducted on college or university campuses. These may be students involved with federally funded programs like Upward Bound or students in programs that target underserved populations. Librarians at Ohio University delivered information literacy workshops to high school sophomores and juniors who were participating on their campus in Minority Men and Women in Engineering and Technology, programs designed to promote careers in the sciences and engineering (Huge, Houdek, and Saines 2002). Adeyemon (2009) reported on librarians mentoring high school juniors during a four-week learning and work experience, which culminated in groups of students producing videos on local historical events. Another example comes from Wake Forest University (Collins 2009). The author explores the opportunities for collaboration available through summer programs at universities and details experiences of a library collaboration with a summer debate program, during which librarians provided orientation and instruction to participating high school students.

The third category of high school students is comprised of those currently enrolled in dual credit programs, or postsecondary enrollment option (PSEO) students. PSEO students take college classes while still in high school and receive both college and high school credit. This educational strategy, while not new, has seen a rise in popularity in response to the pressures of educational reform and the need to shorten the pathway to a college degree (Allen 2010). PSEO programming may also represent a major opportunity for librarians, as little has been reported in the literature. Bruch and Frank (2011) reported on establishing the Senior-to-Sophomore Information Literacy Program at Colorado State University–Pueblo. A LSTA grant-funded collaboration between librarians, program directors, and writing instructors, the program focused on training instructors in the dual credit program to integrate information literacy with their courses. These instructors then gave information literacy assignments to their students and connected them to university library databases and resources.

Transition Tools and Resources

Tools and resources supporting the transition movement are included in this chapter under Models of Collaboration and Outreach because they can be instrumental in aiding and furthering collaborative efforts; additionally, many of them were developed collaboratively. Much of this development has grown from the *Blueprint for Collaboration*. The AASL/ACRL Interdivisional Committee on Information Literacy was formed in 2002 to continue the work of the 1998 AASL/ACRL Task Force on the Educational Role of Libraries. The committee focuses on preparing students in K-20 to become information literate through information sharing and professional development. The Library Instruction Round Table (LIRT) of ALA has a Transitions to College Committee that also seeks to extend this work. The LIRT committee builds and supports partnerships between school, public, and academic librarians to assist students in their transition to the academic library environment. At recent ALA annual conferences, they regularly organized round table discussions focused on high school to college transitions. Since 2005, the INFOLIT discussion list, an AASL/ACRL collaboration devoted to discussion between K-12 and higher education librarians, has served as a critical resource in building partnerships and information sharing for librarians. Many other association-based tools, such as information literacy standards, have already been mentioned earlier in this chapter. Conference presentations as well as panel and other round table discussions about supporting the high school to college transition have appeared regularly on program schedules at regional and national conferences over the past decade. Likewise, this discussion has referred to the professional literature numerous times throughout this chapter. The literature surrounding the transition movement is indeed an excellent resource. Another example is the frequently cited article "A Transition Checklist for High School Seniors" by Patricia Owen (2010), whose title speaks for itself. See a selected, annotated bibliography by Tammy J. Eschedor Voelker in Chapter 22 of this book for a more detailed discussion of the literature.

Beyond the literature and professional associations, some important web-based resources have been developed. Most notably, two web-based projects supported by the Institute for Library & Information Literacy Education (ILILE) and Kent State University Libraries have become popular tools for librarians supporting student transitions. *TRAILS: Tool for Real-Time Assessment of Information Literacy Skills* is a freely available information literacy assessment tool, offering assessments targeted not only at high school grades 9 and 12, but also at the earlier grades of 3 and 6. With over 13,000 registered users in 50 states and over 30 countries, TRAILS is not only highly used, but highly relevant. Its assessment items are based on the AASL's *Standards for the 21st Century Learner* and *Ohio Academic Content Standards*. A second project developed at Kent State University is called *Transitioning to College: Helping You to Succeed*. This web site, inspired by the transition needs of high schools challenged by budgetary constraints and their lack of proximity to colleges, presents a wide array of resources for students, school librarians, and teachers working on college preparation. The site is headlined by a series of videos about first-year college students interacting with the academic library. Additional resources include worksheets, suggested activities, sample college syllabi, and a list of web links to other helpful sites. For a more complete discussion of resources for the high school to college transition see Kate Zoellner's "Supporting the High School to College Transition on a Shoestring," which is Chapter 11 in this book.

IMPACT AND CHALLENGES

Has the transition movement made an impact? Has the collaborative work of librarians across the educational continuum benefited students? The answer is a not very straightforward, "Yes, but we don't know for sure." The librarians' answer would be, "Yes." They have a rich, informal understanding of the success and impact of their efforts. As we have seen and will see throughout this book, the professional life of librarians reveals many successful, active collaborative projects and programs that contribute to the transition movement. Funding agencies like the Institute of Museum and

Library Services continue to support this work. Information literacy is a valued 21st-century skill. We know that instructors at high schools and universities highly value information literacy (ACT 2009) and that many students are not prepared for college research (Achieve 2005). The value is evident, the need has been identified, and librarians and educators are committed to it. But are these efforts to ease transitions and prepare students for success working?

Educational administrators and others outside the educational system would probably go with the "We don't know for sure" answer. Despite the work of the transition movement, we lack clear, compelling evidence that these efforts make a difference. The literature is absent of broad, systematic studies of how libraries and librarians have impacted transition efforts. Instead, we find small-scale studies that at most provide only a narrow snapshot of this work. In a 1991 study, Goodin found that information literacy instruction had a significant impact on the performance and attitudes of college-bound high school students, but a clear case for the transferability of these skills and attitudes was not established. Smalley (2004) found that college students who came from high schools with school librarians demonstrated higher information literacy abilities than students entering from high schools lacking school librarians. In efforts to better understand how students are being prepared for college, several authors at universities have studied school librarian perceptions of their own information literacy curriculum (Islam and Murno 2006; Zoellner and Potter 2010; Nix, Hageman, and Kragness 2011), but these studies are developmental in that they help librarians learn about the instructional needs of their students.

Lacking direct evidence, we can look indirectly. Yet libraries in general, especially academic libraries, have long struggled with validating their impact on the success and learning of students at their own institutions (Oakleaf 2010). School libraries are a bit of an exception. "School library literature is dominated by efforts to demonstrate the impact of school libraries and librarians on student learning" (Oakleaf 2010, 58). Among these efforts are several large-scale studies, some correlating school libraries and success on statewide standardized tests (Oakleaf 2010; Hamilton-Pennell et al. 2000). While school librarians and researchers have done a good job of showing their impact on student success, the literature lacks longitudinal data connecting this work to the transition experience.

Clearly, broad-based, systematic studies of this work are needed, but perhaps we are asking the wrong question for now. Perhaps the better question to ask is about the extent the transition movement has accomplished what it set out to do. Has the *Blueprint for Collaboration* been articulated? Here we have a firmer answer, "We've made a good start." The joint task force that authored the *Blueprint* was charged with "Recommending ways of initiating and fostering . . . ways and means of affecting closer collaboration between librarians in K-12 and post secondary education to the benefit of the constituencies they serve" (AASL and ACRL Task Force on the Educational Role of Librarians 2000, paragraph 1), and it is hard to argue that progress has not been made. In each of the *Blueprint*'s four recommendation areas—Collaboration, Joint Association Activities, Continuing Education for Librarians, and Outreach—much has been accomplished. Many of these efforts were discussed earlier in this chapter. Yet a few important recommendations remain unfulfilled, like "develop an award for collaboration on information literacy projects among libraries, school districts and Colleges of Education" (2000, IV.A)

So a good start is just that, a good start. Certainly there is more work to be done, but to understand how next steps could be taken, we must understand the challenges that librarians face, and as we shall see, the challenges for the transition movement are in many ways the same challenges that our educational systems face. Carr (2012) identifies these challenges, or barriers to collaboration, as differences between K-12 and academic librarians:

- **Professional identity:** Teaching is a core focus of the AASL. Instruction is one section out of 17 within the ACRL.
- **Role and status:** School librarians usually belong to the same job category as the teachers they work with and often work in the same building. In higher education, librarians may or may not have similar status as classroom faculty, and academic librarians and classroom faculty usually do not have offices in the same building.
- **Organizational structure:** Schools usually are part of a system within a district. Colleges and universities come in all shapes and sizes, and differ in funding, mission, and the types of students they serve.
- **Authority structure:** K-12 is rigid and authoritarian in structure. The curriculum is often dictated by state and local standards. Parents can be informed of issues directly. Higher education is much more loosely structured. Students can decide whether to go to class. Curriculums are largely created by the faculty of the institution, with minimal input from outside agencies. Communication to parents is limited by the Federal Educational Rights and Privacy Act (FERPA).
- **Role of the student:** Students in K-12 are part of their class or community. They have limited choices and learn within a highly structured and guided environment. Students in college have autonomy to make choices about what institutions to attend, courses to register for, and classes to attend. (Carr 2012, 167–168). Students in higher education view themselves more as consumers (Maringe 2006).

FUTURE STEPS: WE THOUGHT WE WERE BUILDING A BRIDGE, BUT IT IS REALLY A HIGHWAY

Where do librarians go from here? How can obstacles be overcome and transition efforts moved forward? What can be done to ensure that the strong collaborations already established are sustained and strengthened? This last question is especially important at a time when we find school and academic libraries and librarians experiencing staffing cutbacks and severe budget challenges in many states and in Canada (Stewart 2012; AASL 2011; Maimann 2011). The good news is that in many ways, librarians are uniquely prepared to participate in and facilitate broader discussions on aligning curricula and creating streamlined student experiences. If librarian reflect on and recognize how they can fit into larger reform efforts, they may truly be able help align K-12 and higher education and foster student success, while at the same time creating value for their educational work. It is clear that what was once thought of as a bridge needed to traverse the skill gap between high school and college is really a highway that connects student educational experiences not only throughout their formal schooling, but throughout their lives. What follows are a number of potential steps that librarians can consider to help drive the transition movement forward.

Plug into Educational Reform Efforts

Many states are active in the federally funded Race to the Top grant program. For example, in Ohio, the Ohio Department of Education (ODE) is collaborating with the Ohio Board of Regents on the High School–Higher Education Alignment Initiative (ODE 2012). This program seeks to lower postsecondary remediation by aligning the curriculum for English and mathematics. It also aims to align teacher preparation programs to new Ohio content standards and to create data structures for information sharing between K-12 and higher education. Librarians in secondary schools and colleges need to be aware of these reform initiatives in their states and consider how they might participate. They need to learn about the agendas of the P-16 councils in your state or region. School librarians are likely already well aware of the Common Core Standards, but academic librarians should likewise learn how they fit into their transition work and work to support their own students. These standards are aligned with college and work expectations.

Renew and Streamline Information Literacy Standards

It is probably time for the ACRL to revise its conception of information literacy and renew its standards. As the AASL's *Standards for the 21st Century Learner* state, "Information literacy has progressed from the simple definition of using reference resources to find information. Multiple literacies, including digital, visual, textual, and technological, have now joined information literacy as crucial skills for this century" (2007, 3). The AASL standards are probably a good starting place for consideration. This would also provide an opportunity to better align information literacy standards in higher education with other outcomes-based learning reforms in higher education, like the AAC&U's *Essential Learning Outcomes* (2007).

And librarians, school and academic, should consider how to formally recognize and articulate transition outcomes between their standards. Here we refer to the holy grail of the seamless information literacy curriculum. For those interested you might also examine the alignment and gaps between current standards. See Oakleaf's (2011) work in which she maps the *ACRL Information Literacy Standards for Higher Education* to 10 other major standards, including the AASL's and the Common Core. Interestingly, until recently, no standards formally recognized transitional outcomes. However, a *New Curriculum for Information Literacy (NCIL)*, a report by the Arcadia Project at Cambridge University, has changed that (Secker and Coonan 2011). The NCIL aligns its outcomes along 10 strands, presenting an innovative vision for articulating information literacy throughout the undergraduate curriculum. Strands 1 and 10 are rooted in transitions, identifying outcomes related to the high school to college transition and others related to workplace information literacy and lifelong learning. Although this work originates in the United Kingdom, it offers a great model for librarians in North America to consider.

Unify the Teaching Role of Librarians

As Carr suggests, "ALA should improve the coordination of information literacy efforts . . . by making information literacy an ALA level priority" (2012, 171). She goes on to suggest the creation of an information literacy division within the ALA. While the

AASL and ACRL have a great record of collaboration, a centralized organizational structure would likely ease the alignment of standards and further the goal of creating a seamless information literacy curriculum. Instead of having to constantly learn about each other's identities, librarians could begin to develop a shared identity.

Focus on Local and State-Level Partnerships

While librarians have shared information with and established transition resources for national and international audiences, it is what happens in their local communities as well as states and provinces that will make a difference. Librarians are already well engaged in partnerships focused on students transitioning in their local educational systems. They need to continue this work and give special attention to aligning this with the goals of their institutions in order to make a value connection with administrators.

Invest in Research

Just as the ACRL seeks to advance its value in the research agenda at academic libraries, librarians should coordinate across states to develop a transition research agenda. It likely would involve developing a series of model community-based research studies that could be replicated in a variety of states and school districts. The ability to share data across educational systems can be a difference maker for adding longitudinal dimensions to these studies, and librarians should investigate what data structures already exist within their states. Ultimately, librarians could draw these studies together to present a broader and more large-scale view of their transition efforts.

A MOVEMENT OR NOT A MOVEMENT?

We return to an unanswered question posed earlier: Does the work of librarians in supporting the high school to college transition really constitute a formal movement? *Merriam-Webster's Online Dictionary* defines the word "movement" in one sense to mean: "a series of organized activities working toward an objective" (2012). Based on this broad definition, it would seem that we could make the argument that this work is a movement, but even if we stop short of this admission, we certainly can agree that this conception of a movement provides a helpful scaffold for considering the transition efforts of libraries and librarians. Perhaps, as hinted at earlier, what we are really talking about is the intersection of the information literacy and the P-16 movements. Whatever the case, librarians should take a moment to reflect on and recognize the progress they have made with the *Blueprint for Collaboration* and their collaborative efforts to support student transitions. But they should not delay too long before putting their figurative hard-hats back on. Much work remains, and librarians can play a valuable role in helping to construct new collaborations focused on a common information literacy curriculum and student success.

BIBLIOGRAPHY

Abilock, Debbie, ed. "Information Literacy K-20." Special issue, *Knowledge Quest* 32, no. 4 (2004).

Achieve, Inc. *Rising to the Challenge: Are High School Graduates Prepared for College and Work?* Washington, D.C.: Author, 2005.

ACT. *The Condition of College Readiness 2009*. Iowa City: Author, 2009.

Adeyemon, Earnestine. "Integrating Digital Literacies into Outreach Services for Underserved Youth Populations." *Reference Librarian* 50, no. 1 (January 2009): 85–98.

Allen, Drew. *Dual Enrollment: A Comprehensive Literature Review and Bibliography*. New York: City University of New York, 2010.

Ameika, Martha. "Introducing College Research at the High School Level: A Jump Start on Success." *Voice of Youth Advocates* 31, no. 5 (2008): 408–409.

America COMPETES Reauthorization Act of 2010. Title 20 U.S. Code, Pt. 9871. 2011. http://www.gpo.gov/fdsys/pkg/USCODE-2011-title20/pdf/USCODE-2011-title20-chap78-subchapIV-sec9871.pdf.

American Association of Colleges & Universities (AAC&U). "Liberal Education and America's Promise: Essential Learning Outcomes." Washington, DC: AAC&U, 2007. http://www.aacu.org/leap/documents/EssentialOutcomes_Chart.pdf (accessed November 4, 2012).

American Association of School Librarians (AASL). "AASL President Releases Statement on School Library Position Cuts." Chicago: ALA, 2011. http://www.ala.org/news/pr?id=6632 (accessed May 19, 2012).

American Association of School Librarians (AASL). *Crosswalk of the Common Core Standards and the Standards for the 21st-Century Learner*. Chicago: American Library Association, 2011. http://www.ala.org/aasl/guidelinesandstandards/commoncorecrosswalk (accessed May 1, 2012).

American Association of School Librarians (AASL). *Information Power: Building Partnerships for Learning*. Chicago: American Library Association, 1998.

American Association of School Librarians (AASL). *Information Power: Guidelines for School Library Media Programs*. Chicago: American Library Association, 1988.

American Association of School Librarians (AASL). *Standards for the 21st Century Learner*. Chicago: American Library Association, 2007.

American Association of School Librarians and Association for Educational Communications and Technology National Guidelines Vision Committee. *Information Literacy Standards for Student Learning*. Chicago: American Library Association, 1996.

American Association of School Librarians (AASL) and Association of College and Research Libraries (ACRL) Task Force on the Educational Role of Librarians. *Blueprint for Collaboration*. Chicago: American Library Association, 2000. http://www.ala.org/acrl/publications/whitepapers/acrlaaslblueprint.

American Library Association (ALA). *Presidential Committee on Information Literacy: Final Report*. Chicago: Author, 1989.

Association of College & Research Libraries (ACRL). *Information Literacy Standards for Anthropology and Sociology Students*. Chicago: American Library Association, 2008.

Association of College & Research Libraries (ACRL). *Information Literacy Competency Standards for Higher Education*. Chicago: American Library Association, 2000.

Association of College & Research Libraries (ACRL). *Information Literacy Standards for Teacher Education*. Chicago: American Library Association, 2011.

Association of College & Research Libraries (ACRL). *Information Literacy Competency Standards Review Task Force Recommendations*. Chicago: American Library Association, 2012. http://www.ala.org/acrl/sites/ala.org.acrl/files/content/standards/ils_recomm.pdf (accessed November 4, 2012).

Bruch, Courtney, and Katherine Frank. "Sustainable Collaborations: Libraries Link Dual-Credit Programs to P-20 Initiatives." *Collaborative Librarianship* 3, no. 2 (2011): 90–97.

Burhanna, Kenneth J. "Instructional Outreach to High Schools." *Communications in Information Literacy* 1, no. 2 (2007): 74–88.

Burhanna, Kenneth J., and Mary Lee Jensen. "Collaborations for Success: High School to College Transitions." *Reference Services Review* 34, no. 4 (2006): 509–519.

Burrell, Allison, and Linda Neyer. "Helping High School Students Transition to College-Level Work: Can Collaboration between Librarians make a Difference?" *Learning & Media* 38, no. 3 (2010): 8–9.

Bushong, Sara, and Colleen Boff. "Information Literacy for Teaching and Learning: A Course for Teacher Practitioners." *Education Libraries* 31, no. 2 (2008): 12–18.

Cahoy, Ellysa Stern. "Will Your Students be Ready for College?" *Knowledge Quest* 30, no. 4 (2002).

Carr, Jo Ann. "Crossing the Instructional Divide: Supporting K-20 Information Literacy Iniatives." In Carroll Wetzel and Courtney Bruch, eds., *Transforming Information Literacy Programs: Intersecting Frontiers of Self, Library Culture, and Campus Community* (pp. 153–178). Chicago: Association of College and Research Libraries, 2012.

Carr, Jo Ann, and Ilene F. Rockman. "Information-Literacy Collaboration: A Shared Responsibility." *American Libraries* 34, no. 8 (September 2003): 52–54.

Carr, Jo Ann, and Kenneth Zeichner. "Academic Libraries and Teacher Education Reform: The Education of the Professional Teacher." In Patricia Senn Breivik and Robert Wedgeworth, eds., *Libraries and the Search for Academic Excellence* (pp. 83–92). Metuchen, NJ: Scarecrow Press, 1988.

Collins, Bobbie L. "Integrating Information Literacy Skills into Academic Summer Programs for Precollege Students." *Reference Services Review* 37, no. 2 (2009): 143–154.

Common Core State Standards Initiative. "Common Core State Standards." Washington, DC: Author, 2011. http://www.corestandards.org/about-the-standards (accessed May 1, 2011).

Cosgrove, John A. "Promoting Higher Education: (Yet) Another Goal of Bibliographic Instruction of High School Students by College Librarians." *College & Undergraduate Libraries* 8, no. 2 (2001): 17.

Craver, Kathleen W. "Use of Academic Libraries by High School Students: Implications for Research." *RQ* 27 (Fall 1987): 53–66.

Davis, R. P., and J. L. Hoffman. "Higher Education and the P-16 Movement: What Is to Be done?" *Thought & Action: The NEA Higher Education Journal* (Fall 2008): 123–134.

Dobie, Dawn, Nancy T. Guidry, and Jan Hartsell. "Navigating to Information Literacy: A Collaboration between California High School and College Librarians." *California School Library Association (CSLA) Journal* 34, no. 2 (2010): 6–9.

Eisenberg, Michael B., Carries A. Lowe, and Kathleen L. Spitzer. *Information Literacy: Essential Skills for the Information Age*, 2nd ed. Westport, CT: Libraries Unlimited, 2004.

Emmons, Mark, Elizabeth B. Keefe, Veronica M. Moore, Rebecca M. Sánchez, Michele M. Mals, and Teresa Y. Neely. "Teaching Information Literacy Skills to Prepare Teachers Who Can Bridge the Research-to-Practice Gap." *Reference & User Services Quarterly* 49, no. 2 (Winter 2009): 140–150.

Ewbank, Ann Dutton, Melissa Guy, Julie Tharp, and Ellen Welty. "Collaboration and Connection: A University Outreach Program for High School Librarians and English Teachers." *Library Media Connection* 30, no. 2 (2011): 28–30.

Fernekes, William R., and Harlene Z. Rosenberg. "Building a High School Archives Program: A Case Study in School–University Collaboration." *Journal of Archival Organization* 6, no. 3 (2008): 151–168.

Fitzgerald, Mary Ann. "Making the Leap from High School to College: Three New Studies about Information Literacy Skills of First-Year College Students." *Knowledge Quest* 32, no. 4 (2004): 19–24.

Fuson, Courtney, and Jenny Rushing. "Climbing Out of the 'Ivory Tower': Conversations between Academic and School Librarians and Teachers." *College & Research Libraries News* 70, no. 10 (2009): 566–569.

Goodin, M. Elspeth. "The Transferability of Library Research Skills from High School to College." *School Library Media Quarterly* 20 (Fall 1991): 33–41.

Gratch-Lindauer, Bonnie. "Comparing the Regional Accreditation of Academic Librarianship: Outcomes Assessment and Other Trends." *Journal of Academic Librarianship*, 28, no. 1 (2002): 14–25.

Guidry, Nancy and Dawn Dobie. "Library Skills for New College Students." Bakersfield, CA: Bakersfield College, 2010. http://www.bakersfieldcollege.edu/library/survival.asp (accessed November 4, 2012).

Hamilton-Pennell, Christine, Keith Curry Lance, Marcia J. Rodney, and Eugene Hainer. "Dick and Jane Go to the Head of the Class." *School Library Journal* 46, no. 4 (2000): 44.

Huge, Sharon, Bob Houdek, and Sherri Saines. "Teams and Tasks: Active Bibliographic Instruction with High School Students in a Summer Engineering Program." *College & Research Libraries News* 63, no. 5 (2002): 335–337.

INFOhio and OhioLINK Special Task Force. *Preparing 21st Century Ohio Learners for Success: The Role of Information Literacy and Libraries*. Columbus, OH: INFOhio, 2008.

Institute for Library & Information Literacy Education (ILILE). "About ILILE." http://www.ilile .org/ about.html (accessed May 20, 2012).

International Society for Technology in Education. "National Educational Technology Standards for Students." http://www.iste.org/ standards.aspx (accessed May 19, 2012).

Islam, Ramona L., and Lisa Anne Murno. "From Perceptions to Connections: Informing Information Literacy Program Planning in Academic Libraries through Examination of High School Library Media Center Curricula." *College & Research Libraries* 67, no. 6 (2006): 492–514.

Jesudason, Melba. "Academic Libraries and Outreach Services through Precollege Programs: A Proactive Collaboration." *Reference Services Review* 21, no. 4 (1993): 29–36.

Johns, Sara Kelly. "AASL Standards for the Twenty-First-Century Learner: A Map for Student Learning." *Knowledge Quest* 36, no.4 (March/April 2008): 4–7.

Katz, Irvin R. "Testing Information Literacy in Digital Environments: ETS's iSkills Assessment." *Information Technology & Libraries* 26, no. 3 (2007): 3–12.

Kent State University. "ILILE, Institute for Library and Information Literacy Education." http://www.ilile.org/ (accessed May 1, 2012).

Kent State University Libraries. "TRAILS: Tool for Real-Time Assessment of Information Literacy." Kent State University. http://www.trails-9.org/ (accessed May 19, 2012).

Kent State University Libraries. "Transitioning to College: Helping You to Succeed." Kent State University. http://www.transitioning2college.org/ (accessed May 19, 2012).

Kern High School and Bakersfield College. "Information Literacy Skills Groups and Accompanying Assignments." Bakersfield, CA: Kern High School District, 2012. (http://www .kernhigh.org/instruction/instruction/informationliteracy.aspx (accessed November 45, 2012).

Kirst, Michael, and Andrea Venezia. "Bridging the Great Divide between Secondary Schools and Postsecondary Education." *Phi Delta Kappan* 83, no. 1 (2001): 92.

Kirst, Michael, and Andrea Venezia, eds. *From High School to College: Improving Opportunities for Success in Postsecondary Education*. San Francisco: Jossey-Bass, 2004.

Kovalik, Cindy L., Mary Lee Jensen, Barbara Schloman, and Mary Tipton. "Information Literacy, Collaboration, and Teacher Education." *Communications in Information Literacy* 4, no. 2 (2010): 145–169.

Lupton, Mandy. "Evidence, Argument and Social Responsibility: First-Year Students' Experiences of Information Literacy when Researching an Essay." *Higher Education Research & Development* 27, no. 4 (2008): 399–414.

Maimann, Trevor. "School Library Cuts Not Good for Students: Library Association." *Epoch Times* (June 16, 2011). http://www.theepochtimes.com/n2/canada/school-library-cuts-not -good-for-students-library-association-57783.html (accessed November4, 2012).

Manuel, Kate. "National History Day: An Opportunity for K-16 Collaboration." *Reference Services Review* 33, no. 4 (2005): 459–486.

Marcoux, Betty. -New Standards—Refreshing our Work, AGAIN!" *School Library Media Activities Monthly* 24, no. 7 (2008): 18–20.

Maringe, Felix. "University and Course Choice." *International Journal of Educational Management* 20, no. 6 (2006): 466–479.

Martorana, Janet, Sylvia Curtis, and Sherry DeDecker. "Bridging the Gap: Information Literacy Workshops for High School Teachers." *Research Strategies* 18, no. 2 (2001): 113–120.

Merriam-Webster's Online Dictionary, (appearing under the word). "Movement." http://merriam -webster.com/ dictionary/movement (accessed May 15, 2012).

National Commission on Excellence in Education. *A Nation at Risk: An Imperative for Educational Reform*. Washington, D.C.: Government Printing Office, 1983.

National Center for Higher Education Management Systems (NCHEMS). "Student Pipeline: Transition Completion Rates from 9th Grade to College." Boulder, CO: NCHEMS, 2012. http://www.higheredinfo.org/dbrowser/?year=2008&level=nation&mode=graph&state=0 .&submeasure=119 (accessed May 12, 2012).

Nichols, Janet W., Lothar Spang, and Kristy Padron. "Building a Foundation for Collaboration: K-20 Partnerships in Information Literacy." *Resource Sharing & Information Networks* 18, no. 1 (2005): 5–12.

Nix, Donna, Marianne Hageman, and Janice Kragness. "Information Literacy and the Transition from High School to College." *Catholic Library World* 81, no. 4 (2011): 268–281.

Oakleaf, Megan. *The Value of Academic Libraries: A Comprehensive Review and Report*. Chicago: Association of College and Research Libraries, 2010.

Oakleaf, Megan. "Are They Learning? Are We? Learning Outcomes and the Academic Library." *Library Quarterly* 81, no. 1 (2011): 61–82.

Ohio Department of Education (ODE). "High School–Higher Education Alignment Initiative." http:// www.education.ohio.gov/GD/Templates/Pages/ODE/ODEDetail.aspx?page=3&TopicRelationID =1887&ContentID=112628&Content=123674 (accessed May 19, 2012).

Owen, Patricia. "A Transition Checklist for High School Seniors." *School Library Monthly* 26, no. 8 (2010): 20–23.

Partnership for 21st Century Skills. *Framework for 21st Century Learning*. Washington, D.C.: Author, 2011. http://www.p21.org/overview/skills-framework (accessed November 4, 2012).

Pearson, Debra, and Beth McNeil. "From High School Users College Students Grow: Providing Academic Library Research Opportunities to High School Students." *Knowledge Quest* 30, no. 4 (March/April 2002): 24–28.

Salisbury, Fiona, and Sharon Karasmanis. "Are They Ready? Exploring Student Information Literacy Skills in the Transition from Secondary to Tertiary Education." *Australian Academic & Research Libraries* 42, no. 1 (2011): 43–58.

Saunders, Laura. "Perspectives on Accreditation and Information Literacy as Reflected in the Literature of Library and Information Science." *Journal of Academic Librarianship* 34, no. 4 (2008): 305–313.

Schein, Christine, Linda Conway, Rebecca Harner, Sue Byerley, and Shelley Harper. "Bridging the Gap: Preparing High School Students for College Level Research." *Colorado Libraries* 36, no. 1 (2011): 1-4.

Secker, Jane, and Emma Coonan. *A New Curriculum for Information Literacy.* Cambridge, England: Arcadia Project, Cambridge University Library, 2011.

Shinew, Dawn M. and Scott Walter, eds. Information Literacy Instruction for Educators: Professional Knowledge for an Information Age. Binghamton, NY: Hawthorn Information Press, 2003.

Smalley, Topsy N. "College Success: High School Librarians Make the Difference." *Journal of Academic Librarianship* 30, no. 3 (2004): 193–198.

Stewart, Penni. "Academic Libraries Are Under Attack." *Canadian Association of University Teachers (CAUT) and Association canadienne des professeures et professeurs d'université (ACPPU) Bulletin* 59, no. 5 (2012). http://www.cautbulletin.ca/en_article .asp?articleid=2958 (accessed November 4, 2012).

Stover, Mark. Special issue, *Behavioral & Social Sciences Librarian* 22, no. 1 (2003).

U.S. Department of Education (DOE), National Center for Education Statistics. *The Condition of Education 2004 (NCES 2004–077).* Washington, D.C.: Government Printing Office, 2004.

Walsh, Erin J. "P-16 Policy Alignment in the States: Findings from a 50-State Survey." In *States, Schools, and Colleges: Policies to Improve Student Readiness for College and Strengthen Coordination between Schools and Colleges* (National Center Report #09-2). San Jose, CA: National Center for Public Policy and Higher Education, 2009. http://www .highereducation.org/reports/ssc/index.shtml (accessed November 2, 2012).

Witt, Steve W., and Julia B. Dickinson. "Teaching Teachers to Teach." *Behavioral & Social Sciences Librarian* 22, no. 1 (2003): 75–95.

Zoellner, Kate, and Charlie Potter. "Libraries across the Education Continuum: Relationships between Library Services at the University of Montana and Regional High Schools." *Behavioral & Social Sciences Librarian* 29, no. 3 (2010): 184–206.

2

Closing the 12-13 Gap Together: School and Academic Librarians Supporting 21st Century Learners

Megan Oakleaf and Patricia L. Owen

INTRODUCTION

Both teacher-librarians and academic librarians require evidence to tailor instruction to 21st century skills and dispositions. One recent syllabus study reveals what students need to know and do to be successful in their first semester at college. By forming partnerships, teacher-librarians and academic librarians can duplicate this study and focus on the needs of students at individual high schools and colleges. When teacher-librarians and academic librarians collaborate to gather evidence, they build sustaining partnerships, share their workload, and reveal important information that can be used to improve instruction and increase student success during the 12-13 transition.

CLOSING THE GAP

In recent years, teacher-librarians and academic librarians have made strides in closing the gap between the senior year of high school and the first year of college. They've surveyed college faculty about what they expect from students and gathered anecdotal descriptions of student skill deficiencies noted by both teacher-librarians and academic librarians. These opinion surveys and anecdotes provide only a partial picture of what students need to know to be successful in college. However, evidence-based studies provide concrete data that can be used to advocate for increased information literacy instruction on both sides of the 12-13 gap.

Academic librarians at one university studied the syllabi of first semester, first year students in an effort to determine which 21st century skills and dispositions are needed

Originally published as Oakleaf, Megan and Patricia L. Owen, "Closing the 1213 Gap Together: School and College Librarians Supporting 21st Century Learners," *Teacher Librarian* 37, no. 4 (April 2010), 52–58. Reprinted with permission.

to perform inquiry-based research. At the college level, the results of this study can be used to argue for increased librarian access to students for information literacy instruction, fine tune the topics covered in those information literacy instruction sessions, increase librarian instructional skills, and improve student learning (Oakleaf 2009).

This study also has implications in the high school context. First, high school teacher-librarians can use the results to provide concrete evidence of the 21st century skills and dispositions their college-bound seniors will be required to exhibit in their first semester of college—information of interest to students, parents, teachers, and school administrators. Second, some teacher-librarians may wish to tailor the results by completing a similar study in partnership with academic librarians at the college and universities their students attend. Either way, the evidence can be used to improve 21st century skills instruction at individual high schools.

THE SYLLABUS STUDY

Recently, a syllabus study was conducted at North Carolina State University (NCSU), a university that admits over 4,000 first year students each year (VanScoy and Oakleaf 2008, 569). During the fall semester, two academic librarians began the study by requesting course enrollment information about a random sample of 350 first year students' course schedules from the university registrar. Names and other personally identifiable information were stripped from the data to ensure student privacy. Next, the academic librarians created a list of courses in which at least one student in the sample was enrolled. Then, the librarians checked course websites and emailed instructors to collect syllabi and assignment sheets for the courses; ultimately, the librarians were able to locate information on all the courses of 139 of the students.

In the next step of the study, the librarians examined course syllabi for the presence of inquiry-based research assignments in order to determine the required research tasks. Research tasks were categorized as follows:

- Use articles
- Use books
- Use websites
- Use reference books
- Use data and statistics

All of the students included in the study had applied critical thinking skills to interact with at least one information source to create a new inquiry-based research product. Ninety-five percent interacted with websites, 94% interacted with articles, and 85% interacted with books (see Figure 2.1). Forty percent interacted with reference books, and 40% interacted with data and statistics. A majority of students interacted with multiple source types (see Figure 2.2), and 26% of the students studied interacted with them all!

The evidence produced by this study reveals a gap. First semester, first year college students must interact with information using 21st century skills and dispositions they may not have been taught in high school. Considering the inadequate student-to-librarian ratio at most colleges, these students may not have been taught them in college yet either. Consequently, first-year students must demonstrate flexibility by adapting their traditional information-seeking strategies. For example, when students use

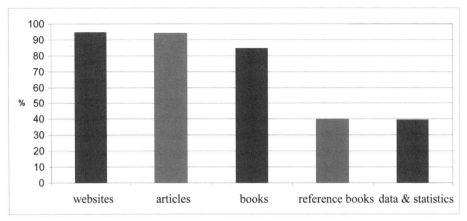

Figure 2.1.
Percentages of Students Required to Use Source Types

websites, they must choose a search engine, construct an effective search, critically evaluate website quality, incorporate website information, and cite the website ethically and responsibly (see Figures 2.3 through 2.6 for alignment to AASL, ISTE, ACRL, and Partnership for 21st Century Skills standards). Using articles also requires first year students to employ a number of high-level inquiry-based research skills. They must navigate a library website, choose an appropriate database, construct an effective search, distinguish popular and scholarly articles, evaluate article quality, and incorporate and cite article information ethically. Furthermore, critical-thinking students must display emotional resilience by persisting despite challenges. For instance, to use circulating books, students must navigate a library website and online catalog, construct a search, use LC classification, evaluate book quality, and incorporate and cite book information ethically. To use reference books, students must complete the aforementioned tasks, as well as employ challenging search strategies that identify reference books within the

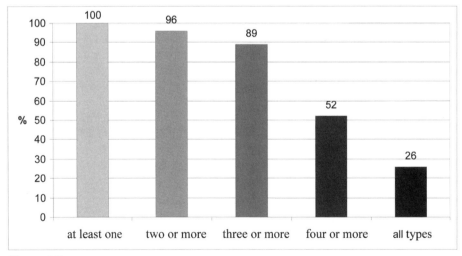

Figure 2.2.
Percentages of Students Required to Use Multiple Source Types

SOURCES STUDENTS USE IN COLLEGE

WEBSITES	ARTICLES	BOOKS	REFERENCE BOOKS	DATA & STATISTICS	
Skills Required to Use Websites →	Skills Required to Use Articles →	Skills Required to Use Books →	Skills Required to Use Reference Books →	Skills Required to Use Data & Statistics →	AASL STANDARDS FOR THE 21st CENTURY LEARNER
Choose a search engine	Navigate a library website; choose an article database	Navigate a library website and online catalog	Navigate a library website, online catalog	Identify and locate sources of data and statistics	1.1.4 Find, evaluate, and select appropriate sources to answer questions.
Construct an effective web search	Construct an effective database search	Construct an effective online catalog search; use LC classification	Construct search strategies that identify reference books within the rest of the collection	Construct an effective search of data and statistics sources	1.1.8 Demonstrate mastery of technology tools for accessing information and pursuing inquiry. 1.2.5 Demonstrate adaptability by changing the inquiry focus, questions, resources, or strategies when necessary to achieve success. 1.2.6 Display emotional resilience by persisting in information searching despite challenges. 1.2.7 Display persistence by continuing to pursue information to gain a broad perspective. 2.2.1 Demonstrate flexibility in the use of resources by adapting information strategies to each specific resource and by seeking additional resources when clear conclusions cannot be drawn.
Evaluate website quality	Distinguish popular and scholarly articles; evaluate article quality	Evaluate book quality	Distinguish among a variety of reference books; use evaluation criteria specific to reference books	Interpret and evaluate data and statistics	1.1.5 Evaluate information found in selected sources on the basis of accuracy, validity, appropriateness for needs, importance, and social and cultural context. 1.2.4 Maintain a critical stance by questioning the validity and accuracy of all information.

					AASL Standards
Incorporate website information into an assignment	Incorporate article information into an assignment	Incorporate book information into an assignment	Incorporate reference book information into an assignment	Incorporate data and statistics information into an assignment	2.1.1 Continue an inquiry-based research process by applying critical thinking skills (analysis, synthesis, evaluation, organization) to information and knowledge in order to construct new understandings, draw conclusions, and create new knowledge. 2.1.2 Organize knowledge so that it is useful. 2.1.6 Use the writing process, media, and visual literacy, and technology skills to create products that express new understandings. 3.1.1 Conclude an inquiry-based research process by sharing new understandings and reflecting on the learning. 3.1.3 Use writing and speaking skills to communicate new understandings effectively. 3.1.4 Use technology and other information tools to organize and display knowledge and understanding in ways others can view, use, and assess.
Cite the website according to style guidelines	Cite the article according to style guidelines	Cite the book according to style guidelines	Cite the reference book according to style guidelines	Cite the data and statistics according to style guidelines	3.1.6 Use information and technology ethically and responsibly.
Use multiple source types					1.2.3 Demonstrate creativity by using multiple resources and formats.

Excerpted from *Standards for the 21st-Century Learner* by the American Association of School Librarians, a division of the American Library Association, copyright © 2007 American Library Association. Available for download at www.ala.org/aasl/standards. Used with permission.

Figure 2.3.
Sources students use in college and corresponding AASL standards

SOURCES STUDENTS USE IN COLLEGE

WEBSITES	ARTICLES	BOOKS	REFERENCE BOOKS	DATA & STATISTICS	ISTE NATIONAL EDUCATIONAL TECHNOLOGY STANDARDS (NETS-S) AND PERFORMANCE INDICATORS FOR STUDENTS
Skills Required to Use Websites →	Skills Required to Use Articles →	Skills Required to Use Books →	Skills Required to Use Reference Books →	Skills Required to Use Data & Statistics →	
Choose a search engine	Navigate a library website; choose an article database	Navigate a library website and online catalog	Navigate a library website, online catalog	Identify and locate sources of data and statistics	3b. Students locate . . . information from a variety of sources and media. 6b. Students select . . . applications effectively and productively.
Construct an effective web search	Construct an effective database search	Construct an effective online catalog search; use LC classification	Construct search strategies that identify reference books within the rest of the collection	Construct an effective search of data and statistics sources	3a. Students plan strategies to guide inquiry. 6b. Students . . . use applications effectively and productively.
Evaluate website quality	Distinguish popular and scholarly articles; evaluate article quality	Evaluate book quality	Distinguish among a variety of reference books; use evaluation criteria specific to reference books	Interpret and evaluate data and statistics	3b. Students . . . evaluate . . . information from a variety of sources and media. 3c. Students evaluate and select information sources and digital tools based on the appropriateness to specific tasks.

Incorporate website information into an assignment	Incorporate article information into an assignment	Incorporate book information into an assignment	Incorporate reference book information into an assignment	Incorporate data and statistics information into an assignment	1a. Students apply existing knowledge to generate new ideas, products, or processes. 1b. Students create original works as a means of personal or group expression. 2b. Students communicate information and ideas effectively to multiple audiences using a variety of media and formats. 3b. Students . . . synthesize . . . information from a variety of sources and media. 4c. Students collect and analyze data to identify solutions and/or make informed decisions.
Cite the website according to style guidelines	Cite the article according to style guidelines	Cite the book according to style guidelines	Cite the reference book according to style guidelines	Cite the data and statistics according to style guidelines	3b. Students . . . ethically use information from a variety of sources and media. 5a. Students advocate and practice safe, legal, and responsible use of information and technology.
Use multiple source types					4d. Students use multiple processes and diverse perspectives to explore alternative solutions.

Figure 2.4.
Sources students use in college and corresponding ISTE standards

SOURCES STUDENTS USE IN COLLEGE

WEBSITES	ARTICLES	BOOKS	REFERENCE BOOKS	DATA & STATISTICS	PARTNERSHIP FOR 21st CENTURY SKILLS
Skills Required to Use Websites →	**Skills Required to Use Articles** →	**Skills Required to Use Books** →	**Skills Required to Use Reference Books** →	**Skills Required to Use Data & Statistics** →	
Choose a search engine	Navigate a library website; choose an article database	Navigate a library website and online catalog	Navigate a library website, online catalog	Identify and locate sources of data and statistics	• Accessing information efficiently and effectively. (Information, Media & Technology Skills)
Construct an effective web search	Construct an effective database search	Construct an effective online catalog search; use LC classification	Construct search strategies that identify reference books within the rest of the collection	Construct an effective search of data and statistics sources	• Using technology as a tool to research. (Information, Media & Technology Skills) • Using digital technology, communication tools and/or networks appropriately to access . . . information in order to function in a knowledge economy. (Information, Media & Technology Skills)
Evaluate website quality	Distinguish popular and scholarly articles; evaluate article quality	Evaluate book quality	Distinguish among a variety of reference books; use evaluation criteria specific to reference books	Interpret and evaluate data and statistics	• Evaluating information critically and competently. (Information, Media & Technology Skills) • Using technology as a tool to . . . evaluate information. (Information, Media & Technology Skills) • Using digital technology, communication tools and/or networks appropriately to . . . evaluate . . . information in order to function in a knowledge economy. (Information, Media & Technology Skills)

Incorporate website information into an assignment	Incorporate article information into an assignment	Incorporate book information into an assignment	Incorporate reference book information into an assignment	Incorporate data and statistics information into an assignment	• Framing, analyzing and synthesizing information in order to solve problems and answer questions. (Learning & Innovation Skills) • Articulating thoughts and ideas clearly and effectively through speaking and writing. (Learning & Innovation Skills) • Using information accurately and creatively for the issue or problem at hand. (Information, Media & Technology) • Using technology as a tool to . . . organize . . . and communicate information. (Information, Media & Technology Skills) • Using digital technology, communication tools and/or networks appropriately to . . . manage, integrate . . . and create information in order to function in a knowledge economy. (Information, Media & Technology Skills)
Cite the website according to style guidelines	Cite the article according to style guidelines	Cite the book according to style guidelines	Cite the reference book according to style guidelines	Cite the data and statistics according to style guidelines	• Possessing a fundamental understanding of the ethical/legal issues surrounding the access and use of information. (Information, Media & Technology Skills) • Using technology as a tool to research . . . and the possession of a fundamental understanding of the ethical/legal issues surrounding the access and use of information. (Information, Media & Technology Skills) • Demonstrating integrity and ethical behavior (Life & Career Skills)
Use multiple source types					• Understanding the interconnections among systems. (Learning & Innovation Skills)

Partnership for 21st Century Skills, 2012, www.p21.org

Figure 2.5.
Sources students use in college and corresponding 21st Century Skills

SOURCES STUDENTS USE IN COLLEGE

WEBSITES	ARTICLES	BOOKS	REFERENCE BOOKS	DATA & STATISTICS	ACRL INFORMATION LITERACY COMPETENCY STANDARDS FOR HIGHER EDUCATION ↓
Skills Required to Use Websites ↓	**Skills Required to Use Articles** ↓	**Skills Required to Use Books** ↓	**Skills Required to Use Reference Books** ↓	**Skills Required to Use Data & Statistics** ↓	
Choose a search engine	Navigate a library website; choose an article database	Navigate a library website and online catalog	Navigate a library website, online catalog	Identify and locate sources of data and statistics	2. The information literate student accesses needed information effectively and efficiently. 2.1 The information literate student selects the most appropriate investigative methods or information retrieval systems for accessing the needed information.
Construct an effective web search	Construct an effective database search	Construct an effective online catalog search; use LC classification	Construct search strategies that identify reference books within the rest of the collection	Construct an effective search of data and statistics sources	2. The information literate student accesses needed information effectively and efficiently. 2.2 The information literate student constructs and implements effectively-designed search strategies. 2.4 The information literate student refines the search strategy if necessary.
Evaluate website quality	Distinguish popular and scholarly articles; evaluate article quality	Evaluate book quality	Distinguish among a variety of reference books; use evaluation criteria specific to reference books	Interpret and evaluate data and statistics	3. The information literate student evaluates information and its sources critically and incorporates selected information into his or her knowledge base and value system. 3.2 The information literate student articulates and applies initial criteria for evaluating both the information and its sources.

Incorporate website information into an assignment	Incorporate article information into an assignment	Incorporate book information into an assignment	Incorporate reference book information into an assignment	Incorporate data and statistics information into an assignment	2.5 The information literate student extracts, records, and manages the information and its sources. 3.1 The information literate student summarizes the main ideas to be extracted from the information gathered. 3.3 The information literate student synthesizes main ideas to construct new concepts. 4. The information literate student, individually or as a member of a group, uses information effectively to accomplish a specific purpose. 4.1 The information literate student applies new and prior information to the planning and creation of a particular product or performance. 4.3 The information literate student communicates the product or performance effectively to others.
Cite the website according to style guidelines	Cite the article according to style guidelines	Cite the book according to style guidelines	Cite the reference book according to style guidelines	Cite the data and statistics according to style guidelines	5. The information literate student understands many of the economic, legal, and social issues surrounding the use of information and accesses and uses information ethically and legally. 5.3 The information literate student acknowledges the use of information sources in communicating the product or performance.
Use multiple source types					1.2 The information literate student identifies a variety of types and formats of potential sources for information.

Information Literacy Competency Standards. Chicago: Association of College & Research Libraries, 2000. http://www.ala.org/acrl/standards/informationliteracycompetency

Figure 2.6.

Sources students use in college and corresponding ACRL standards rest of the collection, distinguish among a variety of reference books, and use evaluation criteria specific to reference books. Additionally, students must construct understandings, draw conclusions, and create new knowledge. In situations calling for data and statistics, students must formulate a strategy to guide their search for organizations that care enough to compile data. They must interpret and evaluate the data and statistics, integrate the information and cite it ethically. The evidence produced by this study suggests that, if students do not adapt and learn these 21st century skills and dispositions before leaving high school, it's likely they won't be adequately prepared to participate in college-level inquiry-based research.

FINDING OUT WHAT YOUR SENIORS NEED TO KNOW

Although being aware of the 21st century skills and dispositions first semester, first year students at one university need to conduct inquiry-based research is informative, extending this study to uncover the skills your seniors need may be substantially more useful for improving information literacy instruction. While tailoring the study to the seniors at your high school may seem daunting, you don't have to go it alone. By partnering with academic librarians, you can share the evidence-gathering workload needed to implement instructional improvements and launch your college-bound seniors over the 12-13 gap.

1. Form Partnerships

While you probably acknowledge the general value of collaboration (see Figure 2.7), you may be uncertain about how to partner in ways that are directly related to 21st century student learning and achievement. One strategy is a syllabus study. The first step in a syllabus study is to identify a college connection. To get the most relevant evidence, partner with an academic librarian at a college that your students attend. If you don't already know what colleges most of your seniors attend, ask them. Or, for a more complete picture, query your school guidance counselors. In preparation for writing this article, the authors cold-called several high schools and asked for the guidance office. Then they posed the question, "What colleges are your graduating seniors most likely to attend?" In less than five minutes, each school provided a list.

Once you create a list of possible colleges, identify a partner at one of them. You may already have established a connection or know a colleague who can recommend a college reference and instruction librarian. If not, visit college library websites or call college library reference desks to identify a first point of contact. Many college libraries have a first year experience librarian or instruction coordinator; nearly all have a head of reference services. Any of these librarians can get you started. Once you identify a collaborator at the college level, share the following steps.

2. Get the Syllabi

The second step in a syllabus study is collecting course syllabi, and this task is best completed by your academic library partner. To begin, the academic librarian investigates the human subjects or institutional review procedure at their college. If you or your colleague plans to publish results, the academic librarian completes an institutional review board (IRB) application, consisting of a form and approval process. After

Teacher-librarians and academic librarians should collaborate to help students bridge the gap between high school and college (Daniel 1997, 53, 59; Martorana et al. 2001, 114; Ford 1996, 48). They share a common vision of student success, information literacy program goals (Carr and Rockman 2003, 53), and challenges to achieving those common goals (Donham 2003, 32). According to the AASL and ACRL Task Force on the Educational Role of Libraries (2000), teacher-librarians and academic librarians, "share the goals of fostering life-long learning and ensuring that students at all educational levels are prepared to meet the challenges of the 21st century." They have similar user populations and the same need to work with subject area faculty (Muronaga and Harada 1999; Jackson and Hansen 2006). Also, teacher-librarians need to increase student achievement, and academic librarians need to demonstrate their impact on student learning, increased student retention, and degree completion (Carr and Rockman 2003, 52). For all these student learning-focused reasons, teacher-librarians and academic librarians should form partnerships to support the students they share.

In addition to the advantages to students, collaborative partnerships also benefit librarians. When teacher-librarians and academic librarians form meaningful, lasting connections, they learn from each other, extend their current knowledge, and develop new skills. The *NBPTS for Library Media* (2001, 44) recognizes the benefits as well: "With a goal of strengthening library media programs and expanding information literacy, accomplished library media specialists welcome partnerships with cultural and educational institutions such as . . . university libraries." AASL (2009, 20) agrees: "The school library media specialist . . . collaborates with an extended team that includes . . . academic . . . libraries . . . to include the expertise and assistance in inquiry lessons and units." Indeed, when teacher-librarians partner with academic librarians, they develop learning communities that offer rich self-initiated professional development opportunities.

Figure 2.7.
Rationale for collaboration of teacher-librarians and academic librarians

receiving IRB approval, the academic librarian contacts the university registrar and requests a random sample of first year students with personally identifying information (name, student identification number, etc.) removed. Next, adjust the sample size depending on available time and overall number of first year students. In the NCSU study, the random sample was equal to 10% of the first year class.

Next, the academic librarian begins the process of collecting course syllabi by accessing them via learning management systems (WebCT, Blackboard, Moodle) or by calling departmental offices. In preparation for this article, the authors cold-called academic departments at four institutions. At three of the four, the departmental administrative assistant offered syllabi in binders. The remaining institution supplied readily available online syllabi.

3. Get a Plan

With syllabi in hand, you and the academic librarian devise a plan for analyzing them. At NCSU, librarians created a short checklist of 21st century inquiry-based tasks aligned with the AASL *Standards for the 21st Century Learner* (2007) and the ACRL *Information Literacy Competency Standards for Higher Education* (2000). The *Framework for 21st Century Learning* (2009), the *ISTE National Educational Technology Standards (NETS-S) and Performance Indicators for Students* (2007), state-determined academic content standards, or another local framework would also be a good foundation. Once you and the academic librarian agree on a plan for analyzing the syllabi, divide them for efficiency. Ideally, you should double-check at least a portion of each other's work.

4. Sum It Up & Apply the Evidence

After all the syllabi are examined and analyzed, summarize the evidence together. What are your results? What does a 21st century college learner look like? What skills and dispositions do your ready-to-graduate, high school seniors need to exhibit as first semester, first year college students?

After completing the summary, determine what changes and enhancements to teaching and learning are suggested by the evidence. What implications do your findings have for teaching your high school seniors? For teaching students in grades 9–11? For the instruction offered to first semester, first year students in college? How does a high school or higher education context impact the implementation of 21st century instruction? What are the interconnections between the two contexts?

5. Share the Evidence

Simple percentages tell a convincing story and are intuitively understood by your stakeholders including students, parents, teachers, and administrators. After considering stakeholder needs, determine the best way to format the findings. Will a bar chart tell your story? A comparison to local curriculum content? An alignment between the evidence provided by the study and the library lessons your high school or college offers? What vehicle will best describe the evidence, demonstrate the need for improvement, and advocate for your school library? A brief PowerPoint slide show for administrators? A 1-page summary? A brochure for parents? A newsletter story for teachers? More than one approach may work, depending on the audience.

CONCLUSION

Evidence-based research is one method for revealing the 21st century skills and dispositions your students need to be successful in their first semester of college. The step-by-step process described in this article can help both you and your academic library partner improve the critical areas of instruction 21st century learners deserve. By sharing new understandings gleaned from this article, teacher librarians can initiate professional partnerships with academic librarians, encourage each other to gather syllabi information, analyze the tasks required of students, and use the resulting data to improve instructional efforts—in short, use this article to close the 12-13 gap.

BIBLIOGRAPHY

American Association of School Librarians (AASL). *Empowering Learners: Guidelines for School Library Media Programs.* Chicago: American Library Association, 2009.
American Association of School Librarians (AASL). "Standards for the 21st Century Learner." http://www.ala.org/ala/mgrps/divs/aasl/guidelinesandstandards/learningstandards/AASL _Learning_Standards_2007.pdf (accessed July 20, 2009).

American Association of School Librarians and Association of College and Research Libraries Task Force on the Educational Role of Libraries. "Blueprint for Collaboration." Chicago: American Library Association, 2000. http://www.ala.org/ala/mgrps/divs/acrl/publications/whitepapers/acrlaaslblueprint.cfm (accessed July 20, 2009).

Association of College and Research Libraries (ACRL). "Information Literacy Competency Standards for Higher Education." http://www.ala.org/ala/mgrps/divs/acrl/standards/informationliteracycompetency.cfm (accessed July 20, 2009).

Carr, J., and Rockman, I. F. "Information Literacy Collaboration: A Shared Responsibility." *American Libraries* 34, no. 8 (2003): 52–54.

Daniel, Eileen. "High School to University: What Skills Do Students Need?" In Lynne Lighthall and Ken Haycock, eds., *Information Rich but Knowledge Poor? Emerging Issues for Schools and Libraries Worldwide. Research and Professional Papers Presented at the Annual Conference of the International Association of School Librarianship held in Conjunction with the Association for Teacher-Librarianship in Canada, July 6–11, 1997.* Vancouver, British Columbia, Canada, 1997.

Donham, Jean. "My Senior Is Your First-Year Student: High School Transition to College." *Knowledge Quest* 32, no. 1 (2003): 32.

Ford, Barbara J. "All Together Now." *School Library Journal* 42 (1996): 48.

International Society for Technology in Education. "The ISTE National Educational Technology Standards (NETS-S) and Performance Indicators for Students." http://www.iste.org/Content/NavigationMenu/NETS/ForStudents/2007Standards/NETS_for_Students_2007_Standards.pdf (accessed July 20, 2009).

Jackson, Lydia, and Julia Hansen. "Creating Collaborative Partnerships: Building the Framework." *Reference Services Review* 34, no. 4 (2006): 575–588.

Martorana, Janet, Curtis, Sylvia, and Sherry DeDecker. "Bridging the Gap: Information Literacy Workshops for High School Teachers." *Research Strategies* 18, no. 2 (2001): 113–120.

Muronaga, Karen, and Violet Harada. "Building Teaching Partnerships: The Art of Collaboration." *Teacher-Librarian* 27, no. 1 (1999): 9–14.

National Board for Professional Teaching Standards (NBPTS). *NBPTS Library Media Standards.* Arlington, VA: NBPTS, 2001. http://www.nbpts.org/userfiles/File/ecya_lm_standards.pdf (accessed July 20, 2009).

Oakleaf, Megan. "The Information Literacy Assessment Cycle: A Guide for Increasing Student Learning and Improving Librarian Instructional Skills." *Journal of Documentation* 65, no. 4 (2009): 539–560.

Partnership for 21st Century Skills. "Framework for 21st Century Learning." http://www.21stcenturyskills.org/documents/framework_flyer_updated_jan_09_final-1.pdf (accessed July 20, 2009).

VanScoy, Amy, and Megan Oakleaf. "Evidence vs. Anecdote: Using Syllabi to Plan Curriculum-Integrated Information Literacy Instruction." *College and Research Libraries* 69, no. 6 (2008): 566–575.

3

Research Skills: What College Professors Expect Incoming Students to Know

Jennifer Sigalet, Leslie Barton, and Sherri Savage

INTRODUCTION

Student preparedness at the time of transition from high school to university is a major concern for educators, as is demonstrated in mainstream transition literature (Brinkworth et al. 2009, 158). Recent surveys (OCUFA 2009) have indicated there is a widening gap between the information literacy skills of high school students and the information literacy skills expectations postsecondary professors have of incoming first-year college students. Information literacy, as defined by the Association of College and Research Libraries (1989), is a set of abilities requiring individuals to "recognize when information is needed and have the ability to locate, evaluate, and use effectively the needed information (paragraph 3)." This chapter reports on a project between high school and academic librarians in British Columbia, Canada that investigated the expectations of college professors for information literacy skills possessed by incoming first-year students.

PROJECT AIMS AND OBJECTIVES

In response to the recent literature on perceived gaps in the information literacy skills of first-year students, a teacher-librarian from Pleasant Valley Secondary School pitched to the librarian at Okanagan College Vernon Campus (Vernon, British Columbia, Canada) a film interview initiative that would explore the information literacy skills university professors expect incoming first-year university students to have. Pleasant Valley Secondary School, a public high school with ninth through twelfth grades, is located in the rural town of Armstrong, British Columbia (Canada) Okanagan College, a multi-campus institution with a student population of approximately 8,000 full-time equivalent students (FTES), delivers postsecondary programs on four campuses throughout the Okanagan Valley in British Columbia. The college also offers adult upgrading, continuing studies, vocational studies, international education, and trades programs.

In the fall of 2008, the two librarians and an Okanagan College educational technology film technician launched a collaborative video interview project, *Research Skills: Bridging the Gap between High School and Post-Secondary,* which sought to explore the information literacy skills university professors expect incoming first-year university students to have.

The initial motivating goals of the *Research Skills* film project (and a subsequent iterative *Library Research Skills Survey* conducted in 2011), were grounded in the quest to:

- Identify and document postsecondary professors' information literacy skills expectations of incoming students
- Highlight perceived shortfalls in the information literacy skills incoming students have
- Create a means for sharing the results with local secondary and postsecondary educators and administrators

While one of the major driving goals of the film project was to share transition concerns with key players in the local educational community, other secondary objectives aimed to:

- Bring together useful information on the current state of transition between high school and postsecondary education
- Reinforce the necessity to support teaching information literacy skills in high school in preparation for postsecondary education
- Share best practices with information literacy colleagues at various professional forums to help support awareness of the need for a K-16 information literacy continuum
- Support the collaborative transition efforts of teacher-librarians and postsecondary librarians
- Help foster cooperation and collaboration in the development and promotion of information literacy awareness

The *Research Skills* interview film project and the subsequent companion *Library Research Skills Survey* have together provided important feedback on college professors' information literacy skills expectations of incoming first-year students. Based on key findings of the interviews and the surveys, this chapter aims to highlight these research skills expectations and identify the gaps in these skills as perceived by college professors.

BACKGROUND AND CONTEXT: *RESEARCH SKILLS* FILM PROJECT

The *Research Skills* film project was planned in the fall of 2008, and interviews were conducted and filmed shortly after. Six Okanagan College professors from six core academic disciplines (anthropology, biology, English, history, psychology, and sociology) responded to a series of questions addressing their information literacy skills expectations of first-year university students. The interviews were documented in the 16-minute video titled *Research Skills: Bridging the Gap between High School and Post-Secondary* filmed by Educational Technology, Okanagan College (see

Bibliography for link to streaming a version of the film by Barton, Sigalet and Tessier.) The primary overarching question was "What are your research skills expectations of first-year students?" which in turn also provided responses relating to what the perceived gaps in these research skills were.

The word "gap" in the film's title refers to a disparity between the research skills graduating high school students have and the skills they need for the successful completion of academic coursework. The word "bridge" refers to the interest in the collaboration between librarians at different levels of education for a smoother transition from high school to university. A term associated with such collaboration is "transition literacy." "Transition literacy is not a new concept but it is gaining momentum as a concept in schools and universities as students need to be ready to enter the next step in their academic life in an information rich environment" (Beaudry 2009, 47). Librarian Richard Beaudry outlines some concrete *need-to-know* areas to ensure new student success at the postsecondary level:

- New knowledge: Students graduating from high school need to be aware that they are changing library classification systems from the Dewey decimal to the Library of Congress classification used in college and university libraries.
- New resources: Colleges and universities offer access to numerous databases and search tools that are not always available to public school students.
- Web 2.0 technology tools: New tools such as blogs or wikis enable students to collaborate with classmates and participate in group discussions. Other Web 2.0 tools will assist students in creating and sharing their projects online.
- Learning how to search for information and writing papers: New students have to understand the importance of information literacy skills in their own lives. They're more likely to do so if they understand how the skills relate to their immediate and future success. College and university assignments require in-depth research skills (Beaudry 2010, 47).

In the *Research Skills* film project interviews, the six participating postsecondary professors were asked the following guiding questions (Barton, Sigalet, and Tessier 2010):

- Ideally, what research skills would you like first-year college students to come equipped with (that they often don't have)?
- What typical use is made of the college library by your classes (perhaps example[s] of a research project you might assign)? What is the role of the librarian in the process?
- What are your expectations in regards to quality of information sources?
- Subtopics could include peer reviewed material, print resources, online resources, databases (online, CD ROM), number of sources used, research notes or rough drafts of work, and citation of sources.
- What is your policy in regards to plagiarized words and ideas? What is the policy of the college? How do you know when/if something is plagiarized?

The emerging themes from the filmed interviews (Barton and Sigalet 2010) were that the majority of students in first-year university courses are not familiar with:

- The research process
- Where to look for appropriate resources for first-year research
- What a peer-reviewed article is

- How to evaluate the sources they find
- How to cite the resources they have used
- The difference between "opinion" and "informed opinion"

The skills deficiencies identified by the six professors send a strong message pointing to the necessity for students to acquire these skills before entering postsecondary
education, and consequently bring to light the necessity to support the role and retention of teacher-librarians as information and critical thinking skills experts who prepare
high school students for first-year university coursework and beyond. The film has
proven to be an impactful tool for sharing these expectations with key players in the
educational arena (in particular high school administrators, teachers, teacher-
librarians, student teachers, parent groups, university/college professors and librarians,
and college administrators) and for creating an awareness of the disparity between the
expectations of postsecondary educators and the shortfalls that exist in the information
literacy skills of first-year university students. Furthermore, the *Research Skills* interviews confirm the results of ongoing studies, surveys, and reports on the significant
gap between high school and first-year university students' preparedness for postsecondary education in Canada. The Ontario Confederation of University Faculty
Associations (OCUFA 2009) survey suggests that postsecondary educators are finding
first-year students:

- Have lower levels of maturity
- Lack required writing, mathematical, and critical thinking skills
- Demonstrate poor research skills as evidenced by an overreliance on Internet tools such as
  Wikipedia as external research sources
- Expect success without the requisite effort
- Display an inability to learn independently

Furthermore, the OCUFA study reports that over 55 percent of responding professors
and librarians perceive that first-year students are less prepared than they were three
years ago in 2006 (2009).

Similar studies have been conducted outside Canada, finding related gaps between
high school and postsecondary education. A pilot survey of science students at the University of Ulster (Cook and Leckey 1999) in Northern Ireland confirmed that student
study habits formed in secondary school persist to the end of the first semester of university life. Based on the results of this study, authors Lowe and Cook conclude that
students are not bridging the gap between high school and university quickly and effectively, and students as well "find themselves ill-prepared for higher education" (Lowe
and Cook 2003, 53).

Two companion 2006 U.S. national surveys conducted by the *Chronicle of Higher
Education* (Sanoff 2006) compared the views of college faculty members with those
of high school teachers about students' overall preparation for college and found
related gaps. Over 9,000 teachers and 7,000 faculty members were surveyed, with a
75 percent rate of return. While this study did not focus specifically on research skills,
the findings in the area of general preparedness—including study habits, critical thinking skills, organization, and writing—all show a difference in perception at the two levels of education. The study finds differing gaps of perception for different subjects and
finds also some agreement between college and high school educators in their

assessment of student completion of homework and motivation, but generally concludes that high school teachers are, as a whole, more positive about student preparedness than their postsecondary counterparts.

Since its inaugural screening at the Research Skills Roundtable at the 2010 British Columbia Library Association Annual Conference, the grassroots film—*Research Skills: Bridging the Gap Between High School and Post-Secondary*—has proven to be a powerful tool for stimulating lively discussions among teacher-librarians and postsecondary librarians at professional conferences and workshops locally, provincially, nationally, and internationally British Columbia Library Association (BCLA), British Columbia Teacher-Librarian Association (BCTLA), International Federations of Library Associations and Institutions (IFLA), and Workshop for Instruction in Library Use (WILU), and has served as a promotional tool for bridging opportunities between school districts and postsecondary institutions.

The ongoing goals of the *Research Skills* project are to continue to:

- Increase awareness among educators institutional, district, provincial, national, and international levels
- Develop collaborative strategies for seeking and obtaining formalized support for the teaching of K-16 information literacy skills
- Develop formalized information literacy programs to help ease the transition to postsecondary education
- Create a more structured and collaborative approach to bridging this troubling gap in information literacy skills

BACKGROUND AND CONTEXT: LIBRARY RESEARCH SKILLS SURVEY

In the spring of 2011, Okanagan College Library embarked on a survey study that further explored the question, "What research skills do college professors expect first-year students to have?" The Okanagan College Vernon Campus librarian and a San Jose State University Master of Library and Information Science (MLIS) distance student working at Okanagan College Library collaborated on the development of an institutional survey, *Library Research Skills Survey*. The survey was distributed to all Okanagan College faculty members by email; participation was voluntary. Survey responses were based on opinion and expanded upon the questions of the film project, which were grounded in the Association of College and Research Libraries (ACRL) standards as laid out in the *Information Literacy Competency Standards* (ACRL 2000). While the *Research Skills* film project participants consisted of a sampling of Okanagan College professors, the *Library Research Skills Survey* aimed to widen the data field by inviting all university and business faculty to participate. Approximately 35 percent of faculty members responded to the survey.

The results of the *Library Research Skills Survey* (Savage and Sigalet 2011) were consistent with and showed a similar trend to the *Research Skills* film interviews as well as other recent surveys and reports on transition and information literacy. The survey indicated that professors perceived that most students are not prepared for the demands of first-year university coursework. When asked, "Do you think first-year students transitioning from high school have the research skills needed to succeed in first-year university?" 73 percent answered "no," 10.8 percent answered "yes," and 16.2 percent answered "other" (see Figure 3.1) (Savage and Sigalet 2011, 4).

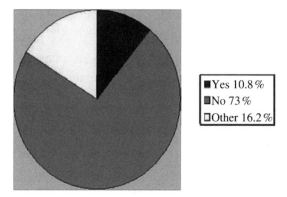

Figure 3.1.
Do You Think First-Year Students Transitioning from High School have the Research
Skills Needed to Succeed in First-Year University

The majority of the faculty instructors (73 percent) thought that students did not
have the research skills needed to succeed in postsecondary education. When asked to
explain why, the responses included (Savage and Sigalet 2011, 4):

• Students think that a search on the Internet using Google, Google Scholar, or Wikipedia is
  adequate research.
• They do not know where to begin research or to organize, prepare, or evaluate information.
• They generally believe that writing papers is about expressing their opinion, not researched
  proof to support an argument.
• They have no idea how to search databases, understand peer-reviewed articles, or properly cite works.
• Students have no preparation for finding research that is used to support an argument. They can
  Google, but they cannot organize, prepare, or evaluate that information.
• That is what we teach in first year college. I do not expect them to already know it.

Table 3.1 shows the results of the survey, which ranked the top 10 research skills
expectations postsecondary professors have of incoming first-year students.

While the majority of the faculty instructors (73 percent) believed that students did
not have the research skills needed to succeed, only half of the instructors took advantage of librarian-led in-class research instruction. In the next question in the survey—
"Do you contact a librarian to provide in-class research instruction?"—51.4 percent
answered "yes" and 48.6 percent answered "no." Those who said they did not contact
a librarian to provide in-class research instruction were also asked why not (see Figure
3.2) (Savage and Sigalet 2011, 5).

The majority of the replies focused on the factor of time. The professors responded
that class time should be spent on course content. Therefore, there is not enough time
for librarian-led research instruction in class, and the professors prefer that students
go to the library during their own time to improve research skills. Some of the professors themselves taught research instruction to the students, and others assumed that
other professors would cover it or already had. Conclusions can be made that instructors require librarian-led research instruction outside of class time or in-class
librarian-led sessions that last for short durations.

Table 3.1.

Top 10 Research Skills

Expectations Okanagan College professors have of incoming first year students (Savage and Sigalet 2011, 6).	
1	How to locate and access information
2	How to avoid plagiarism and recognize the importance of citing and referencing sources
3	How to recognize when information is needed
4	How to evaluate the credibility and authority of information
5	How to organize and apply information effectively
6	How to differentiate between popular and scholarly sources
7	How to differentiate between primary and secondary sources
8	How to create a research strategy or keep a research journal
9	How to synthesize and build on existing information
10	How to develop these skills

Faculty instructors were then asked to propose other ideas about how librarians can improve students' research skills. Common responses included easy reference handout sheets and the ability to access librarians in the library for quick demonstrations or more in-depth help either at the information desk or at a requested meeting in a study room. Professors had mixed opinions about continuing in-class sessions or focusing on workshops held outside of class time. In-class sessions should be tailored to the course content and provide examples of a typical research assignment. Workshops held outside of class time should be thematically organized throughout the term, attendance should be tracked, and credit should be given toward students' course grade so that the workshop is meaningful for students.

One professor responded to the question of in class library instruction versus outside of class workshops as follows:

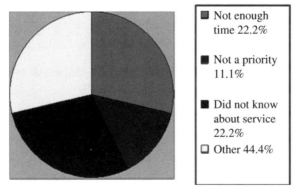

Figure 3.2.

No, You Do Not Contact a Librarian to Provide In-Class Research Instruction. Why Not?

I think it is great that the librarians are interested in doing this—but to be honest, I think the problem is greater and we need to begin teaching students these skills in high school. I also strongly believe that there should be required seminars or a course on basic academic skills.

(Savage and Sigalet 2011, 7)

The preceding sentiment and the results provided by the *Library Research Skills Survey* strengthen the argument for the necessity of a collaborative effort to improve students' information literacy skills. These skills need to be addressed by teacher-librarians at the secondary level and academic librarians at the postsecondary level. School districts and postsecondary decision makers need to formally support K-16 bridging endeavours that advance lifelong learning and the development and enhancement of information literacy programs at both the high school and postsecondary levels.

CONCLUSIONS

Reaching beyond the walls of her high school, a teacher-librarian initiated a fruitful collaboration with a college librarian that has resulted in an ongoing investigation of information literacy transition issues locally and beyond. The original film collaboration *Research Skills: Bridging the Gap between High School and Post-Secondary* in 2008 provided fodder for further investigations of research skills expectations in the institutional *Library Research Skill Survey* at Okanagan College in the spring of 2011. The motivating goals behind both projects were to identify and document professors' information literacy skills expectations, find the gaps in these expected skills, create an impactful means of communicating the results of the findings, stimulate discussion among the educational community, and seek support for formalized bridging initiatives as well as K-16 information literacy collaborations.

The conclusions of the two-pronged project point to the need for increased discussions between secondary and higher education systems to ease student transition. The highlights of the project will be used to:

• Encourage discussions and collaborations between high school and college/university librarians
• Communicate with school administrators and college administrators the significant role information literacy skills play in easing the transition between high school and postsecondary education
• Continue the development and enhancement of information literacy programs in high school and postsecondary libraries

The ongoing goals of the project include:

• Continuing to identify perceived gaps in the research skills of students entering their first year of university
• Involving students in the information literacy process in preparation for postsecondary education
• Creating institutional awareness and commitment to transition opportunities
• Creating sustainable collaborations between secondary schools and postsecondary institutions
• Creating a lobby group in support of funding for teacher-librarians locally and beyond
• Collaborating on the development of instruction programs to ensure a more seamless transition

- Including academic librarians in professional development events as presenters and participants
- Inviting postsecondary librarians to address local school boards and promote information literacy and the role it plays in preparing students for college success.
- Identifying and working with other groups who are focusing on supporting student transitions
- Continuing the development of a presentation package based on the *Research Skills* video and survey for the purpose of increasing the awareness of gaps in information literacy skills of first-year university students

Some of the challenges (Barton and Sigalet 2010, 8) the authors faced in carrying out these ongoing goals are:

- Budgetary/funding issues (school visits, field trips)
- Cutbacks in educational funding.
- Cutbacks in teacher-librarian time and library clerical support
- Curriculum demands on subject teachers
- Added clerical demands on teacher-librarians' time and resources
- Assessment-driven curricula time, workloads, and resources.

Interestingly, the Okanagan Mainline Transitions Partnership (OMTP), a new transition collaboration between Okanagan College and seven School Districts in British Columbia (Thomson 2010) has allowed Okanagan College to deliver a selection of dual-credit and concurrent enrollment programs for high school students from these districts. This innovative initiative is studying and identifying important collaborations in student transition work of professionals in the K-12 and postsecondary systems.

The *Research Skills* project team has briefly shared transitions concerns with the OMTP, which in turn has noted the role libraries could play in supporting transitions, and also that information literacy is an important piece of the transition picture that has possibly been overlooked in mainstream transition literature. Connections like this, between educators located near each other but formerly in separate and disconnected worlds, can be both encouraging and inspiring, as they can work together to seek ways of easing student transitions. Certainly information literacy professionals need to continue using collaborative strategies to help bridge the gap between high school information literacy preparedness and the expectations of first-year postsecondary instructors. It is clear from the projects and research discussed in this chapter that more collaboration is needed. Through collaboration, educators can continue identifying common concerns and seeking methods of intervening in the support and development of the teaching and learning of these transferrable information literacy skills in high school and first-year university curricula in support of students' lifelong learning. Support and leadership is required in this field, as teachers, teacher-librarians and postsecondary librarians come to professional development days, workshops, and conferences and want to talk about how we can all be involved and work together on information literacy issues and transitions.

BIBLIOGRAPHY

Association of College & Research Libraries (ACRL). *Information Literacy Competency Standards for Higher Education.* Chicago: American Library Association, 2000.

Association of College and Research Libraries (ACRL). *Presidential Committee on Information Literacy. Final Report.* Chicago: American Library Association, 1989. http://www.ala .org/ala/mgrps/divs/acrl/publications/whitepapers/ presidential.cfm.

Barton, Leslie, and Jennifer M. Sigalet. "Research Skills: Bridging the Gap between High School and Post-Secondary." Presentation, annual conference for the British Columbia Teacher-Librarians Association, Kelowna, British Columbia, October 21–22, 2010.

Barton, Leslie, Jennifer M. Sigalet, and Karen Tessier. *Research Skills: Bridging the Gap between High School and Post-Secondary.* DVD. Directed by Leslie Barton. Kelowna, BC: Okanagan College Educational Technology, 2010. Also available as streaming video, http:// library-1.okanagan.bc.ca.ezproxy.okanagan.bc.ca/vwebv/holdingsInfo?bibId=290130.

Beaudry, Richard. "Transition Literacy in High Schools: A School Model." *School Libraries in Canada* 26, no. 3 (2009): 44–52. http://search.ebscohost.com/login.aspx?direct =true&db=tfh&AN=36836548&site=ehost-live.

Brinkworth, Russell, Ben McCann, Carol Matthews, and Karin Nordström. "First Year Expectations and Experiences: Student and Teacher Perspectives." *Higher Education: International Journal of Higher Education and Educational Planning* 58, no. 2 (2009): 157–173.

Cook, Anthony, and Janet Leckey. "Do Expectations Meet Reality? A Survey of Changes in First-Year Student Opinion." *Journal of Further and Higher Education* 23, no. 2 (1999): 157–171.

Lowe, Houston, and Anthony Cook. "Mind the Gap: Are Students Prepared for Higher Education?" *Journal of Further and Higher Education* 27, no. 1 (2003): 53–76.

Ontario Confederation of University Faculty Association (OCUFA). "Students Less Prepared for University Education Than in 2005, According to Ontario University Faculty." *OCUFA Press* Release, http://notes.ocufa.on.ca/OCUFApress.nsf/A97A540CA9EEC6D68 52573B00053F099/DA2506597AEEBA378525759000497B01?OpenDocument (accessed April 6, 2009).

Sanoff, Alvin P. "A Perception Gap over Students' Preparation." *Chronicle of Higher Education* 52, no. 27 (2006): B9–B14.

Savage, Sherri B., and Jennifer M. Sigalet. *Library Research Skills Survey Report: What Research Skills Do College Professors Expect First-Year Students to Have?* Kelowna, BC: Okanagan College, 2011.

Thomson, Diana. "Transitions." *Enhancing the Practice of Learning and Teaching: Institute for Learning and Teaching at Okanagan College* 1, no. 6 (2010). http://illt.okanagan.bc.ca/ wp-content/uploads/2010/12/illt_fall_10.pdf

ADDITIONAL READINGS

Burhanna, Kenneth J. "Instructional Outreach to High Schools: Should You Be Doing It?" *Communications in Information Literacy* 1, no. 2 (2007): 74–88.

Burhanna, Kenneth J., Julie A. Gedeon, Mary Lee Jensen, and Barbara F. Schloman. "Reaching Forward: Three High School Outreach Initiatives at Kent State University." In Nancy Courtney, ed., *Academic Library Outreach: Beyond the Campus Walls* (Chapter 2, pp. 9–20). Westport, CT: Libraries Unlimited, 2009.

Burhanna, Kenneth J., and Mary Lee Jensen. "Collaborations for Success: High School to College Transitions." *Reference Services Review* 34, no. 4 (2006): 509–519.

Burkhardt, Joanna M., Mary C. MacDonald, and Andrée J. Rathemacher. *Creating a Comprehensive Information Literacy Plan: A How-to-Do-It Manual and CD-ROM for Librarians.* New York: Neal-Schuman, 2005.

Cahoy, Ellysia S., and Leslie Moyo. "K-16 Outreach: Creating Connections that Matter." In Nancy Courtney, ed., *Academic Library Outreach: Beyond the Campus Walls* (Chapter 3, pp. 21–30). Westport, CT: Libraries Unlimited, 2009.

Hayden, Katharine Alix. 2010. "Together We Are Stronger: K-16 Information Literacy Collaborations." *Treasure Mountain Canada,* http://tmcanada.pbworks.com/TM-Canada-Papers (accessed January 20, 2011).

Nichols, Janet W., Lothar Spang, and Kristy Padron. "Building a Foundation for Collaboration: K-20 Partnerships in Information Literacy." *Resource Sharing and Information Network* 18, no. 102 (2005): 5–12.

Sigalet, Jennifer M. 2011. *Research Skills: Bridging the Gap between High School and Post-Secondary LibGuide.* Okanagan College, http://libguides.okanagan.bc.ca/js-bridging (accessed October 25, 2011).

Sigalet, Jennifer M., and Sherri B. Savage. 2011. "Grassroots Collaborations: Bridging the Gap between High School and Post-Secondary." Presentation, annual conference for the Workshop for Instruction in Library Use, Regina, Saskatchewan, June 1–3, 2011. Also available online: http://www2.uregina.ca/wilu2011/wp-content/uploads/2011/06/WILU-T8-Sigalet-Grassroots-1.98MB.pdf.

Theijsmeijer, Heather R. "Translating High School to University: What to Expect from Your First-Year Students." *CASCA Education*, http://www.cascaeducation.ca/files/proAstro_translating.html (accessed October 23, 2012).

4

Boundary Spanning by Librarians to Support the College Transition for Students with Disabilities

Anne Marie Perrault

Any life transition is a dynamic and complex journey. Young people of varying abilities face many new challenges as they move from high school to college and navigate uncharted waters. Transition planning involves building the academic and life skills of students with disabilities in college and beyond. Individuals with a range of cognitive, emotional, and physical disabilities represent a growing number of students attending college and also represent one of the largest groups of diverse learners. About 12 percent of the school-age population, or more than 5.7 million students between the ages of three and 21, have a disability (U.S. Department of Education, 2009).

Yet early, mid, and late career education professionals report ongoing challenges in making learning accessible and inclusive for all students. Academic, school, and public librarians are among a cadre of educators, including even special education teachers, who feel their knowledge and skills to support students with disabilities are either lacking or dated. These challenges must be overcome because it is both a federal right and an ethical imperative by educational professionals that all students are supported. Librarians' knowledge of best practices in teaching and learning as well as strategies to collaborate with others who may be internal or external to the organization, and an understanding of available assistive and adaptive technologies can make a difference in supporting learners with varying abilities. This chapter aims to help prepare librarians for these challenges by defining their role and the role of information literacy, sharing best practices and support strategies, and pointing out quality resources.

BOUNDARY SPANNER ROLE

Boundary spanning by librarians offers a means to contribute and draw on the resources and knowledge within an ecology, or network, that support the transition process. The term "orchestrator" or "linker" has also been used in describing this role.

Boundary spanning goes beyond collaboration, although collaboration is a valuable component. Librarians who are boundary spanners go across interorganizational boundaries to access information and resources so that they can bring back information and resources for their patrons. Acquiring information and resources may also result in forming relationships that are mutually beneficial through different initiatives and partnerships. Linking the user to appropriate resources, people, and opportunities is common practice for librarians. Boundary spanning complements this task by broadening the scope of network to draw upon.

Just as it would be difficult for any one school or community organization to meet the needs of all youth in transition, it is vital to reconceptualize how librarians can cross boundaries to support youth with disabilities in the transition process to postsecondary education. A review of research in the area of transitions to college by students with disabilities supports the concept of boundary spanning. For example, factors such as interagency and interdisciplinary collaboration are identified as being best practices for transition services for students with varying abilities (Zhang et al. 2005). Research has also confirmed that a range of stakeholders who demonstrate active involvement and commitment are vital to the successful transition process (Benz, Lindstrom, and Halpern 1995).

To meet the broad and diverse needs of students with disabilities , an ecology, or network, of support must be the new norm. Librarians are vital stakeholders in a vast network of resources required to empower students with the lifelong skills and knowledge necessary to be successful in college and careers. Yet a tremendous amount of knowledge, experiences, and resources exists in disparate entities—in different types of professionals in different organizations and institutions. To meet the diverse information and learning needs of all of our students, our professional community must be expanded to include a wide range of professionals who are involved in working to support the transition process of young adults going from high school to college. For example, members might include special education teachers, staff from the accessibility office on a college campus, experts in assistive and adaptive technologies, staff from local community agencies, faculty from special education departments, staff from teaching and learning centers, and differentiation specialists.

INFORMATION ECOLOGIES

While the responsibilities of academic, school, and public librarians vary, they share a common focus—helping library users learn the skills necessary to effectively and efficiently use information. Young adults reach out to librarians in various settings for a myriad of educational and personal information needs. Yet often their interactions with librarians are, in a sense, "siloed" experiences. Their experiences with libraries tend to be independent events and often the natural and potentially synergistic relationship among libraries and librarians is not evident. Library professionals who are faced with increased workloads and fiscally constrained work environments may also fail to take into account the power of scale.

Librarians are naturally part of the organizational network where they are employed. However, there exists a potentially wider network from which they could leverage resources to improve practices and services. Librarians are part of what Nardi and O'Day call an "information ecology," or a system of people, practices, values and technologies (1999, 49). Librarians who take a systems perspective are cognizant that they are part of an information network that is dynamic and expansive. It is the scale of the ecology that allows for points of intersection and openings for points of leverage. Consider the potential of a network and its resources that purposefully includes librarians in multiple types of settings. That information network would be a boundary-free ecology available to be leveraged for the benefit of students transitioning to college.

INFORMATION LITERACY SKILLS FOR DIVERSE LEARNERS

Developing proficiency in the ability to access, evaluate, and use information plays a part in all students' transition from high school to college. Students enter postsecondary education settings with varying degrees of experience and proficiency in information literacy skills and resources. However, gaps and areas for growth emerge within the first few weeks of college classes. Significant attention and effort have been made by academic and school librarians to collaborate in ways that that will coordinate a K-16 development of information literacy skills.

The *Blueprint for Collaboration* document is representative of a joint effort by the Association of College and Research Libraries (ACRL) and the American Association of School Librarians (AASL). The document offers a framework to guide a more seamless transition of information literacy skills through the K-16 level. The document highlights the need for increased collaboration among the two groups of professionals, more interaction between the two professional associations, ongoing professional development, and increased outreach efforts. Examples of existing partnerships and a list of other organizations involved in building information literacy collaborations are provided in the appendix of the document.

A report that reflects a broader ecological perspective in considering academic libraries and their services is Megan Oakleaf's *Value of Academic Libraries: A Comprehensive Research Review and Report* (2010). In the report, Overleaf not only draws on the research of academic libraries to understand how best to understand and articulate the value of libraries, but reports on and makes connections to existing best practices in school, public, and special (e.g., corporate, medical, law) libraries. Oakleaf cites the importance of cultivating an awareness of developments in K-16 learning standards and assessment initiatives, and she cites the Common Core State Standards for College and Career Readiness (98) as being one tool for understanding the learning background of incoming college students. In suggesting steps to help create a positive role for libraries to play in bolstering student enrollment, Oakleaf outlines a concept of proactive services that are tailored to individual user needs.

AASL offers support for the Common College and Career Readiness Standards in a 2010 position statement and encourages school librarians to address the integration of the information literacy standards outlined in AASL's *Standards for the 21st Century Learner* and also take an active role in the process of implementation.

The beginning of the 21st century saw a concerted articulation across professional library communities to provide equitable access to all individuals. For example, the Library Services for People with Disabilities Policy was unanimously approved in 2001 by the American Library Council (ALC), the governing body of the American Library Association (ALA). The policy was written by the Americans with Disabilities Act (ADA) assembly, a representational group administered by the Association of Specialized and Cooperative Library Agencies (ASCLA), a division of the American Library Association. The Library Services for People with Disabilities Policy addresses key areas in equitable library access such as library services, facilities, collections, and assistive technologies. Ensuring equal access to library resources, programs, and services through a variety of strategies and modifications is at the heart of the policy.

The policy recognizes the significant range of challenges individuals with disabilities may face in terms of equal access to information, programs, resources, and services. The policy notes the "catalytic role" libraries play in the lives of individuals with disabilities. The policy explicitly states that the principles of universal design should be used by libraries to ensure that library policy, services, and resources are inclusive.

The policy also puts clear emphasis on collaborating with others as a viable strategy and notes collaborative relationships between the ALA and its various divisions and units as well as with other professional associations and community agencies, as a means to improve inclusion and accessibility. The belief in equitable access to books and reading, information, and information technology is also echoed throughout the AASL *Standards for the 21st Century Learner.*

INFLUENCES OF FEDERAL AND STATE MANDATES

The federal categories of disabilities are as follows: autism, deafness, deaf-blindness, emotional disturbance, hearing impairment, mental retardation, multiple disabilities, orthopedic impairment, other health impairment, specific learning disability, speech or language impairment, traumatic brain injury, visual impairment, and developmental delay. Increasing numbers of students with varying abilities transitioning to higher education coincides with changes in federal and state legislation as well as public policy initiatives for individuals with disabilities and advances in assistive and adaptive technologies. Federal laws such as the Americans with Disabilities Act (ADA) and Section 504 of the Rehabilitation Act of 1973 are intended to provide equitable access to facilities and services for individuals with disabilities.

Academic, public, and school library facilities fall under the reach of Section 504 in the Rehabilitation Act of 1973 and the ADA. Specific to schools is the Individuals with Disabilities Education Act (IDEA) (formerly called P.L. 94-142, or the Education for all Handicapped Children Act of 1975), which requires public schools to provide to all eligible children with disabilities a free appropriate public education (FAPE) in the least restrictive environment (LRE) appropriate to their individual needs. Both the intent and practices put in place because of IDEA have positively influenced how students with disabilities access and use libraries. In the reauthorizations of IDEA in 1997 and 2004, the requirement to include transition planning in the individualized education programs (IEPs), sometimes also called an individualized education plan, beginning at age 14 for students with disabilities was added. A student's transition outcomes might range from postsecondary education to vocational education to employment. It is important to note that although IDEA does not have a postsecondary application, the planning leading up to the transition requires collaborative partnerships and support.

DIFFERENCES AT THE POSTSECONDARY LEVEL

A particular distinction between disability services in secondary and postsecondary school experiences for youth with disabilities is that to receive accommodations or supports in postsecondary settings, students first must disclose or "self-identify" a disability to their school. The responsibility to self-identify, present valid documentation, and make formal requests for services is one key change young people in the move from high school to college do face. These processes are part of the 504 and ADA.

The National Longitudinal Transition Study-2 (NLTS-2) funded by the U.S. Department of Education provides an in-depth, national look at the experiences of secondary school students with disabilities as they go through their early adult years. The 10-year study collected data at five points, beginning in the 2000 to 2001 school year with study participants who ranged from 13 to 16 years old and received special education services in grade seven or above, under the Individuals with Disabilities Education Act (IDEA). Researchers found that within eight years of leaving high school, about 60 percent of the young adults with disabilities that were studied continued on to postsecondary education. Approximately 44 percent of these youth enrolled in community college; 32 percent in vocational, business, or technical schools; and about 19 percent at four-year colleges or universities (Newman et al. 2011, xv). Also of relevance for librarians in their own professional development and development of instructional strategies is the finding from this study that 60 percent of post-secondary students, previously identified by their secondary schools as having a disability, no longer considered themselves to have a disability. Only 28 percent of these students self-identified and made their post-secondary schools aware of their disability, and only 19 percent requested accommodations or supports (Newman et al. 2011). The numbers of students receiving supports in a postsecondary setting is starkly less than those receiving supports when they were in a high school setting.

Reports such as NLTS-2 provide librarians with a deeper understanding of the complexity of the makeup of incoming classes. Details on the changing landscape of student demographics can serve as a catalyst to refine and improve instructional strategies and services that differentiate and meet the needs of a variety of learners.

PEDAGOGICAL PRACTICES AND THE LIBRARY PROFESSIONAL

Society's shift toward more inclusionary thinking and practices involves both a change in mindset and in practices. In secondary educational settings, this shift is reflected by efforts to educate learners with exceptionalities alongside their peers and provide them with supports and services as needed. A school librarian, as part of an instructional team serving students, is eligible to review a student's Individualized Education Plan (IEP). An IEP offers important information about the type of disability and accommodation(s) deemed appropriate for a particular individual to achieve educational success. However, a surprising number of librarians report that they are unaware of their right and responsibility to access this document. Academic and public librarians who have no access to guiding documents such as IEPs, or in many cases, even the knowledge that a particular student has a disability, often find themselves in an information vacuum and must devise other strategies.

Developing a proficiency in instructional strategies that address the various learning styles of students is one approach any type of librarian can use. Currently, few librarians—even school librarians—leave their graduate programs with a solid grounding in educational pedagogy. Nationally, there is talk of integrating the topic of pedagogy into the curriculum of library and information schools; however, it is not yet a widespread occurrence. Professional associations such as ALA and AASL are raising the bar on awareness of the librarian's need for pedagogical skills and many offer a

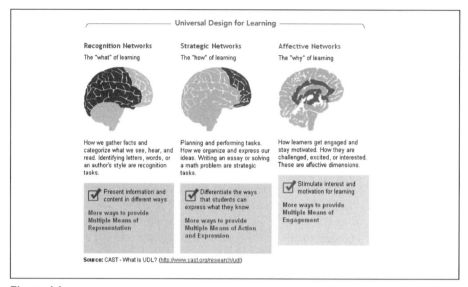

Figure 4.1.
Center for Applied Special Technology (CAST): What is Universal Design for Learning (UDL)?

range of professional development opportunities. New best practices continuously emerge. Our understanding of cognition changes. Resources and technologies develop and improve. Teaching and learning are truly dynamic processes. Librarians must make it a priority to develop and continuously refine their instructional skills. Understanding and using the principles of Universal Design for Learning (UDL) is one place to start.

UNIVERSAL DESIGN FOR LEARNING: A TOOL TO REACH ALL LIBRARY USERS

All students learn differently and bring with them a wide range of interests, needs, and skills. Universal Design for Learning (UDL) offers a flexible framework for librarians across the continuum to use in creating instructional goals, methods, and materials that can be tailored for individual needs (Rose and Meyer 2002). UDL is intended to give all individuals an equal opportunity to learn.

Three primary principles guide the development of curriculum that is accessible to all learners: (1) provide multiple means of representation, (2) provide multiple means of action and expression, and (3) provide multiple means of engagement (CAST 2011). These principles are based upon neuroscience research and help educators create curricula to meet the needs of all learners. Three primary brain networks are considered in the UDL framework. Figure 4.1 outlines the three networks and connects them to the UDL principles.

Table 4.1 is a detailed overview of the UDL guidelines. The guidelines expand on the three principles of recognition, strategy, and affectivity to provide assistance to librarians in planning information literacy curriculum, including identifying goals, methods, materials, and assessments that reduce barriers and increase support for all learners to be successful. The guidelines help librarians evaluate existing curriculum in terms of existing barriers (CAST 2011).

Table 4.1.

Universal Design for Learning Guidelines for Developing an Accessible Curriculum

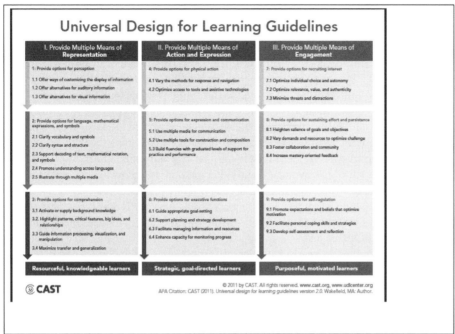

Educator-friendly examples and resources related to the implementation of the UDL guidelines and check points are offered at the National Center on Universal Design for Learning (NCUDL) web site (see the "Starting Points for Professional Learning" section at the end of this chapter). Exploring these examples and resources not only helps to clarify what is meant by each of the checkpoints, but also gives educators tangible ideas of ways to implement UDL in their classrooms and libraries so as to better meet the needs of all students.

PROFESSIONAL DEVELOPMENT

The Common Core Standards Initiative (2011) is a national K-12 framework of curriculum standards intended to prepare students for college and careers. It provides educators, parents, and students with a mutual understanding of what is to be learned and offers benchmarks for learning to assist all students. The standards recognize that specific supports and services tailored to the needs of students with disabilities are necessary for them to access the general curriculum and that they should be based on the principles of UDL. Instructional accommodations as well as assistive technology devices and services are noted as key tools to provide access and improving student success within the framework of the standards.

This Common Core Standards Initiative, along with the changing student demographics, represents a significant influence on the professional lives of librarians. An essential question for the library and information profession is how best to educate current and future librarians and foster within them the knowledge and skills necessary to serve a diverse student population. The *Library Services for People with Disabilities Policy* addresses the need for all graduate programs in library and information studies to require students to learn about accessibility issues, assistive technology, and the needs of people with disabilities both as users and employees. Graduate students should understand the crucial role libraries play as a resource to some individuals with disabilities. Students and practitioners need to be aware of the laws applicable to the rights of people with disabilities as they impact library services (American Disabilities Act Assembly 2001). The policy also states that libraries have a responsibility to offer their employees and volunteers training related to disability awareness and appropriate services. It is vital to create awareness of free accessibility features that are built into most computers, and certainly newer computers, which can support learning for students with disabilities. Even most online databases offer many features to make their content more accessible. Assistive technologies go far beyond wheelchairs and products beyond of the reach of the average library. Personal mobile devices are creating new vistas in individuals' access to information, and many low-cost and free accessibility options are available to be used with them. Increasingly, different types of assistive technologies that address the needs of students with high-incidence disabilities are readily available for free and at low cost.

Establishing a mission and tone for inclusion and advocacy by professional associations is a vital step. With the profession in flux, we need to draw from a wide range of resources to foster professional growth and change. Ongoing professional development is needed to build the capacity of all librarians who are naturally part of the transition process of young adults.

Professional development should foster in librarians the knowledge and skills to:

- Strive to continuously increase the knowledge and skills needed to meet the learning needs of all students.
- Be a model for using people-first language.
- Understand the categories of disabilities and relevant vocabulary and concepts.
- Develop a shared framework and focus among stakeholders of what is involved in the transition process for young adults with disabilities. This involves creating awareness and understanding of different types of disabilities within the context that each person is unique.
- Serve as a boundary spanner and seek out peers in other organizations and institutions that play a role in the transition process. Learn about areas of need, areas of strength, and resources to be shared.

STARTING POINTS FOR PROFESSIONAL LEARNING

American Library Association, the American Association of School Librarians (AASL)
(http://www.ala.org/aasl/)
Professional development opportunities include conferences and workshops and well as continuing education opportunities. The organization also serves as an advocate for the profession and provides extensive advocacy resources for school librarians to use in their own schools.

Association of College and Research Libraries (ACRL)
(http://www.ala.org/acrl/)
Offers resources and professional development opportunities focused on learning, teaching, and researching in higher education. Professional development opportunities include conferences, workshops, webinars, articles, and a mentoring program. Refer to the "Get Involved

with ACRL" section of the web site for a more extensive list of professional development opportunities.

Center for Applied Special Technology (CAST)
(http://www.cast.org/)
Professional development opportunities through CAST include online learning and training, on-site consultations and programs, and summer institute programs.

Council for Exceptional Children (CEC)
(www.cec.sped.org)
The CEC is a professional association dedicated to improving educational opportunities for students with disabilities. Its web site offers a range of resources and professional development tools to increase knowledge and awareness about different disabilities and specific strategies and resources to use to meet students' instructional needs. Nonmembers can also use many resources at the site. Professional standards and guidelines are also highlighted.

National Center for Universal Design for Learning (NCUDL)
(http://www.udlcenter.org/)
The UDL Center, a part of CAST, is focused on providing resources and training for educators and information professionals to effectively incorporate the Universal Design for Learning ideas and guidelines into their curriculum. Online professional development opportunities are available on their web site and include online modules, examples, and toolkits.

National Center on Secondary Education and Transition (NCSET)
(http://www.ncset.org/)
The NCSET site provides resources and assistance concerning transition services for youth with disabilities. Professional development opportunities include conferences, workshops, and webinars for educators on awareness, inclusion, planning, and transition services.

National Dissemination Center for Children with Disabilities (NICHCY)
(http://nichcy.org/)
NICHCY focuses on providing information and resources related to children with disabilities of all ages. Resources provided endeavor to clarify national laws and standards as they apply to the classroom, as well as a listing of state-specific resources and organizations.

Public Library Association (PLA)
(http://www.ala.org/pla/)
The PLA offers resources and educational opportunities for professionals in public libraries. Online resource highlights include tips on dealing with current issues public libraries are facing as well as advocacy resources and toolkits. Professional development opportunities include conferences, workshops, interest committees, and online learning opportunities in the form of webinars, workbooks and virtual conferences.

BIBLIOGRAPHY

American Association of School Libraries (AASL) and Association of College & Research Libraries (ACRL) Task Force on the Educational Role of Libraries. *Blueprint for Collaboration*. Chicago: Association of College and Research Libraries, 2000.

American Library Association (ALA). *AASL Standards for the 21st Century Learner*. Chicago: American Association of School Librarians, 2008.

Americans with Disabilities Act (ADA) Assembly. *Library Services for People with Disabilities Policy.* Chicago: American Library Association, 2001.

Benz, Michael R., Lauren E. Lindstrom, and Andrew S. Halpern. "Mobilizing Local Communities to Improve Transition Services." *Career Development for Exceptional Individuals* 18, no.1 (1995): 21–32.

Center for Applied Special Technology (CAST). *Universal Design for Learning Guidelines, Version 2.0.* Wakefield, MA: Author, 2011.

Nardi, Bonnie, and Vicki O'Day, *Information Ecologies: Using Technology with Heart.* Cambridge, MA: Massachusetts Institute of Technology (MIT) Press, 1999.

National Governors Association Center for Best Practices (NGA Center) and the Council of Chief State School Officers (CCSSO). "Common Core State Standards Initiative," (2009). http://www.corestandards.org (accessed October 23, 2012).

Newman, Lynn, Mary Wagner, Anne-Marie Knokey, Camille Marder, Katherine Nagle, Debra Shaver, and Xin Wei. *The Post-High School Outcomes of Young Adults with Disabilities up to 8 Years after High School: A Report from the National Longitudinal Transition Study-2 (NLTS2)*, September 2011. http://ies.ed.gov/ncser/pubs/20113005/pdf/20113005.pdf (accessed October 24, 2012).

Oakleaf, Megan. *Value of Academic Libraries: A Comprehensive Research Review and Report.* Chicago: Association of College and Research Libraries, 2010.

Rose, David H., and Anne Meyer. *Teaching Every Student in the Digital Age: Universal Design for Learning.* Alexandria, VA: Association for Supervision and Curriculum Development (ASCD), 2002.

Zhang, Dalun, Joy G. Ivester, Li-Ju Chen, and Antonis Katsiyannis. "Perspectives on Transition Practices." *Career Development for Exceptional Individuals* 28 (2005): 15–25.

Section II: Conversations and Collaborations

5

College Readiness at the Grassroots Level

Ken W. Stewart and Laurie Hathman

It began in line at the coffee kiosk at American Librarian Association (ALA) annual conference in Washington, D.C. in June 2010. A school librarian was talking with an academic librarian, and the conversation turned to communication between high schools and colleges and universities. As the high school librarian walked away, he wondered, "Why couldn't I just invite some people over to talk?" When he returned from the conference, he met with his principal about the idea. "This fits right in with our college readiness initiative we're beginning this year," the principal said. Permission was granted, and a date was established. The school librarian then went to a mentor of his who happened to be the library director of a nearby university. She readily agreed to cohost, and the school librarian happily went back to see his principal. "I've got a cohost for our college readiness dialogue," he said, "and I'm going to invite a few more people."

The recognition of a gap in preparation for higher education is not new to librarians, but how to initially address this issue was the challenge. Without knowing what the experience was for students in the formative middle and high school years, when communication arts and social sciences were a significant part of their curriculum, it would be difficult for academics to make changes in existing information literacy programs or courses for incoming freshmen. It is typical for many academic libraries to work with high schools seniors enrolled in advance college credit courses, more commonly in English composition. Since the assignments for these types of courses were identical or, at the minimum, closely followed the same curriculum of freshmen English composition courses, it was not clear if these assignments were typical of what high school seniors would experience in the traditional high school communication arts course, which included composition. It seemed apparent that to identify the gaps in competency development, deeper conversation would need to take place between secondary and postsecondary educators. Cohosting an event such as this would give the academic librarians direct access to high school educators, including those not involved in advanced college credit programs. When the opportunity arrived to join forces in this venue, it was a natural match.

Academic librarians routinely experience incoming freshmen not prepared with what would be considered basic information literacy skills. Several years ago, two of the American Library Association's (ALA) divisions, the American Association of School Librarians (AASL) and the Association of College and Research Libraries (ACRL), individually established what are considered desired information literacy outcomes for both high school and college graduates to prepare them to be lifelong learners in both their personal and professional lives. The AASL's *Standards for The 21st-Century Learner in Action* states that students "Inquire, think critically and gain knowledge; Draw conclusions, make informed decisions, apply knowledge to new situations, and create new knowledge; Share knowledge and participate ethically and productively as members of our democratic society; and Pursue personal and aesthetic growth" (2009, 12–39). The ACRL information literacy competency standards (2000) state that students should be able to identify the need for information, access information effectively, evaluate information and its sources, effectively use information for a purpose, and understand the legal and ethical issues associated with information. While recognizing that there are competency outcomes shared by AASL and ACRL, secondary and academic librarians felt that there was common ground to explore collaboration.

COLLEGE READINESS DIALOGUE I

The first College Readiness Dialogue, held on October 15, 2010, was planned specifically to be an opportunity for face-to-face discussion between high school and academic educators, rather than a planned program typical of conferences. Ken Stewart, school librarian at Blue Valley High School (BVHS) in Stilwell, Kansas, and Laurie Hathman, library director at Rockhurst University in Kansas City, Missouri, organized the free-to-attend event. The metropolitan Kansas City area includes cities and counties in both Missouri and Kansas, so it seemed likely there was a large audience in the region that could attend. The event, which hosted over 90 librarians, classroom teachers, and administrators from 60 schools, districts, and organizations as well as 12 colleges and universities, drew professionals from public, private, and alternative schools in both Kansas and Missouri. The dialogue was purposely scheduled to be held on the afternoon of a staff development day for the Blue Valley school district so that teachers and administrators could attend.

As the program was developed, the cohosts of the event wanted to know what kind of questions or preconceived ideas those attending the event might have. It was important that the attendees be able to continue to share information and make contact after the event in order to continue the dialogue begun on that day. It was decided to build a College Readiness Dialogue wiki for the event and allow others to sign up and share information on the wiki after advertising it at the event. SurveyMonkey, online survey software, was utilized to create registration and evaluation forms. The questions and concerns gathered before the event identified key themes for the small group discussions. A school improvement specialist at the district level was utilized to create a matrix that would allow the registrants to break into small groups (see figure 5.1) and then rotate so that each group had the opportunity to meet with academic librarians from a variety of higher education institutions, (public, private, four-year, and

Figure 5.1.
A Small Group Discussion at the First College Readiness Dialogue Held on October 15, 2010 at Blue Valley High School in Stilwell, Kansas.

community colleges) while at the same time meet new secondary educators and librarians in each setting.

Each group had a recorder so that comments could be gathered, and the last session of the afternoon brought all participants back together to share these comments.

Many of the initial discussions focused on areas such as the mechanics of writing research papers, presentation styles, and the location and evaluation of source materials. How were secondary school librarians instructing students about sources of information and their appropriateness for research? How were academic librarians orientating incoming freshmen as to required literacy skills for higher education?

Three predominant lessons were learned from this event. First, few secondary school librarians have direct access to the students for teaching information literacy skills. Unless they are collaborating with the teacher on a specific unit, these skills are not incorporated into the curriculum. Second, filtering persists in schools. For the academic librarians, this was a key point in understanding the challenges high school educators face by not having open access to the Internet in their classrooms. Often, permission had to be granted from the information technology (IT) personnel at the administrative level to allow access to specific web sites needed during instruction. Obtaining access to these sites often took days, eliminating the "aha" moment of evaluation that often takes place during a lesson. Teachers had to plan well in advance. Internet filtering has, at times, proved detrimental to the development of critical thinking skills, a desired outcome of web site evaluation. Third, not all colleges and universities (including two-year institutions) offer incoming freshmen research orientation classes. Secondary school librarians wondered if orientation classes were not offered, where would freshmen receive the specifics on research in their individual disciplines? The academic librarians shared the variety of methods used by institutions of higher education to foster information literacy development, such as course embedded instruction, first-year experience courses, for-credit courses, course management software, and tools such as *LibGuides*.

It was evident from this event that participants wanted additional opportunities for collaborative experiences and discussion. Evaluations were gathered, assessed, and discussed by the event's cohosts. At that time, planning for a future dialogue began.

COLLEGE READINESS PANELS

In January 2011, a follow-up event took place during which academic librarians from four institutions formed a panel that met with all of the communication arts and social sciences teachers from the Blue Valley school district at the middle and high school levels, as well as with invited district office personnel. This initial grouping, requested by district office personnel who had attended the prior dialogue, was comprised of the departments with whom school librarians most often and most closely interact. Initially, the discussion was approached from two often diverse angles: (1) the basic mechanics of citation styles used for research in colleges and universities and (2) the skills necessary to evaluate relevant information from a variety of formats such as books, periodical articles, and web sites. Library anxiety on both levels was identified as a common experience for both secondary students and incoming freshman. Strategies for mitigating this anxiety were shared. Outcomes from this dialogue included future site visits to regional schools by the academic librarians (both with individual classes and departments) and the purchase of *EasyBib* (an online subscription service for formatting both citations and research strategies) by BVHS. Before this purchase, the agreed-upon format for all papers in the building was that of the Modern Language Association (MLA), and a significant amount of library instruction time consisted of the mechanics of formatting research papers. After the initial dialogue, the Social Science and Science departments opted to change to APA (American Psychological Association) formatting to more closely work with those formats required on the postsecondary level. Formatting instruction was still provided, but the purchase of *EasyBib* allowed the instruction time to be more closely focused on research content. Students were now becoming more aware of the different styles required at colleges and universities. Although they had been introduced to various formatting styles during prior instruction, they now were putting them into practice with understanding.

An overall increased interest in the subject of college readiness became apparent to the authors as their proposals to speak on this topic were repeatedly selected for state, regional and national conferences. This interest became more apparent over the summer. In September 2011, when the new school year began, a panel discussion was held for the entire senior class at BVHS for one period during the school day. A college panel was formed consisting of academic librarians from four area colleges and universities. Two days prior, the seniors were prepared with a worst-case scenario dealing with last-minute research at the postsecondary level. The panel presented to the seniors and followed up with a question and answer period. Ken Stewart returned to the senior English classes the next day and presented them with a survey form. They kept the form and were instructed to self-evaluate their papers and projects throughout the semester after they were submitted to their teachers. The forms would be gathered at the end of

November; their anonymous comments would consist of items that they felt needed additional time or information (e.g., evaluation of web sites, formatting papers, presenting to a group). Depending on their responses, the library would begin to offer morning seminars called Senior Chat & Chew. Interested seniors would come to the library at 7:00 a.m., 45 minutes before classes began. Bringing their breakfast with them, the seniors, the librarian, and any other interested educators would have breakfast while being entertained with presentations on a variety of subjects that were designated by the seniors on the survey. Some sessions, such as presentation skills, evaluating web sites, and the differences between APA, MLA, and Chicago-Turabian had already been scheduled. Based on current remarks from students, more sessions would follow. At BVHS, the transition from school librarian–driven college readiness to student-driven readiness has started. This move has proven positive thus far.

COLLEGE READINESS DIALOGUE II

In the spring of 2011, more focused planning began for the next College Readiness Dialogue to be held the following fall. Results from the evaluations submitted after the initial event indicated the need to broaden the scope of the dialogue. Participants wanted more discussion, more variety, and more networking time. The next event had to be a full-day affair.

On November 12, 2011, the second College Readiness Dialogue took place. This event was also free to attend thanks to contributions from the Blue Valley school district, BVHS, and Rockhurst University. The day began with two Skype sessions. The first was with Carl Harvey, the school librarian at North Elementary School in Noblesville, Indiana. A published author and current president of AASL, Harvey began the day with views on college readiness at the national level and its relationship with the new Common Core elements that are currently being adopted by many state educational departments. The second session featured Lynda Duke, the academic outreach librarian at Illinois Wesleyan University's Ames Library in Bloomington, Illinois. Duke has most recently coedited with Andrew D. Asher a new book entitled *College Libraries and Student Culture: What We Now Know.*

Duke led an active discussion on student use of college libraries (see Figure 5.2). During the discussion, it became apparent that others areas of the country were also deeply concerned about the need for college readiness skills instruction at the secondary level. Incoming college and university freshmen continue to have problems with the mechanical aspects of research in source location, evaluation, and formatting. These types of problems are not specific to any one geographic area; they seem to be common across our nation. The second part of the day consisted of a free-float period where attendees moved independently between three classrooms, the library, and the commons area where discussions were either discipline focused (communication arts, social studies, science) or used for professional networking. A bring-your-own-lunch period continued the discussion with various table topics, which were shared at the end of the day. The third session was a presentation by three area public library systems on their outreach programs to high school and college students with heavy emphasis on the research databases and tutoring that the staff provides. The day concluded with a discussion on assessment and best practices, followed by sharing experiences of the day's events.

Participants in the latest event have begun to take ownership of this grassroots effort in the development of future collaborative opportunities. These will include a library

Figure 5.2.
Participants Speaking with Lynda Duke, Academic Outreach Librarian at Illinois
Wesleyan University.

camp "unconference" around the theme of college readiness; use of the wiki for sharing
resources and ideas among school, academic and public librarians; as well as outreach
to academic faculty in the areas of communication arts, social sciences, and the sciences. Academic, school, and public librarians identified ways to further collaborate
in order to close the circle for supporting student information literacy skill development. Additional school visits by the academic and public librarians will provide an
opportunity to share resources from their collections, which could be accessed at school
or at home. Likewise, academic and public librarians welcomed school librarians and
teachers to bring their students to visit their campuses and libraries for an introduction
to resources unique to academic and public library collections. These visits can have
the additional benefit of allowing students to start to develop personal relationships
with academic and public librarians as research experts. For college readiness, this also
may result in reducing the library anxiety often experienced by incoming freshmen.

BIBLIOGRAPHY

American Association of School Librarians (AASL) Learning Standards Rewrite Task
    Force (2006–2007) and AASL Learning Standards Indicators and Assessment Task Force
    (2007–2008). *Standards for the 21st-Century Learner in Action.* Chicago: American
    Association of School Librarians, 2009.

Association of College & Research Libraries (ACRL). "AASL/ACRL Interdivisional Committee on Information Literacy." American Library Association. http://www.ala.org/ acrl/ aboutacrl/directoryofleadership/committees/aas-ilc (accessed February 28, 2012).

Association of College and Research Libraries (ACRL). *Information Literacy Competency Standards for Higher Education*. Chicago: American Library Association, 2000.

Duke, Lynda M., and Andrew D. Asher, eds. *College Libraries and Student Culture: What We Now Know*. Chicago: American Library Association, 2012.

Hathman, Laurie, and Ken Stewart. "College Readiness Dialogue Wiki." CollegeHighSchoolLibrarians, College Readiness Dialogue Wiki. September 1, 2010. http://collegehighschool librarians.pbworks.com/w/page/30847868/College_Readiness_Dialogue_Wiki (accessed October 24, 2011).

Stewart, Ken W., and Laurie Hathman. College Readiness Dialogues Kansas City. October 31, 2012. http://bvhlearningcommons.bluevalleyk12.org/collegereadinessdialogues (accessed November 01, 2012).

6

Go Further: The College and Career Readiness INFOhio OhioLINK P20 Task Force

Paula Nespeca Deal

This chapter shares the work of the joint College and Career Readiness INFOhio OhioLINK P20 Task Force in Ohio. Comprised of librarians from K-12 and higher education, the task force has been a powerful and persuasive advocate for libraries collaborating across the educational continuum to ensure student success. Beginning with the creation of a white paper and action plan, task force activities have opened dialogues, provided professional development resources, and provided learning tools for teachers and students.

BACKGROUND AND HISTORY

Ohio has a strong tradition of library system collaboration and coordination. Emblematic of this is Libraries Connect Ohio (LCO), a consortium of consortiums that has helped the state coordinate strategy across all its major library systems. LCO is comprised of INFOhio, the Information Network for Ohio schools; OhioLINK, the Ohio Library and Information Network (serving higher education); OPLIN, Ohio Public Library Information Network; and the State Library of Ohio. Working together, the consortia have ensured that Ohio students have a continuity of resources and a seamless means of locating and using research journals. The continuity provided by having students access the same product from kindergarten through graduate school provides a comfort level as students change buildings and advance to higher level work.

Through the vision and leadership of INFOhio's executive director Theresa Fredericka and OhioLINK's former executive director Tom Sanville, the 12-13 Transition Task Force was born in 2007. These leaders wanted this new group to tackle a formidable challenge—find ways to encourage and advance collaboration between school librarians and academic librarians in order to better prepare students for the rigors of college-level work. The task force's work would be in direct response to recent state developments, including the adoption of the Common Core State Standards and the push for career to college readiness for all students. Their work would also leverage the importance of information literacy and 21st-century skills as well as the tools needed for teaching and assessing these skills that are so critical to student success. Originally named the 12-13 Transition Task Force or the Go Further Task Force, the group rebranded itself in 2012 as College and Career Readiness INFOhio OhioLINK P20 Task Force

The call to join this new task force went out in mid-2007. INFOhio targeted two groups of librarians. First, invitations were sent to high school librarians who were already actively preparing their students for college-level research and teaching information literacy skills. Second, the call went out to academic librarians who had worked with high school librarians, who were designated as first-year experience librarians, or provided research skill training to students and preservice teachers. In addition, other interested nonschool or academics were approached and readily accepted. A glance at the current transition Task Force roster will give an idea of the scope, breadth, and experience of the committee: http://www.infohio.org/PreparingOhioLearners/TaskForceRoster.html. It also reflects the current emphasis on pre-kindergarten (pre-K) through higher education, which dovetails with the Ohio Department of Education's "Career and College Readiness" emphasis as reflected in the Ohio Revised Academic Content Standards and Model Curriculum. These revisions bring Ohio content standards into alignment with the Common Core State Standards (http://www.corestandards.org/the-standards) and the Partnership for Assessment of Readiness for College and Careers (http://www.parcconline.org), to which Ohio belongs.

The task force's project has come to be been known by several names, including the Transition Task Force, the Go Further Task Force, (the Go Further title being used on the INFOhio webpages) or more commonly the 12-13 Task Force. Most recently, it has been called the PreK-20 Initiative. Then in 2012, in light of the adoption of the Common Core Standards and other career-college readiness initiatives in Ohio, the task force was formally renamed the College and Career Readiness INFOhio OhioLINK P20 Task Force.

From the beginning, the task force has been action oriented. The group began its work by creating a foundation document, a joint white paper of INFOhio and OhioLINK, that could be used to set goals and action items for the committee and provide background and groundwork necessary when approaching influential stake holders. Released in September 2008, the original white paper included a review of the literature as well as a discussion of the importance of information literacy and 21st-century learning skills to college success. Most importantly, the report provided an explanation of the task force's mission not just for fellow librarians, but also for teachers and professors, school administrators, deans, boards of education, parents, and legislators (INFOhio and OhioLINK 2008, 3).

From the introduction to the white paper, the determination of the task force to make a difference is apparent:

In order to be successful in school, college, and the workforce, Ohio's 21st century students must be equipped with the necessary skills to explore and exploit new information. Students must be able to: identify what information they need to be successful in life and work, know how to find information efficiently, evaluate the quality of information, and use information effectively and ethically.

Ohio's school and academic librarians already work within their individual organizations to prepare young people for an information-intensive world and are uniquely positioned to influence student success. INFOhio, the PreK-12 school library information network, and OhioLINK, the academic library network, currently support teaching and learning by providing quality information that serves student needs across PreK-20. However, an even greater effort to teach students to use these resources effectively must be coordinated if Ohio is to return to its place as an economically competitive giant in the global marketplace.

State decision makers need to ensure that all Ohio students, regardless of economic means or geographic location, have access to a robust, high quality information infrastructure that prepares students to be astute and productive consumers of information. To properly prepare Ohio's students for success in college and to grow and maintain a strong 21st century workforce, Ohio must mandate that information literacy is a critical lifelong skill that every Ohio student needs. As the first step toward that future, INFOhio and OhioLINK urge the Ohio Department of Education and Board of Regents to endorse the six goals identified in this report. (INFOhio 2008, 8)

Most importantly, the white paper urged the Ohio Department of Education and Ohio Board of Regents to endorse the six identified goals and provided action steps to accomplish the goals. Called *Goals Ensuring Ohio's Information Literate Future* (INFOhio 2008, 7), they are:

1. **Development of 21st century skills:** Teach all Ohio high school students the 21st-century information literacy skills needed for transition from high school to college and into the world of work.
2. **Incorporate research experiences:** Incorporate robust research experiences into classroom teaching strategies to better prepare Ohio's juniors and seniors for college-level research.
3. **Deliver research resources:** Provide students and educators with free and equitable access to an essential academic core collection of online and physical library materials appropriate to PreK-20 research.
4. **Prepare student teachers:** Inform Ohio's education faculty that the preparation of student teachers must include 21st-century information literacy skills and how collaboration with school librarians can contribute to these instructional objectives.
5. **Partner with groups statewide:** Partner with state initiatives and advocacy groups to encourage them to incorporate information literacy skills within their own goals.
6. **Enable collaboration:** Provide school and academic librarians with opportunities to work together to develop collaborations supporting the transition of secondary school students to college-level research.

TOOLS FOR SUCCESS: HELPING TODAY'S STUDENTS AND TOMORROW'S TEACHERS

A myriad of accomplishments have sprung from the task force white paper and action steps. In the past four years, task force members have given numerous presentations discussing the white paper and sharing the successful collaborations and resources available through the INFOhio web site. Some venues for sharing and discussing the task force's work have included the American Library Association's annual conference (Chicago 2010), the Harrisburg Area Community College (HACC) Information Literacy Symposium (Harrisburg, PA 2009), the Association of College and Research Libraries Conference (2007), the Library Orientation Exchange (LOEX) National

Conference (2006), and numerous state conferences, including the Ohio Educational Library Media Association (OELMA), Academic Library Association of Ohio (ALAO), Ohio eTech (Technology), and Libraries, Learning and Technology (LLT) conferences.

"GO FURTHER, PREPARING OHIO LEARNERS" WEB SITE AND BROCHURE

Perhaps the task force's most visible accomplishments are displayed on the INFOhio web site. In the second year of the task force, the Go Further, Preparing Ohio Learners pages were constructed and went live. To raise awareness, the site (hosted by INFOhio) provides an overview of resources that can aid students, librarians, and teachers: http://www.infohio.org/PreparingOhioLearners.html. Among the resources provided are those that INFOhio provides to students and their parents to ensure that all students within the state have access to appropriate databases. In addition to receiving help with completing homework assignments and devising research topics for projects and papers, students can now improve their skills related to state and college-level testing, for example, SAT, ACT and Advanced Placement (AP) exams.

Thanks to assistance from EBSCOhost, the task force created and disseminated a summary brochure about the initiative. EBSCO graciously provided graphic arts and printing services. Titled INFOhio's Go Further!—Road to Career and College Readiness campaign, the brochure is a handy summary of the rationale and goals of the task force while identifying resources and case studies (called success stories) to help K-12 librarians promote college and career readiness (INFOhio 2011, 2). The brochure is available online: http://www.infohio.org/PreparingOhioLearners/GoFurther201101.pdf.

The task force has fostered other means of communication and collaboration. A new listserv, sponsored by INFOhio, was established specifically for those interested in discussing all types of information literacy, including media literacy. In 2011, this list was incorporated into the general INFOhio elist. Also, task force members became involved with the Ohio P21 movement as reflected in the goals and activities of the national organization Partnership for 21st Century Skills (www.p21), which advocates for 21st-century readiness for every student. One of the most promising tools is the Knowledge Building Community area of the INFOhio 21st Century Learning Commons (learningcommons.infohio.org), which encourages educators to discuss topics of interest and make this social networking site part of one's personal learning network.

TOOLS FOR SUCCESS

The task force is currently working on providing resources to support the educational continuum, from kindergarten through the first years of college, with the goal of helping prepare 21st-century Ohio learners for success. The INFOhio web site links to tools for student and teacher success. The following are some of the most important resources.

Electronic Resource Databases

These resources (http://www.infohio.org/ER/ERcore.asp), which are specifically designed for academic and other postsecondary school research, are available to all Ohio students. These paid premium databases, which are password protected, are known as the INFOhio Core Collection, a useful suite of reference sources that are curriculum-based and appropriate for learner needs. The collection is funded in part by a Museum and Library Services Library Services and Technology Act (LSTA) grant awarded by the State Library of Ohio to INFOhio, OhioLINK, and OPLIN, providing online resources to the three library networks. Students becoming proficient in the uses of the INFOhio databases will transfer those skills when accessing the premium databases at other academic and public libraries.

21st Century Learning Commons

This learning commons (http://learningcommons.infohio.org) provides an online, interactive site for educators, including preservice teachers, to understand how learning has changed, adapt teaching to inspire students to think critically, solve problems, collaborate, innovate, and create. The 21st Century Learning Commons is unique nationally in that it was created and then supported by a state library network. It includes 21 Essential Things for 21st Century Learning, self-paced, interactive online modules for teachers to learn 21st-century skills. The Knowledge Building Community, an area of the 21st Century Learning Commons, provides teachers and school librarians with a professional social network that is not usually blocked by Internet filters, to discuss issues pertaining to information literacy, research, 21st-century learning, and libraries. This piece of teachers' personal learning network features posts, blogs, and sharing of information in the form of links, videos, photos, and documents.

LearningExpress Library

This resource, part of the INFOhio Core Collection, contains more than 100 programs to learn about as well as practice and prepare for tests on a variety of subjects, including college entrance exams. It includes the Job & Career Accelerator for researching careers and job-hunting. This service is funded by the LSTA grant and is also a password-protected premium database.

Research Project Calculator (RPC)

Based on the student's type of assignment (research paper, presentation or video) and due date, the RPC (http://www2.infohio.org/rpc) provides a step by step plan for completing the research process on time. The plan includes key questions, establishes suggested milestones and points out helpful resources. The RPC is a free interactive online tool that provides a research process model for students and curriculum along with lesson plan help for teachers who are instructing on the research process from fourth grade and higher. Teachers can access the accompanying materials, which include useful handouts and lessons. Originally designed by the University of Minnesota Libraries, which generously gave permission for INFOhio to use and revise the calculator, the RPC takes the mystery out of research (University of Minnesota Libraries 2012).

Tool for Real-Time Assessment of Information Literacy Skills (TRAILS)

TRAILS (http://trails-9.org), developed at Kent (Ohio) State University Libraries, is an online student knowledge assessment with multiple-choice questions targeting a variety of information literacy skills for grades 3, 6, 9, and 12. Initial support for

TRAILS was provided through the University Libraries' grant partnership with the Institute for Library and Information Literacy Education (ILILE), which was a federally funded initiative of the Institute of Museum and Library Services (IMLS) and the U.S. Department of Education. TRAILS provides teachers and librarians a formative assessment tool so often missing from the teaching of information literacy. Results can be used to make data-driven decisions about what skills are taught and how.

Transitioning to College (T2C)

T2C (http://transitioning2college.org), another web site supported by Kent State University, provides a multitude of ways for students to learn more about Ohio college libraries and college research skills, including five learning modules, engaging videos about the libraries, and other helpful resources. Designed for college freshmen, it is an appealing introduction to college libraries for high school students as well.

CASE STUDIES IN COLLEGE AND CAREER READINESS

One of the most exciting results of the task force's action plan is the many high school and college collaborations that were either fostered or highlighted through the group's goals and activities. With the encouragement of the Go Further initiative, many Ohio high school librarians and classroom teachers are working with nearby college and university colleagues to create exciting and valuable opportunities to help students make and effective transition from the K-12 environment to postsecondary experiences.

Some of these success stories are shared on the INFOhio web site as "Success Stories in College and Career Readiness" (www.infohio.org/PreparingOhioLearners/TransitionStudies.html). The page collects examples of collaborations around the state, telling how urban, suburban, and rural high school students visited (in person or virtually) private and public college libraries. College librarians shared the experience of college-level research and many times, high school students were given the privilege of using college library resources. Students got a real taste of reality, often marveling at the vastness of a large college library. Teachers too were part of the collaboration, working with their building librarians on ways to help their students understand how to carry out college-level research assignments.

One collaboration in particular epitomized the mission of the task force. At Southern State Community College (Hillsboro, Ohio), Louis Mays, professor and librarian, encourages various high schools to take part in a program that gives their students access to college and library resources without leaving the confines of their own school. Via videoconference, students are guided through OhioLINK research databases. "Our high school students have valuable exposure to the technology . . . This will allow them a successful transition to college," remarks Laurel Marion, media specialist at Zane Trace High School in the Zane Trace (Ohio) local schools (INFOhio 2011).

About her high school class visits to Cleveland State University, high school librarian Joanna McNally said, "This opportunity introduces students to the same resources they will use if they attend any Ohio college or university . . . We believe this experience will assist the students in successfully transitioning to college. That's where my expertise as a licensed school librarian comes in. The INFOhio research databases offer a good starting point to find reliable information" (INFOhio 2011).

In 2010 the Task Force consolidated its goals and concentrated its focus on four areas: students, teachers, resources, and partnerships. These four goals were most likely to be realized based on the resources of the committee, the members, INFOhio, and OhioLINK:

1. **Focus on students: developing 21st century skills:** Teach all Ohio high school students the 21st century information literacy skills needed for transition from high school to college and into the world of work.
2. **Focus on teachers: incorporating research experiences:** Provide professional development that helps create and provide opportunities and collaborations for pre-service and service teachers that incorporate robust research experiences into classroom teaching strategies to better prepare Ohio's juniors and seniors for college-level research while promoting those opportunities to education faculty and state teacher organizations and school districts.
3. **Focus on resources: delivering research resources:** Provide students and educators with free and equitable access to an essential academic core collection of online and physical library materials appropriate to preK-20 research
4. **Focus on partnerships: enhancing partnerships and collaborations statewide:** Collaborations of statewide, regional and local K12 and higher education and advocacy groups will continue to work toward student high school and college success through 21st-century information literacy skills (INFOhio 2011, 2).

WHAT NEXT? FUTURE PROJECTS

What is next for the College and Career Readiness INFOhio OhioLINK P20 Task Force? More of the same practical, proven ways of helping our students gain the skills they need to succeed in high school and higher education. In the spring of 2012, the task force began planning for the 2012–2013 school year. The first step included the process of rebranding the initiative to more accurately reflect Ohio's preK-12 college and career readiness emphasis and revising the Go Further pages to provide more relevant resources for students and teachers. Most of the current pages and/or content developed by the task force will be incorporated into new pages, but its history and background will be preserved and available on the site.

Another current project began in 2011 and aimed to devise a set of "transition checklists" inspired by Patricia Owen's work at Eastwood (Ohio) local schools. Owen created a handy list of information literacy skills high school seniors must master to be successful at college research (Owen 2010). After the first drafts, the task force changed its focus to a critical partner in the transitions process—parents. The task force is now creating a flyer "Top 10 Ways to Help Your Children with Research Projects" to assist parents in helping their children with the research process. Plans to distribute the brochure include the P16 councils, school counselors, and public libraries. The flyer will coincide as well with the revamping of the INFOhio parent pages, http://www .infohio.org/Parent/

INFOhio has been developing other significant resources that will impact student transitions. Funded by a grant from the Ohio Department of Education, a student portal guides middle and early high school students to web tools and databases of online journal articles and reference books to help them learn to use the tools necessary for thorough academic research. Go! INFOhio: Ask, Act, Achieve (http://go.infohio.org) went live in February 2012. The colorful, interactive site breaks the research process into three components to help students learn to use the tools necessary for academic research and includes a collection of helpful web sites and documents for both students and teachers. To complement Go! Ask, Act, Achieve, INFOhio has developed a high school information literacy course funded through an Institute of Museum and Library Services LSTA grant awarded by the State Library of Ohio. Debuting in the fall of 2012, R4S: Research for Success (http://www.infohio.org/index.php/course) is designed to be used in either face-to-face instruction or in a blended learning environment by high school teachers or college educators. R4S is may be utilized by students via the R4S site or via a learning management system (LMS) using widgets that easily integrate the content from each module into the LMS. The six-part course may be taken as a whole or may be used module-by-module.

Launched in the fall of 2012, the IPowered Matrix (http://imtrix.infohio.org) is another interactive, online tool available at the INFOhio web site. It is designed for teachers and links to the Ohio Academic Content Standards, the INFOhio DIALOGUE Model for the 21st Century Skills, and INFOhio Core Collection resources. The Research Project Calculator is also in the revision stage; when completed, it will reflect the functionality and personalization now in the Minnesota calculator. Plans are to incorporate the calculator into the Go site to make it more accessible.

Collaboration, always a top priority for the task force, continues as well. Plans are to contact academic librarians at all Ohio colleges that are involved with information literacy training or instructing students and preservice teachers to share the work of the task force and foster similar projects. The task force will highlight the many available resources and urge their college-level colleagues to establish collaborations with local school librarians. The committee also plans to make connections with local P16 councils, which are local committees of academic, government, and business people working towards Ohio students' college and career readiness, and other regional and state organizations, including the Ohio Department of Education and the Board of Regents.

Through the College and Career Readiness P20 Task Force, this creative partnership of INFOhio and OhioLINK has attempted to bridge the gap between high schools and higher education, and it has succeeded. The partnership has connected academic librarians with high school librarians, has gathered and posted stories of successful collaborative ventures, and has connected students and teachers with academic resources such as the Research Project Calculator and the 21st Century Learning Commons. INFOhio's Go Further initiative is just one component in a larger collective of statewide organizations, initiatives, and programs that are essential to providing Ohio students with the best educational opportunities possible. INFOhio, through leadership of this collaboration of academic librarians and P-20 school librarians, is dedicated to preparing Ohio's future leaders by paving the way for all Ohio's students as they journey down the road of education and beyond.

BIBLIOGRAPHY

American Association of School Librarians (AASL). *Standards for the 21st Century Learner.* Chicago: American Library Association, 2007.

Common Core State Standards Initiative. "The Standards." http://www.corestandards.org/the -standards (accessed March 18, 2012).

INFOhio. "21st Century Learning Commons." http://learningcommons.infohio.org (accessed September 15, 2011).

INFOhio. "DIALOGUE Model for the 21st Century Skills." http://learningcommons.infohio.org/index.php?option=com_content&view=article&id=298&Itemid=132 (accessed September 15, 2011).

INFOhio. "Go! INFOhio: Ask, Act, Achieve." http://go.infohio.org (accessed March 22, 2012).

INFOhio. "iMatrix." "http"//imatrix.infohio.org (accesses September 10, 2012).

INFOhio. *INFOhio's Go Further! Road to Career and College Readiness.* Columbus: INFOhio, 2011. http://www.infohio.org/PreparingOhioLearners/GoFurther201101.pdf (accessed October 24, 2012).

INFOhio. "Preparing 21st Century Ohio Learners For Success, Transition Task Force Members." http://www.infohio.org/PreparingOhioLearners/TaskForceRoster.html (accessed Aug. 15, 2011).

INFOhio. "Research4Succss." http://www.infohio.org/index.php/course (accessed October 20, 2012).

INFOhio. "Success Stories in College and Career Readiness." http://www.infohio.org/PreparingOhioLearners/TransitionStudies.html (accessed September 15, 2011).

INFOhio and OhioLINK Special Task Force. *Preparing 21st Century Ohio Learners for Success: The Role of Information Literacy and Libraries.* Columbus: INFOhio, 2008.

Ohio Department of Education. "Revised Academic Content Standards and Model Curriculum Development." http://www.ode.state.oh.us/GD/Templates/Pages/ODE/ODEDetail.aspx?page=3&TopicRelationID=1696&ContentID=83819&Content=121448 (accessed March 18, 2012).

Owen, Patricia. "A Transition Checklist for High School Seniors." *School Library Monthly* 26, no. 8 (April 2010): 20–23.

Partnership for Assessment of Readiness for College and Careers. "Implementation." http://www.parcconline.org/implementation (accessed March 18, 2012).

University of Minnesota Libraries. "Research Project Calculator Classic." 2012. http://rpc.elm4you.org/classic (accessed October 31, 2012).

7

Conversations for Collaboration: Librarians and the High School to College Transition in Louisiana

Debra Cox Rollins, Anthony J. Fonseca, Mitchell J. Fontenot, and Kathryn B. Seidel

THE K-20 INITIATIVE

In 2006, Mitch Fontenot, outreach librarian at Louisiana State University (LSU), noticed a surge in the number of high school and middle school students visiting Middleton Library at LSU, what these students called a "big and real" library. Surprised at such sudden interest, he spoke to students, teachers, and high school librarians, learning that many high school students were concerned about their lack of research skills and lack of access to a fully functional library. Fontenot began seeking committee appointments through the Louisiana Library Association (LLA) and the American Library Association to take part in significant conversations on connecting high school and college librarians, as well as the first-year or transitional year student (TYS). He found himself at the nexus of a statewide questioning of how best to prepare Louisiana's high school, middle school, and even elementary school students for later research and analytical/critical thinking at the college level, which proved timely. In December 2009, the Louisiana Board of Regents drafted a new *Master Plan for Public Postsecondary Education in Louisiana*, calling for stronger "collaboration among the state's education systems . . . to develop beneficial partnerships, to simplify student transitions from one level to the next, and to improve the quality of teaching and learning at all levels . . . " (1). Although this plan was finalized in 2011 with little reference to the aforementioned collaboration, in 2010, the Louisiana Chapter of the Assocation of College & Research Libraries (ACRL-LA) had recognized that information literacy skills are essential to successful transitions and had responded by creating the K-20 Committee. Fontenot was recruited by then chair Debra Cox Rollins.

The high school to college transition experience has been termed variously as "the freshman experience," "the first year experience," and "the transitional year experience," resulting in various articulations of "your seniors are my freshmen" programs and presentations, such as the creation of the National Resource Center for the First Year Experience and Students in Transition, as well as the Common Core State Standards Initiatives.[1] All indicate that the transitions issue has been persistent since the beginning of this century, becoming an essential part of the college experience today. Members of ACRL-LA's renamed Successful Transitions to Academic Research (STAR) Committee found that the current efforts in Louisiana mirrored the national conversation on successful transitions. STAR decided to focus its effort on statewide conversations between academic and high school librarians, as both must play a role in TYS success. This article will discuss the evolution of that conversation.

EARLY LIGHT

Early on, STAR focused on creating a well-informed discussion about the preparation of college-bound students to serve as a foundation for early academic success. Committee members set out to explore ways librarians could apply ACRL's *Information Literacy Standards for Higher Education* to focus on the needs of the TYS, agreeing that a diverse set of developmental experiences fed into information literacy competencies. Members wanted to emphasize that librarians represented only one type of information literacy educator, although they realized that the committee's first public discussions would engage librarians. Rollins created an outcomes-based graphic (see Figure 7.1), which also served to focus the committee's decision to explore ways to strengthen the transitional "foot bridge" between high school and the first year of college experiences. STAR reviewed the literature of academic and school librarianship, as well as that of first year experience (FYE) and TYS instruction, consulting high school and college librarians, as well as a School of Library and Information Science professor who specializes in school librarianship. The review of salient literature enabled STAR to identify issues common to librarians working with the TYS, and this information was used to generate a set of broad questions that committee members studied at their first meeting in 2008.

The questions, listed here, gave the committee its initial direction:

- Are K-12 classroom teachers, higher education teaching faculty, and administrators adequately aware of the role of libraries and abilities of librarians, which can improve outcomes-based instruction programs?
- Are K-12 classroom teachers and higher education teaching faculty so "curriculum bound" that they have no time to collaborate with librarians?
- If the lines of communication between academic, public, and school libraries were improved, how might this improve student success?
- Is the first year of college the best time for academic librarians to support TYS research activities, or should they postpone involvement until later in the transitional period?
- Is there a better way to connect the traditional understanding of library skills with critical thinking?
- Are school and academic librarians too "tool specific"? Should their emphasis be on transferable knowledge and/or skills and critical thinking?
- Are school librarians' energies too heavily diverted to coordinating media and technology? Are students learning computer skills—without learning critical thinking?
- Should school and academic librarians bear sole responsibility for information literacy?

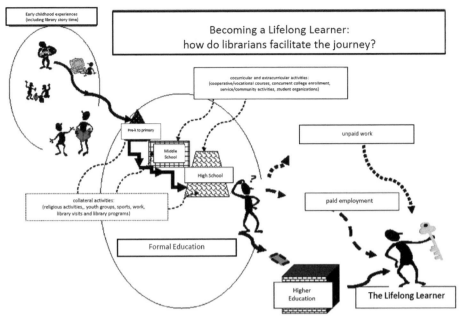

Figure 7.1.
Becoming a Lifelong Learner: How do Librarians Facilitate the Journey?

ILLUMINATION THROUGH LITERATURE

The published literature reflects two preoccupations: a theoretical transitions framework and project examples. Zoellner and Potter (2010) articulate this dichotomy well, citing theoretical studies by Gordon (2002) and Carr and Rockman (2003), and project reports by Tabar (2002), and they note the less common TYS conversations, like Islam and Murno's (2006) nationwide analysis of K-12 information literacy skills assessment and Burhanna's (2007) guidelines for K-12 outreach. Burhanna chronicles the transitions conversation, citing Craver's (1987) tracing of outreach to the 1960s, and he discusses the importance of the FYE librarian; Islam and Murno report their survey on K-12 information literacy skills acquisition, citing budget problems, collaboration issues, and the lack of academic library settings, concluding that collaboration at various levels is necessary—and not just on assignment- or discipline-specific projects, such as those cited by Ercegovac (2003) or O'Sullivan and Dallas (2010). Zoellner and Potter also note the related FYE literature by Cahoy (2002) and Seamans (2002), which look at "comfort" or "confidence" measures, as well as by Dunn (2002) and Fitzgerald (2004) on lifelong learning skills. Other studies include evaluations of the role of high school media centers, such as Kinnersley's (2000) measurement of electronic information resources in Kentucky schools. The need of a skilled approach is hinted at by Boff and Johnson (2002), and more recently by Foster (2006), who found that "college students and high school students preparing to enter college are sorely lacking in the skills needed to retrieve, analyze, and communicate information available online" (A36).

One of the more promising solutions, academic summer camps, is offered by Collins (2009). And as Cosgrove (2001) argues, such collaborative efforts can serve as recruitment tools. Gilbert (2009) discusses another valid solution: a pilot program demonstrating that students benefit from multiple FYE library instruction sessions. Such assessment used routinely would prove essential to an academic library's enriching the transition experience, especially given Lupton's findings that information literacy is almost universally considered a *generic* skill, rather than "as a learning activity situated within a topic, course and discipline" (2008, 400). The idea that information literacy skills will somehow be absorbed in class is particularly problematic, as Sears (2004) argues, calling for faculty to become "more conscious of the skills they want students to develop and of the methods required to learn those skills," positioning *research* as one of those skills which "cannot and will not be developed elsewhere" (166–168). As reported by Schloman and Gedeon (2007), the largest trailblazing transition effort is Kent State's TRAILS program.[2] During its creation, the academic librarians who designed TRAILS consulted with high school librarians, reminding us, as Smalley (2004) notes, that librarians must leave the isolation of the library if they desire to teach information organization and access.

ILLUMINATION THROUGH CONVERSATION

The Louisiana Association of School Librarians (LASL) held a one-day, multiple track conference in January 2010, and STAR was granted a panel ("Successful Transitions: How Librarians Can Help Prepare Students for College Research"). Panelists were Elizabeth Beard, an assistant professor of English; Renee Grantham, a library media specialist; and Jessica Hutchings, an instructional academic librarian. The facilitator was STAR's chair Rollins. The success of this program resulted in an invitation for a second conversation at the annual conference of the Louisiana Library Association (LLA) in March 2010. Panelists at this second conference were Keiren Aucoin, school librarian; Tony Fonseca, an instructional academic librarian; and Shirley McDonald, an adjunct professor of library and information science. The facilitator was Fontenot. In contrast to the first panel, the audience at LLA was made up of school, academic, and a few public librarians. Before each of the two sessions, STAR shared relevant literature with the panelists, inviting them to contribute other readings and questions. The original list of readings is available at http://bit.ly/JD6jP6. Prompts were sent a week prior to the program date. Each panelist was tasked with addressing one overwhelming question: "Speaking from your perspective, what are the most important research skills that entering college students should have?" The panelists and audience tackled difficult issues, for example, the information theory versus practical skills dichotomy, emphasizing that since college freshmen are exposed to one-shot instructional sessions only, such a discussion is essential. All in attendance also discussed the need for a difference in approach with high school versus college students and identified the ideal spectrum of skills for lifelong learning. School librarians emphasized specific skills that prepared students for college, and participants were asked for practical suggestions to improve communication between librarians, classroom teachers, and administrators, with the final discussion being how participants might change their own behaviors.

A third 2010 conversation at the LOUIS (Louisiana Library Network Consortium) Users Conference (LUC) offered a panel featuring a school librarian supervisor with expertise in American Associaton of School Librarians' (AASL) *Standards for the*

21st Century Learner. Panelists were Lance Chance, an academic reference librarian; Cathy Seal, the director for Library Services and Instructional Technology for the East Baton Rouge Parish schools; and Theresa Wozencraft, an assistant professor of psychology. The facilitator was Fontenot. Attracting mostly academic librarians whose common concern was students' lack of library knowledge, this panel discussed a lack of time with students and argued for stronger teacher-librarian communication. All agreed that students did not understand information organization, and all bemoaned the confusion of computer literacy with information literacy. Participants strongly voiced the need for more challenging assignments to foster positive student dispositions toward learning, research, process-oriented thinking, and engagement. The three conversations evidenced that school and academic librarians who worked with the TYS faced common challenges, and that a seamless articulation of the national standards did not exist. School librarians followed the *Standards for the 21st Century Learner.* Academic librarians' conversations were informed by ACRL's *Information Literacy Competency Standards for Higher Education.* While the standards are indeed similar, as STAR moved forward, committee members realized that a closer alignment of the two standards was needed, so to uncover commonalities, members designed a workshop at the 2011 LLA conference. Shown four posters with information literacy standards based on one of the AASL standards on each, each participant was given a piece of paper with one of the five ACRL standards and asked to match it to one of the four poster boards. Encouraged to think heuristically, they were aware that this task was subjective; they were later asked to rewrite the assimilated standards, emphasizing the intention and outcomes, and transcribe these onto new posters.

Discussions during the activity echoed the concerns of the previous conversations: the lack of basic information literacy skills in even the most advanced K-16 students, priorities driven by a predetermined number of units or course credit hours, and technology's shaping of thinking patterns. There was, again, agreement that librarians cannot mandate curriculum change but should lead the information theory versus applicable skills debate, as the two are inseparable—practical exercises are manifestations of higher order skills. Some high school librarians advocated teaching abstract concepts, such as natural language versus controlled vocabulary. All participants expressed concerns with students' reluctance to use anything but online resources, and with students' impatience. However, the rudiments of a common set of performance indicators for the TYS began to emerge. In the two weeks following the workshop, STAR members studied these "first draft" attempts, searching for commonalities and consistencies. The committee members distilled a set of performance objective for the TYS as follows:

The TYS will be able to . . .

- Recognize when information is needed
- Determine how much information is needed
- Use skills, available resources, and tools to retrieve information effectively
- Recognize the librarian as a resource
- Evaluate information
- Draw conclusions
- Make informed decisions
- Synthesize information
- Apply old knowledge to new situations

- Create *new* knowledge (not necessarily original but new to the student)
- Share information ethically
- Use information to foster growth and contribute to society
- Use information to pursue personal and aesthetic grown and development

A fourth conversation, "The Big (and not so) Easy: Missing Voices on the Student Transition to College," resulted from Fontenot's involvement with the Library Instruction Round Table (LIRT). At ALA, LIRT raised versions of STAR questions Fontenot helped author. It featured a biochemistry junior at Louisiana State University, an English graduate student from the University of Connecticut, a local high school English teacher, and the assistant director of the East Baton Rouge Public Library. The facilitator was Carolyn Meier of Virginia Tech. Student expectations of college-level research, faculty expectations of new college students, and the dialogue between high school and public librarians were discussed. Panelists agreed that transferable and basic skills were necessary to address the student fear issue, leading to demystification. Communication between all stakeholders was deemed absolutely necessary, fostering TYS critical thinking and evaluation skills. Specifically, both teaching panelists stated that as a result of the conversation, they now understood the value of sharing assignment/project goals and objectives with librarians to enable them to more effectively help students meet instructors' expectations. Furthermore, they realized the value in sharing students' completed work with librarians. Doing so provided librarians with a model of what a completed assignment would look like as well provided an opportunity for librarians to formatively assess their own contributions to students' research. The students on the panel addressed students' views of research skills, emphasizing evaluation. The panel also advocated that K-12 students must be allowed to choose their own research paths; otherwise, they do not learn the difference between search and research, that research is just a means to an end, and that research tools are practical—while research is theoretical.

CONCLUSION

Over the past three years, ACRL-LA's STAR Committee has sponsored presentations and panel discussions, amounting to four well-attended TYS conversations that generated lively discussion and springboards for thought. STAR's activities mirror some at the national level, such as ALA LIRT's Transitions to College Committee's 2009 brownbag discussions and its panel discussion at ALA Annual Conference (New Orleans) in 2011. These discussions enlightened public, high school, and academic librarians, as well as TYS classroom teachers. The STAR Committee is now using the results of these conversations to move forward on several fronts, to turn theory into practice. To further academic librarian and school librarian collaboration, STAR is soliciting new members from the LASL. With the goal of facilitating successful transitions to college throughout the state, committee members plan to begin several small-scale pilot programs at individual schools. The committee, in conjunction with new partners, will investigate a new electronic resource available throughout Louisiana via academic and public library consortia. It is a tool to design information literacy tutorials and/or videos to help smooth the high school to college transition. Ultimately, the committee will share with others throughout the state challenges and solutions that enhance the academic success of transitional year students. Updates on further STAR

Committee activities can be found on the ACRL-LA website: http://www.acrlla.org/projects/star.

NOTES

1. See Jean Donham. "My Senior Is Your First-Year Student: High School Transition to College." *Knowledge Quest* 32, no. 3 (2003): 32. Donham identifies four areas of importance in transitions research: expectations, collaboration, strategies, and assessment. For other versions of this conversation, see also Betsy O. Barefoot, "Improving the First Year of College: Research and Practice." *Journal of College Student Development* 46, no. 6 (November/December 2005): 699–700; *The National Center for the Study of The Freshman Year Experience*. 2008. http://sc.edu/fye/center/history.html; the New England Library Association's blog for its 2008 conference, "My College Freshman is Your High School Senior." http://nelib.wordpress.com/2008/10/21/my-college-freshman-is-your-high-school-senior/; Martha Ameika. "Introducing College Research at the High School Level: A Jump Start on Success." *Voice of Youth Advocates* 31, no. 5: 408–409, which highlights the "My College Freshman: Is Your High School Senior: Starting the Transition Conversation," presentation by Jennifer Nutefall; Sandy Jenkins and Carol Smith. "My College Freshman is Your High School Senior," presented at the 2009 Missouri Association of School Librarians Conference. http://www.slideshare.net/arabicsmith/my-college-freshman-is-your-high-school-senior. Of particular importance are two resources: (a) The American Diploma Project. *Ready or Not: Creating a High School Diploma that Counts*. Washington, D.C.: Achieve, Inc., 2004. http://www.achieve.org/files/ADPsummary_5.pdf and (b) *Common Core State Standards Initiative*. 2010. http://www.corestandards.org/the-standards. Published in early June, 2010, the *Common Core State Standards*, a state-led effort coordinated by the National Governors Association Center for Best Practices (NGA Center) and the Council of Chief State School Officers (CCSSO), attempt to provide a clear and consistent framework to prepare students for college and the workforce. They have been adopted by the District of Columbia and 35 states, including Louisiana.

2. The TRAILS website can be found at http://www.trails-9.org/. TRAILS is one of the numerous projects of the Institute for Library and Information Literacy Education (ILILE: www.ilile.org). Web sites were last accessed February 16, 2012.

BIBLIOGRAPHY

Bielich, Paul, and Fred Page. "An Information Literacy Partnership." *Knowledge Quest* 30, no. 4 (2002): 31–32.

Boff, Colleen, and Kristin Johnson. "The Library and First Year Experience Courses: A Nationwide Study." *Reference Services Review* 30, no. 4 (2002): 277–287.

Burhanna, Kenneth J. "Instructional Outreach to High Schools: Should You Be Doing It?" *Communications in Information Literacy* 1, no. 2 (2007): 74–88.

Burhanna, Kenneth J., and Mary L. Jensen. "Collaborations for Success: High School to College Transitions." *Reference Services Review* 34, no. 4 (2006): 509–519.

Cahoy, Ellysa S. "Will Your Students Be Ready for College? Connecting K-12 and College Standards for Information Literacy." *Knowledge Quest* 30, no. 4 (2002): 12–15.

Carr, Jo Ann, and Ilene F. Rockman. "Information Literacy Collaboration: A Shared Responsibility." *American Libraries* 34, no. 8 (2003): 52–54.

Collins, Bobbie L. "Integrating Information Literacy Skills into Academic Summer Programs for Precollege Students." *Reference Services Review* 37, no. 2 (2009): 143–54.

Cosgrove, John A. "Promoting Higher Education: (Yet) Another Goal of Bibliographic Instruction of High School Students by College Librarians." *College and Undergraduate Libraries* 8, no. 2 (2001): 17–24.

Craver, Kathleen W. "Use of Academic Libraries by High School Students: Implications for Research," *RQ* 27, no. 1 (1987): 53–66.

Dunn, Kathleen. "Assessing Information Literacy Skills in the California State University: A Progress Report." *Journal of Academic Librarianship* 28, nos. 1/2 (2002): 26–35.

Ercegovac, Zorana. "Bridging the Knowledge Gap between Secondary and Higher Education." *College and Research Libraries* 5, no. 1 (2003): 75–85.

Fitzgerald, Mary Ann. "Making the Leap from High School to College." *Knowledge Quest* 32, no. 4 (2004): 19–24.

Foster, Andrea L. "Students Fall Short on 'Information Literacy,' Educational Testing Service's Study Finds." *Chronicle of Higher Education* 53, no. 10 (2006): A36.

Gilbert, Julie K. "Using Assessment Data to Investigate Library Instruction for First Year Students." *Communications in Information Literacy* 3, no. 2 (2009): 181–192.

Gordon, Carol A. "A Room with a View: Looking at School Library Instruction from a Higher Education Perspective." *Knowledge Quest* 30, no. 4 (2002): 16–21.

Islam, Ramona L., and Lisa Anne Murno. "From Perceptions to Connections: Informing Information Literacy Planning in Academic Libraries through Examination of High School Library Media Center Curricula." *College and Research Libraries* 67, no. 6 (2006): 492–514.

Kinnersley, Ruth T. "Electronic Resources in Kentucky High Schools: A Survey of Availability and Instruction for Students." *Internet Reference Services Quarterly* 5, no. 1 (2000): 7–28.

Louisiana Board of Regents. "Master Plan for Public Postsecondary Education in Louisiana." 2009. http://www.thetowntalk.com/assets/pdf/DK128641217.PDF (accessed October 24, 2012).

Louisiana Board of Regents. "Master Plan for Public Postsecondary Education in Louisiana." 2011. http://www.regents.doa.louisiana.gov/assets/docs/Planning/MasterPlan-FINAL -2011_0901.pdf.

Lupton, Mandy. "Evidence, Argument and Social Responsibility: First-Year Students' Experiences of Information Literacy when Researching an Essay." *Higher Education Research and Development* 27, no. 4 (2008): 399–414.

O'Sullivan, Michael K., and Kim B. Dallas. "A Collaborative Approach to Implementing 21st Century Skills in a High School Senior Research Class." *Education Libraries* 33, no. 1 (2010): 3–9.

Pearson, Debra, and Beth McNeil. "From High School Users College Students Grow: Providing Academic Library Research Opportunities to High School Students." *Knowledge Quest* 30, no. 4 (2002): 24–28.

Schloman, Barbara F., and Julie A. Gedeon. "Creating TRAILS: Tool for Real-Time Assessment of Information Literacy Skills." *Knowledge Quest* 35, no. 5 (2007): 44–47.

Seamans, Nancy H. "Student Perceptions of Information Literacy: Insights for Librarians." *Reference Services Review* 30, no. 2 (2002): 112–123.

Sears, Alan. "Mind the Gap: Prospects for Easing the Transition from High School to University." *Guidance and Counseling* 19, no. 4 (2004): 166–172.

Smalley, Topsy N. "College Success: High School Librarians Make the Difference." *Journal of Academic Librarianship* 30, no. 3 (2004): 193–198.

Tabar, Margaret. "Rite of Passage: A Visit to the University Library." *Knowledge Quest* 30, no. 4 (2002): 29–30.

Zoellner, Kate, and Charlie Potter. "Libraries across the Education Continuum: Relationships between Library Services at the University of Montana and Regional High Schools." *Behavioral and Social Sciences Librarian* 29, no. 3 (2010): 184–206.

8

The DOE/CUNY Library Collaborative: High School to College Transition in New York City

Leanne Ellis, Robert Farrell, Curtis L. Kendrick, Meghann Suzanne Walk, and Barbara K. Stripling

Postsecondary skills and experiences are crucial to students' professional success and opportunities. The good news in New York City is that 61 percent of public school students graduate from high school, up from 52 percent in 2007; the bad news is that of those graduates who continue their education at a City University of New York school, 49 percent must take one or more remediation courses for no credit (Phillips and Gebeloff 2011). In short, students must pay to take high school–level courses over again because they lack the content knowledge and academic skills to transition to college. And it is not just the students who are affected; starting in 2012, all New York City high schools began to be held accountable for how their students fare after graduation—from how many attend college, to the number who graduate, to the number who have to take remediation courses, and so on. In addition, the adoption in New York State of internationally benchmarked Common Core State Standards is ushering in new academic rigor based on evidence and research:

The Common Core standards outline a new definition of and trajectory toward college and career readiness that reflect the demands of the 21st century. These instructional expectations are intended to support schools as we begin to adjust what and how we teach in order to help all students succeed on cognitively demanding tasks and develop along the continuum towards college and career readiness. (New York City Department of Education, "Citywide Instructional Expectations.")

The curriculum focus is on complex texts, higher order skills in reading and writing, using technology and digital media, and building strong content knowledge. In 2014, students will begin taking computerized assessments four times a year on these very skills. This means current assignments will need to be reconstructed and assessments undertaken in the classroom to ensure student mastery of the new standards.

Librarians have a vital role in advancing student achievement by teaching information literacy—the critical thinking, literacy, inquiry, and technology skills that lead to independent and self-directed learning. However, as the statistics listed earlier in this chapter indicate, not enough students are well versed in these skills and content knowledge to guarantee success after high school. The school librarian plays an essential role in changing this: They are unique in that they address the depth and breadth of the entire curriculum and lead in teaching a 21st Century curriculum of inquiry, problem-solving and content creation (Stripling 2011). In addition to the depth of curriculum knowledge, the librarian is in the unique position of interacting with a large percentage of students and educators at both the K-12 and college level. For it is not just the students who will experience a profound shift in academic expectations and required thinking skills because of the college and career expectations as expressed in the Common Core; teachers likewise will undergo a paradigm shift in instructional approach and assessment. They will need to immerse students in the analysis of information texts, focus on text-based answers as students evaluate evidence to build arguments from sources rather than drawing on their own experiences through personal narratives, emphasize vocabulary building, and finally, build in scaffolds to help students of all reading levels approach complex texts (EngageNY "Common Core"). Thus librarians not only work with K-12 teachers to increase student college and career readiness, but they are at the center of helping to ensure continued student achievement at the college level.

The City University of New York (CUNY) and the New York City School Library System (NYCSLS) formed a Collaborative to foster librarians as information literacy leaders and to support them through professional development opportunities, conferences, curriculum guidelines, and collaboration with outside partners. Both CUNY and NYCSLS are the natural organizations to guide a professional development series for librarians, teachers, and professors, with an emphasis on the fundamental role of librarians in student achievement. The aim of this professional development is to increase collaborative partnerships between New York City high schools and CUNY colleges to design aligned curriculum that prepares students to be college and career ready. Studies have shown that these types of partnerships lead to higher graduation rates than the national average and cultivate students who are more likely to have better attendance and be more engaged (Rosenbaum and Becker 2011, 15).

NEW YORK CITY SCHOOL LIBRARY SYSTEM

NYCSLS is a six-member team of library coordinators that supports hundreds of school librarians and more than a million students in over 1,600 schools through multiple approaches: guiding documents, mini-grants, professional development opportunities, site visit consultations, and collaborative partnerships with outside organizations like the New York Public Library and the City University of New York. NYCSLS's mission is to help librarians support and build the intellectual, social, and personal development of all students so that they become independent learners who acquire strong background knowledge, seek evidence, use digital media strategically, and understand other perspectives and cultures.

NYCSLS empowers school librarians to become instructional leaders in their schools with program evaluation rubrics, planning documents, reflective practice instruments, an extensive handbook, and the Information Fluency Continuum Curriculum (New York City School Library System 2012). NYCSLS aligns its programming to the goals of the New York City Department of Education (DOE). For example, in 2008, the DOE launched a middle school achievement initiative, so NYCSLS designed a mini-grant called New Yorkers Read. The goals of the grant were to connect students with real-life reasons to read using nonfiction books and dynamic nonfiction book clubs in libraries, provide schoolwide reading incentive programs, and connect families to students' reading experiences (Stripling 2011).

NYCSLS is likewise grounding the majority of its professional development focus and on-site consultation around the number one academic priority of the DOE and New York State: the Common Core Learning Standards. Workshops at citywide professional development sessions covered analyzing complex texts and building a print and digital collection of primary and secondary materials; aligning information fluency skills with Common Core literacy units; and using the Common Core/Information Literacy Continuum (IFC) alignment to become a leader in the implementation, instructional design, and assessment of these standards in schools (New York City School Library System 2012).

THE CITY UNIVERSITY OF NEW YORK

CUNY is a large urban public university with 21 colleges offering degrees from associate through doctorate. CUNY is mandated to strive for academic excellence as well as provide access to higher education. More than 260,000 CUNY students are enrolled in its degree programs, and 250,000 more are in continuing education and certificate programs. The majority (72 percent) of first time freshmen students at CUNY attended New York City public high schools. Many CUNY students do not have English as their native language (43 percent), and more than 38 percent come from families with household incomes less than $20,000 per year (CUNY Office of Institutional Research and Assessment "A Profile"). And while many New York City high school graduates choose to attend one of the CUNY colleges, CUNY also plays an important role in preparing the students who go on to teach within the city's school system (CUNY Office of Institutional Research and Assessment "Master's Degree"). Among the programs at the university, teacher education is by far the largest (CUNY "The CUNY Value"). Moreover, about one-third of teachers in the New York City public system received their training at CUNY.

CUNY and the New York City DOE have long recognized the need to collaborate in order to provide the best possible public education in New York City. Several recent initiatives have served to strengthen the extent of collaboration and communication between the two systems. However, in spite of the best efforts of CUNY and New York City DOE, success at CUNY has been for many students an elusive goal. The Graduate NYC! College Readiness and Success Initiative was started in August 2010 to address these longstanding concerns. With funding from the Bill & Melinda Gates Foundation, the initiative brings together the resources of New York City's mayor's office, the DOE, the City University of New York, other city agencies, and an extensive group of local community and school-based organizations. New York City leaders have committed to long-term outcomes that align with the Gates Foundation's goals of "doubling the number of college graduates." By 2020, the city will hold its major educational institutions accountable to the following:

- 75 percent of students graduating from high school will meet a basic standard of academic readiness for college-level work.
- 75 percent of students graduating from high school will enroll in college.
- Three-year graduation rates for CUNY associate degree students will increase to 25 percent.
- Four-year graduation rates for CUNY associate degree students will increase to 40 percent.
- Six-year graduation rates for CUNY baccalaureate students will increase to 61 percent.

Graduate NYC!'s activities focus on three key drivers that are necessary for success in order to achieve these goals:

1. Transforming culture in New York City related to college readiness and success
2. Using data to drive change and hold the community accountable for success
3. Changing practices to reflect an orientation toward student success (CUNY Graduate NYC! "Overview")

Since its inception, Graduate NYC! has convened groups of leading practitioners from CUNY, New York City DOE, and community-based organizations to address issues ranging from curriculum alignment, to the quality and availability of academic advisement services for high school and college students, to the need for better coordinated messages about college readiness and success issues to the public. The initiative has also invested significantly in developing a longitudinal tracking database that will enable the city's youth-serving institutions to gain a better understanding of student progress from high school into college.

DOE/CUNY LIBRARY COLLABORATIVE FORMATION AND FOCUS

CUNY's university dean for Libraries and Information Resources, Curtis Kendrick, and the DOE's director of the Office of Library Services, Barbara Stripling, moved to create a joint team comprised of CUNY faculty librarians and DOE librarians focusing on the high school to college transition to build on the Graduate NYC! Initiative. The group began meeting during the 2010–2011 academic year and through several conversations, determined that their work should focus on the area of information literacy because students often struggle with writing requirements and critical thinking skills in college-level courses.

Information literacy has been a priority for both systems for many years, and the DOE/CUNY Library Collaborative has begun to investigate the process of forming a K-16 sequence of information literacy skills. In 2004, CUNY established the Library Information Literacy Advisory Committee (LILAC) to advise senior management in the libraries "with regard to integrating information literacy across the City University curriculum, developing information literacy support materials including assessment tools, and sponsoring information literacy related professional development activities (CUNY Office of Library Services "LILAC Committee Charge"). The group members have been responsible for several professional development programs and presentations at conferences.

One of the most important accomplishments of LILAC to date has been the development of a common set of learning objectives across the university for information literacy (CUNY 2011). These learning objectives ensure that regardless of where a student may first be enrolled, there will be a common expectation of the skills that students are developing with respect to information literacy by the time that achieve sixty credit hours.

CUNY's librarians have been working arduously to build information literacy programs at each of the colleges. Several colleges offer for-credit information literacy–related courses, taught by librarians. In addition, CUNY was the recipient of a grant from the Verizon Foundation to pilot a Critical Thinking Skills Initiative (CTSI), which enrolls students in either a one-credit or three-credit online course. CTSI recognizes that "strong information literacy skills are ever more crucial to academic success, the effective use of information technology in the workplace, and the development of life-long problem solving and critical thinking skills" (CUNY Libraries, "CUNY Critical Thinking Skills Initiative"). CTSI uses the Educational Testing Services' iSkills exam as a pre- and posttest and seeks to connect participating students with internship opportunities in the New York City business community.

Over the past several years, CUNY has made impressive strides in information literacy, and so too have school libraries with support from New York City School Library System. The defining framework for New York City librarians is the IFC, which lays out a grade-by-grade continuum of literacy, inquiry, information, and technology skills. Each grade highlights benchmark skills along with customizable formative assessment graphic organizers for these priority skills (New York City School System 2012).

Also available at the preceding address are documents that lay out the alignment between the IFC and the National Common Core Standards. These alignment documents define the school librarian's role in the Common Core as natural leaders in teaching the skills of inquiry, critical thinking, and research because it unpacks the required learning students need to be able to do in order to be successful in meeting the Common Core Standards.

PROFESSIONAL DEVELOPMENT PROCESS

Early on, the DOE/CUNY Library Collaborative decided to create a professional development initiative as a goal in order to identify how librarians can best collaborate with teachers and professors to help students become successful at college. The Collaborative looked at surveys, research, lesson plans, student work, outcomes, and assessments to identify and assess the specific cognitive and affective skills, strategies, and expectations that define college and career readiness. The Library Collaborative had planned to create a toolkit that would help different constituents integrate the identified skills and assessments into content-area assignments and projects. However, upon further reflection, we decided that professional development was a preferable method to meet our goals: to identify and measure the inquiry and critical thinking skills students need to be successful in college and the workplace, and then, to form partnerships between high schools and CUNY colleges to guarantee skill integration into content areas through the use of best practice implementation and assessment. Participants in an effective professional development workshop need to engage with content, with the ideas presented, and with one another in order for the learning and the change in practice to take place. The passive toolkit model—defined by packaged information—left no mechanisms in place to facilitate partnership formation.

In subsequent conversations and meetings, the collaborative decided to create an interactive professional development series that would initiate the dialogue and critical thinking between secondary teachers, college faculty, and librarians to develop stronger high school curricula and inform college faculty about the Common Core and the challenges of 9-12 education. The workshops have as a goal the formation of lasting partnerships between New York City schools and CUNY colleges, and between subject teachers and teacher-librarians. They are structured on the belief that powerful curriculum is best created by educators in conversation with other educators. A report by the U.S. Department of Education, *Pathways to College Access and Success*, states that "the primary component of an ideal curriculum would be the presence of a clear curricular pathway encompassing high school and developmental course work, aligned with the demands of college course work, and culminating in student enrollment in a college course" (2005, 30).

The Collaborative decided to focus on English language arts, social studies, and science as the three subjects most likely to benefit from this format. The pilot workshops established three working groups, one for each content area. Each working group consisted of a content area secondary teacher, a content area professor, a school librarian, and a CUNY librarian. The task force felt that college faculty would contribute deep subject-area expertise and a sense of where students struggle during their first semesters in college, while K-12 teachers would bring pedagogical methods and assessment techniques to the table, along with a sense of the challenges of preparing students for college level work. Working groups like these present opportunities for educators to learn from each other, share tips, and modify lessons to meet student needs (Rosenbaum and Becker 2011, 17). As such, the task force laid out the following outcomes:

- Developing personal relationships and support between school and college educators through professional/interdisciplinary learning networks
- Promoting cross-conversations and cultural understanding between school and college educators
- Providing a sustainable forum to foster curricular partnerships between schools and CUNY campuses, leading to curricular alignment between secondary schools and college-level work
- Helping K-12 teachers work with librarians through the development of a curricular unit aligned to information literacy standards and college success
- Making librarians a core part of curricular development at both the high school and college level

In the spring of 2012, the task force secured funding for the project, confirmed participants and a location, and selected a facilitator and observer to document the process. The sessions took place in April and May 2012 between the CUNY College of Staten Island and the College of Staten Island High School.

Each working group met twice. Prompted by questions and readings on the Common Core, inquiry and independent learning, and the role of the librarian, the first session allowed members to discuss skill and culture gaps students have upon entering college, what students need to know to succeed in specific disciplines, the role of inquiry, how assignments are constructed, and the challenges of complex texts.

The documentation of the first session served as the basis for the second session. In this session, group members used outcomes of their first meeting to review and comment on high school units from the three disciplines. At the close, participants spoke of the value of reworking a high school curricular unit. They were able to utilize the findings of the first session—high school knowledge demands and task requirements are most often determined by the content and tasks of the state exams, while college faculty struggle to work with students used to being told what to do, and whose content reading largely consists of textbook passages—to inform their feedback and reactions to the high school units. In addition, they were able to articulate where the librarian fits into the role of curricular planning and development, instruction, and assessment. On the college level, faculty become aware of the time and testing restrictions thrust upon high school teachers. On the high school side, teachers were able to gain a sense of the reading and writing demands, types of critical thinking skills, and habits of mind expected of students by college faculty.

Assessment results consisted of a post-workshop evaluative questionnaire followed up by a more extensive survey indicated that participants felt that they benefited from the workshops and viewed their counterparts at the high school or college as future contacts they could draw on and check in with going forward. Perhaps more importantly, teachers came away with a renewed sense of the importance of their school librarian and saw her after the workshops as a partner in curricular development. The one major critique of the workshops was that there was not enough time allocated to fully revising the curricular units.

Next steps are to publicize the task force's work in journals and at conferences in order to secure funding to design a sustainable model at the institutional level. They plan to offer another iteration of this workshop model at a different high school and college with an additional session to develop strategies for addressing the gaps in core skills identified in the first session, and what it means to revise a unit with the Common Core standards in mind. But their hope is that continued collaboration will help spark long-term high school and college partnerships with Graduate NYC! Initiative support and give rise to a network of educators as it expands to other New York City schools and CUNY colleges. These partnerships are already happening in select sites such as Bard High School Early College (Manhattan and Queens, NYC) and International High School at the campus of LaGuardia Community College (Queens, NYC). In these cases, college faculty and secondary teachers design courses together. Unfortunately, these examples are too few in number and need to be expanded.

The advantages of high school and college partnerships are clear: they articulate the role of librarians in this process, increase student awareness and experience of demanding college-level work and expectations, students often attain college credit while in high school, and perhaps most importantly, students raise their self-aspirations. The mission of the DOE/CUNY Library Collaborative is to create true permanence of these partnerships so that we as librarians and teachers can better prepare students for a successful high school to college transition.

BIBLIOGRAPHY

City University of New York (CUNY). "The CUNY Value: What Keeps Us So Affordable?" http://www.cuny.edu/about/info/value/affordable.html (accessed October 3, 2011).

City University of New York (CUNY) Graduate NYC! CUNY/DOE College Readiness and Success Initiative. "Graduate NYC! Overview." http://www.cuny.edu/about/administration/offices/ue/CUNYDOECollegeReadiness/GraduateNYCOverview.pdf (accessed October 4, 2011).

City University of New York (CUNY) Libraries. "Information Literacy Standards for CUNY Students" http://infolit.commons.gc.cuny.edu/aboutinformationliterac/standards// (accessed October 31, 2012).

City University of New York (CUNY) Office of Institutional Research and Assessment. "A Profile of Undergraduates at CUNY Senior and Community Colleges: Fall 2010." http://owl.cuny.edu:7778/portal/page/portal/oira/OIRA_HOME/ug_student_profile_f10.pdf (accessed October 3, 2011).

City University of New York (CUNY) Office of Institutional Research and Assessment. "Master's Degree Granted by College, 2009–2010." http://owl.cuny.edu:7778/DEGR _0004_DEG_MAST.rpt.pdf (accessed October 3, 2011).

City University of New York (CUNY) Office of Library Services. "Library and Information Literacy Advisory Committee (LILAC)." http://infolit.commons.gc.cuny.edu/aboutlilac/ (accessed October 31, 2012).

EngageNY. "Common Core Instructional Shifts." http://engageny.org/common-core (accessed October 20, 2011).

New York City Department of Education (DOE). "Introductions to the Citywide Instructional Expectations for 2011-2012." http://schools.nyc.gov/Academics/CommonCoreLibrary/ Why/NYSStandards/default.htm (accessed October 19, 2011).

New York City School Library System. "Information Fluency Continuum." http://schools.nyc .gov/Academics/LibraryServices/StandardsandCurriculum/default.htm (accessed October 19, 2011).

New York City School Library System "New York City K-12 Information Fluency Continuum and Common Core State Standards" New York:NY: Author, 2012. http://schools.nyc.gov/ Academics/LibraryServices/StandardsandCurriculum/default.htm (accessed March 3, 2012).

Philips, Anna, and Robert Gebeloff. "In Data, 'A' Schools Leave Many Not Ready for CUNY." *New York Times*, June 21, 2011. http://www.nytimes.com/2011/06/22/nyregion/many -from-a-rated-nyc-schools-need-help-at-cuny.html (accessed October 27, 2012).

Rosenbaum, James E., and Kelly Iwanaga Becker. "The Early College Change: Navigating Disadvantaged Students' Transition to College" *American Educator* 35 (2011): 14–20.

Stripling, Barbara. "School Library Services." Strategic Vision Document, New York City School Library System, 2011.

U.S. Department of Education (DOE), Office of Vocational and Adult Education. *Pathways to College Access and Success*. Washington, D.C.: U.S. Department of Education, 2005. http://www2.ed.gov/about/offices/list/ovae/pi/cclo/cbtrans/finalreport.pdf (accessed October 27, 2012).

9

Building a Better Bridge: The Role of the Community College in Information Literacy Efforts

Kathleen Conley

Community colleges in the Commonwealth of Pennsylvania require sponsorship in order to exist as a community college. The sponsorship for Harrisburg Area Community College (HACC) rests on the 22 sponsoring school districts, and in return for this support, it is extremely important for the college to provide services, in addition to a reduced tuition rate, for those sponsoring districts. The libraries provided some benefits, but HACC reference and instruction librarians felt more could be done. They had attended conferences and other professional development sessions focused on high school students and their transition to college and began to think about outreach services to high schools. HACC librarian Kathleen Conley and author of this chapter was fortunate enough to be at the Library Orientation Exchange (LOEX) Conference in 2006 and to attend the session being lead by Ken Burhanna, Mary Lee Jensen, and Barbara Schloman titled Our Transition Mission: Reaching Out to the High School Community. Conley returned to HACC convinced that she and her colleagues needed to do more to support high school student transitions to HACC.

This chapter will discuss the process of creating an open dialogue about information literacy across the curriculum between community college, high school, and four-year college librarians in the Harrisburg area of Pennsylvania. It is imperative these groups communicate to ensure that students develop the necessary information literacy skills needed for success in higher education. Without this conversation, HACC librarians would continue to be unaware of the information literacy skills acquired in the area high schools, as well as the skills necessary for community college students to succeed at four-year institutions. With this conversation, we could all do a better job aligning our work and preparing students for success.

CONNECTING WITH HIGH SCHOOL LIBRARIANS

Conley and HACC librarians across the five-campus region began discussing the idea of dialoging with other librarians, especially those at local high schools. Two librarians from the HACC–Lancaster campus, Sayre Turney and Elisa Weigard, were very interested and enthusiastic about building these collaborations. Sayre, a former high school librarian with connections to school librarians in the Lancaster area, had just been speaking with a high school librarian about ways they could collaborate. Voila, a connection had been made! Since they already had identified some interest, HACC librarians asked to be placed on the agenda for an upcoming Intermediate Unit Thirteen (IU13) librarians meeting. IU13 is an education services agency serving public and nonpublic schools and students from pre-K to adult in Lancaster and Lebanon counties. During the 2006 spring term, HACC librarians from the Harrisburg, Lancaster, and Lebanon campuses attended that meeting to voice eagerness to create a dialogue between the high schools, colleges, and universities in the Lancaster/Lebanon area. They expressed interest in creating a venue to carry on the conversation for those that were interested, and many of the high school librarians in attendance immediately expressed interest. After gathering their contact information, the HACC librarians involved in the project met to discuss the best approach for moving forward.

They decided their next step would be best to host a small event at the Lancaster campus. The idea was discussed with the library director, and with her approval and a small budget for snacks, they began to develop the event. They needed an engaging agenda designed to encourage conversation. Making connections and developing ideas for collaboration was the objective. So they contacted the high school librarians to determine what issues they would like addressed at this small, informal gathering, as well as which four-year institutions they would like to have represented at the meeting. What follows is a list of the questions and issues identified by school librarians.

Expectations for Students

- What information literacy skills are required for incoming students?
- What is each incoming student expected to know?
- How can we stress the need for these skills to our high school students?

Information Literacy and Assessment

- What are the expectations of local academic institutions regarding information literacy?
- Can we discuss the individual standards for information literacy?
- Can we address how technology literacy overlaps with information literacy?
- How can we assess information literacy?
- Are there formal information literacy classes that freshmen must take?
- Do the colleges offer an orientation to college libraries?
- What information literacy skills are necessary? Which skill are lacking?
- Has anyone looked into integrating topics from the ETS ICT Assessment?

College Expectations/Perceptions

- What are the expectations of college professors?
- What resources are considered acceptable by college professors?

- How can we, as librarians, and our faculty members prepare our students for college research?
- What are the outcomes of each information literacy skill? What should students be able to do?
- Do college librarians perceive that freshman are prepared to do research?
- How much information can students use from Internet sources? If it is used, do professors require some kind of evaluation of the site attached to the paper?
- Do professors require books as well as article databases to be used?

Citations and Plagiarism

- Do the local institutions of higher education use plagiarism detection software?
- Should we be preparing our students to be able to cite their sources using various styles?
- Are citations created using automatic citation builders acceptable?
- What are the feelings about librarians teaching citations or allowing students to use online tools to create citations?
- What bibliographic styles are English professors and those in other disciplines requiring?

Outreach and Teacher Training

- In what ways can we educate high school teachers on the expectations of community colleges and four-year institutions?
- How can we emphasize the importance of information literacy to students in teacher preparation programs?
- How are student teachers being educated about the ways to incorporate the library into their lesson plans?
- How can we convince educators of the importance of information literacy in today's high stake state tests?

HACC librarians were excited and intrigued by the questions generated by the high school librarians. Of course, this first three-hour meeting would not be able to address all of these questions, but they certainly would have plenty to discuss. What became evident was that no matter what level of education librarians work with, they have many of the same issues. After examining this feedback, HACC librarians were able to develop a flexible agenda for the first meeting. They looked forward to a spirited dialogue.

INFORMATION LITERACY FORUMS

The date was selected, and the list of those to invite was created. HACC librarians relied heavily upon the input from the high school librarians, and they also gathered statistics on which institutions had the highest number of transfers from HACC to develop the list of four-year college and university librarians to invite. A meeting was held at the HACC Lancaster campus during the 2007 spring term with 10 high school, five HACC, and three college (four-year) librarians in attendance. The meeting began with an opportunity for each attendee to introduce himself or herself and explain what was happening at his or her institution. Each attendee was asked address the following questions during their introductions, and they were welcome to add any additional information.

1. Is instruction being offered at your institution and how is it conducted?
2. Is information literacy being addressed at your institution? How?
3. Does your institution have certain expectations in regards to the assessment of the impact your teaching has on student learning?

The responses were informative, and the attendees often broke into lively discussions as the introductions took place. Here is a summary of the answers to the preceding questions.

1. While most developed customized library instruction sessions based on specific assignments, the demand for and approaches to doing this varied greatly.
2. There were four main strategies expressed for addressing information literacy:
   • A college freshman seminar consisting of many components such as critical thinking, reading, writing, oral presentation, and use of library resources
   • A formal college credit course in information literacy
   • The integration of information literacy into the curriculum
   • The adoption of The Big6™: Information and Technology Skills for Student Achievement (Eisenberg and Berkowitz)
3. With regards to assessment, not much was happening, but many were aware of the buzz that was currently occurring on the topic. Attendees knew the pressure was being placed upon their institutions and more assessment was going to be required soon. Some had already begun developing plans for assessment, while others were waiting to get the official word from administrators. Since the time of these meetings, assessment has become a priority for educators, and the call to action has been heard loud and clear. HACC librarians are now required to consistently ask themselves, "How can this be assessed?" If this question were asked of the attendees today, they would likely give significantly different replies.

After introductions, , the meeting turned its attention to the many questions that were raised about professors' expectations. In order to respond to this topic, librarians representing colleges and universities were asked to bring along some typical assignments for college freshmen. Common needs and expectations were expressed by librarians sharing their experiences supporting those assignments. The discussion also touched on plagiarism as well as various instruction techniques to address specific concepts, such as scholarly versus popular periodicals, evaluating web sites, and creating citations. Most of the participants agreed that they had much in common regarding these issues. It seems that no matter the level of education, students are always struggling with these skills, and the discussion further supported the fact that information literacy is a lifelong process.

Next, one of the attendees was placed in the hot seat. Marjorie Warmkessel had served on the Advisory Panel on Information Literacy for the Middle States Commission on Higher Education and contributed to the content in *Developing Research & Communication Skills: Guidelines for Information Literacy in the Curriculum* (2003). Warmkessel was representing Millersville University at the Lancaster campus meeting. She gave a brief explanation of those guidelines and standards as well as fielded any questions attendees had related to information literacy and accreditation. Warmkessel explained that information literacy is included in the 14 Middle States Standards for Accreditation and should be integrated into all programs of study at an institution. In addition, there was an emphasis placed on assessment. That is, the institutions governed by Middle States were being required to illustrate that their students have information literacy skills. Given the importance of accreditation, this was good news.

An additional question was asked of the representatives from four-year colleges and universities present at both meetings. As community college librarians, HACC librarians were curious to discover what level of literacy the average college junior would be expected to attain to be as successful as other college juniors. The representatives from those institutions expressed that no formal outreach was being made to transfer students in regards to information literacy. However, customized library instruction sessions were often requested for research methods courses at the four-year institutions, and subject area library liaisons were available to conduct research consultations with students.

During the 2008 spring term, a similar meeting at the HACC Harrisburg campus was held with the same number of attendees representing the Harrisburg area: 10 high school, five HACC, and three college (four-year) librarians in attendance. The same agenda was used and like in the first meeting, participants engaged in a lively discussion about their students, curriculum and information literacy.

Attendees at both meetings expressed an interest in continuing the conversation. HACC librarian Kathleen Conley proposed the idea of creating a daylong event much like the Information Literacy Summit held annually in Illinois. Using that event as a model, they could select a keynote speaker and have concurrent sessions throughout the day. The ultimate goals of the event would be to provide attendees with information and tools that they could put into practice at their institutions. It was agreed that this idea should be pursued.

BUILDING THE BRIDGE

During the following fall term, Weigard and Conley began working on a grant proposal. They decided to apply for a Special Initiative Grant from the HACC Foundation. Their application explained that this project would create the necessary environment for HACC area high school, college, and university librarians to have an open dialogue on information literacy across the high school and higher education curriculum. They stressed the need for this conversation, being sure to focus on student success. The activities of the event were to center on assessment and preparing students to access resources efficiently, evaluate resources effectively, and use those resources correctly and ethically as defined by the Association of College and Research Libraries, which is also recognized by the American Association of Community Colleges Position Statement on Information Literacy. they reported on the success of the two initial meetings and explained that as a result of those meetings, it became evident that the librarians found the discussion useful and would fully support an effort to extend the conversation during a daylong event.

Included in the grant proposal were a list of project goals and objectives, an explanation of how the project correlated to the college's strategic plan, a timetable, and a list of assessment criteria. The budget proposal for the event covered the cost of an honorarium and accommodations for the keynote speaker, materials for the event and promotion, equipment rentals, supplies, rental fee for the space, and food for 75 attendees. Again, the goal was to make the event free for all attendees. The total amount requested was $5,500. They were awarded the grant and went to work organizing the event, which was held on May 14, 2009.

To coordinate the event HACC librarians needed to collaborate with colleagues in the public relations department, the college bookstore, the conference center, the center for innovation and technology, and the library system. Some of the tools created to add to the success of the event included email blasts, promotional fliers, an online registration form, continuing education credit slips, a social networking page, and a survey to assess the success of the event.

Within the promotional materials, they included a request for volunteers to speak at the event. As a result, they were able to schedule two concurrent sessions in which there was a choice between two presentations, and they ended the day with a lightening session consisting of three short presentations. The speakers at the event addressed the issues of assessment and information literacy best practices at their respective institutions. A research institution, private college, high school, and community college were all represented on the agenda. The keynote speaker for the event was Ken Burhanna, an academic librarian from Kent State University. He had established a significant outreach program to high schools in Ohio and spoken and written extensively on the topic of librarians supporting student transitions to college.

As the day of the event arrived, HACC librarians' last minute to-do list included printing out an extra registration list for the check-in table, including the keynote speaker on the registration list, creating signage for the speaker sessions, and sending the final agenda out to everyone who had registered for the event. Luckily, many HACC librarians were ready and willing to assist and the event was a success. Seventy-five attendees, representing high schools, community colleges and four-year colleges, participated in the event.

Additional information was gathered from a survey that followed the event. Thirty-six of the attendees responded to the survey, and the following assessment criteria were gathered from those results. Ninety-four percent of the survey respondents agreed that they had increased their knowledge of information literacy skills necessary for student success at the secondary and postsecondary levels of education. Seventy-two percent of respondents agreed they had a better understanding of assessment best practices as a result of this event. The survey also asked the respondents if they would be likely to attend another event like this in the future, to which 97 percent responded positively. Of course the information gathered from the surveys is critical, but HACC librarians were just as interested in reading the comments collected from the free response section of the survey. Librarians are so kind and there were many complements given, but the two most helpful comments offered suggestions for future events.

As this chapter was being written, the author was developing a grant proposal to host another event to deepen the conversation. Based on follow-up conversations and those two wonderful suggestions referenced in the preceding paragraph, the next event will focus on developing working groups by connecting librarians at all levels of secondary and postsecondary education within a particular geographical area. One goal would be for those attendees to be able to start planning how they can work together to ensure information literacy across the curriculum. As a result, the day will focus on building relationships, brainstorming, and sharing ideas. HACC librarians look forward to this future event and firmly believe that great things can happen when librarians put our heads together.

BIBLIOGRAPHY

Burhanna, Kenneth J., Mary Lee Jensen, and Barbara Schloman. "Our Transition Mission: Reaching Out to the High School Community." Presentation, 34th Annual LOEX Conference, College Park, MD, May 2006.

Eisenberg, Mike, and Bob Berkowitz. "The Big6™: Information and Technology Skills for Student Achievement." http://www.big6.com/ (accessed October 25, 2011).

Middle States Commission on Higher Education. *Developing Research & Communication Skills: Guidelines for Information Literacy in the Curriculum.* Philadelphia: Middle States Commission on Higher Education, 2003.

ADDITIONAL READINGS

"Being Part of the Library Ecosystem, Part II." *School Librarian's Workshop* 30, no. 6 (January 2, 2010): 16. *Library Literature & Information Science Full Text (H. W. Wilson)*, EBSCO*host* (accessed March 19, 2012).

Burhanna, Kenneth J. "Collaborations for Success: High School to College Transitions." *Reference Services Review* 34, no. 4 (2006): 509–519, ProQuest (accessed March 19, 2012).

Epstein, Sue. "If Only—What a Ten-Year Veteran of the College Classroom Wished Her Students Had Known." *Knowledge Quest* 30, no. 4 (March 2002): 47–48. *Library Literature & Information Science Full Text (H. W. Wilson)*, EBSCO*host* (accessed March 19, 2012).

Gordon, Carol A. "A Room with a View: Looking at School Library Instruction from a Higher Education Perspective." *Knowledge Quest* 30, no. 4 (March 2002): 16–21. *Library Literature & Information Science Full Text (H. W. Wilson)*, EBSCO*host* (accessed March 19, 2012).

Manuel, Kate. "National History Day: An Opportunity for K-16 Collaboration." *Reference Services Review* 33, no. 4 (2005): 459–486, ProQuest (accessed March 19, 2012).

Pearson, Debra, and Beth McNeil. "From High School Users College Students Grow: Providing Academic Library Research Opportunities to High School Students." *Knowledge Quest* 30, no. 4 (March 2002): 24–28. *Library Literature & Information Science Full Text (H. W. Wilson)*, EBSCO*host* (accessed March 19, 2012).

Tipton, Roberta L., and Patricia Bender. "From Failure to Success: Working with Under-Prepared Transfer Students." *Reference Services Review* 34, no. 3 (2006): 389–404, ProQuest (accessed March 19, 2012).

10

Funding the Way: Seeking Grants to Study the High School to College Transition and the Role of Libraries

Rhonda Huisman and Kindra Orr

INTRODUCTION

In light of the many federal and state programs focused on college readiness, including the adoption of common core standards, college and career readiness initiatives, Lumina's 2025 proposal, and NextGen Gates grants, David Lewis, the dean of the Indiana University-Purdue University Indianapolis (IUPUI) University Library, as well as Kindra Orr, director of development, began to consider University Library's role in college readiness. Aware of her background and interest in information literacy and grant management, they approached colleague Rhonda Huisman about a library-focused outreach pilot project with the Indianapolis urban schools. They agreed that there was a gap in their understanding of the information literacy skills of students entering higher education. What they as academic librarians expected of them seemed much different from what they learned (or were evaluated on) at the high school level. They believed they could potentially seek grants to fund their exploration of and outreach to this problem that has both local and national implications.

In this chapter, the authors share their process, discussions, and points for consideration for those who may want to explore funding similar projects in their own libraries or communities. To date, they have scaled back from their original plan and have secured funds from an Indianapolis community group that focuses on supporting local projects. The initial phases of this project included gathering stories and evidence from fellow academic librarians at IUPUI, as well through a listserv discussion and a review of the literature that led the authors to a new appreciation of the difficulties that many incoming freshmen experience in the research and writing processes. They also knew through personal discussions and testimonials from colleagues that many school media specialists, overworked and underfunded, have limited involvement in curriculum and assessment. The idea for a collaborative project grew from a workshop proposal (focused on professional development support for K-12 school media specialists) for a partnership with Arizona State University (ASU). However, as sometimes happens, their project collaborator at ASU moved on, and they focused once again on the story of their local high schools and their media specialists. It has evolved from developing large-scale, sweeping proposals for several substantial national grants that support research on the transition between high school and higher education, to a local Indianapolis story about partnerships between K-12 urban schools, academic librarians, education faculty, and the community. The authors hope this will lead to being in a better position to connect with the community and the opportunity to build upon this local project with hopes of reinvigorating their original proposal for a nationwide study called *College Ready, College Bound.* At the present time, they are explicitly focusing their research on the role of the school media specialist in 9-12 curriculum development, information literacy standards and assessment, and what possible connections academic librarians could have in preparing and supporting these students for postsecondary learning and success.

NEED

There is little doubt of the importance of a college degree. Beere, Vortuba, and Wells (2011) noted in *Becoming an Engaged Campus* that "almost every person who will play a significant role in the country's future will first acquire an education—and most likely a degree—from one of the colleges or universities in the United States" (9). Yet there is a body of literature that discusses a gap between the skills of high school seniors and skills that are needed for college success (ACT 2008). This gap is more pronounced in children from rural and other underserved populations, minority students, and students with a lower socioeconomic status (Barton and Coley 2009). Indianapolis and its surrounding suburbs have over 2 million residents; Indiana's population is around 6.5 million. Over 1 million students attended public and nonpublic schools in the state of Indiana in 2009 and 2010. There were 77,484 twelfth graders in 2010, which could lead to 80,000 potential college students for Indiana's higher education institutions. IUPUI enrolls over 33,000 students. Unfortunately, national SAT reading, writing and math scores have consistently declined from 2006 to 2011 (NCES 2012). The 2009 ACT National Curriculum Survey shows that information literacy ranks in importance between sixth and ninth out of 26 of the 21st-century skills taught by postsecondary instructors, according to both high school teachers and college faculty (ACT 2009). In addition to these college-entry level assessments, information, communications, and technology (ICT) proficiencies are essential to student success in higher education and are factors around which universities and K-12 schools can collaborate. To be successful in higher education, students must be able not only to master information literacy proficiencies (identifying an information need, locating and evaluating information, and synthesizing it into new knowledge), but also communicate this new knowledge, either in a paper, web page, podcast, or some other type of presentation while using technology tools throughout the entire process. For incoming university freshmen to be academically successful, they must have proficiencies in ICT before entering the higher education setting.

According to an American Library Association (ALA) report, when asked about school libraries, 97 percent of Americans agree (224.5 million) that school library programs are an essential part of the education experience because they provide resources to students and teachers, and 96 percent of Americans agree (222 million) that school libraries are important because they give every child the opportunity to read and learn (Davis 2009, 4). However, the state of many of the public high schools across the country, with budget shortfalls, teacher shortages, high-stakes testing, and school takeovers, the library and the librarian may be the least considered ingredient in creating a successful college-bound student. Libraries are a haven for many students, and they provide fundamental resources and support. The good news is that "the number of school libraries has changed by about 6% from the 1999–2000 and 2006–2007 school years. This increase is a result of population growth and the need for more elementary and secondary public schools, as well as consolidation of smaller schools into larger school districts and the need for additional school libraries to serve students and teachers" (ALA, 2010, 10). Nevertheless, many states have lost funding for school media specialists across K-12, have had to merge school media positions with other teaching roles or extra duties, or have eliminated the positions all together.

THE IUPUI STORY

Discussions about a potential research study and grant began in the summer of 2010, and development of a grant proposal included a projected three-year timeline to include extensive research, evaluation of curriculum, standardized testing, Common Core Standards, and community support and involvement. In identifying funding prospects, the authors focused on foundations with an interest in fostering access to and success in higher education. Since their research activities would include gathering data from local high school media specialists and students, we also explored funders that support K-12 initiatives. Their geographic location in central Indiana further defined which foundations might have an interest in the project. In addition, their desire to design a research plan that would gather detailed data across more than two years, from both campus and community populations, dictated that they seek a significant level of funding, which further defined the pool of funders that could reasonably be approached.

In the initial phase, they considered using *TRAILS: Tool for Real-Time Assessment of Information Literacy Skills* testing when gathering preliminary student data, as well as building a matrix that compares benchmarks and standards (state and national) for grades 9 through 12 and higher education, and gathering additional qualitative research from teachers, curriculum directors, and school media specialists. *TRAILS* is a project of Kent State University Libraries and was imagined as an instrument that would provide a "snapshot of high school students' understanding of basic information literacy concepts and as a fitting complement to Libraries' high school outreach program" (Kent State University Libraries). Although the TRAILS assessment is based on Ohio state standards, it aligns well with recently adopted information literacy standards in Indiana. Building upon what was discovered during the first phase of their planning, they hoped that considering the following questions would help them explore strategies, collaborations, and relationships:

- What resources and skills are needed to equip high school and college teachers as well as school media specialists with the skills necessary to support students' transition from high school to college?
- What early approaches or supports could be implemented in grades 7 through 12 to provide essential information literacy skills necessary for college readiness?

• What 21st-century information literacy skills are necessary not only for entry into higher education, but continued success, retention, and degree completion?

When their first letter of inquiry was rejected because the project did not adequately align with the local funding organization's community priorities, they began exploring other prospects that included large national foundations. As they carefully reviewed the guidelines of these foundations and considered how best to describe the project in terms that clearly fit the missions of these organizations, they realized two important things. First, what seemed obvious to them—libraries and library instruction play an integral role in student success at colleges and universities—was not as obvious to the funders. As neither a degree-granting unit of the university, nor an administrative office determining curriculum goals, their position in the academic lives of students is often not clear to external organizations.

The second thing they observed was that these national funders are interested in shaping policy rather than in supporting a single project on one campus in a particular city. While private national and community foundations contributed more than $6.3 billion to higher education between 2007 and 2010, these organizations are increasingly focused on improving performance and capacity in postsecondary education as a field (Kienzl et al. 2011). They prioritize projects and programs that are scalable, can be modeled, and have the potential to be meaningful across a region or the country (Kresge Foundation 2012). These two important realizations significantly informed their thinking about the research plan as it continued to develop. In addition to making a case for their project, they were going to have to make a case for the role of libraries in student success. They were also obliged to rethink the goals of the project. The information and tools the project yielded would have to be relevant beyond the boundaries of the campus, the county, and the state. Despite the challenges presented by these insights, they were determined to continue in the process and had committed to using the TRAILS assessment. They refined the process to include a campus-wide initiative as well, through a limited pre- and post- assessment in the freshmen learning communities on our campus, as well as the development of a faculty community of practice focused on information literacy, to better determine the expectations that higher education faculty have for students making the transition to higher education.

COMMUNICATION AND ENGAGEMENT

The beginning phase of their project involved several meetings to discuss who might be interested in learning about information literacy skills (was it only librarians?), as well as who would offer support in this endeavor. To secure funding and to carry out their research later, they would need the support and collaboration of a number of institutions, from local schools to the Indiana Department of Education. As they began to draft letters of inquiry, it became clear that to make a compelling case for their project to funding agencies, they would need to have these partnerships in place up front with carefully defined roles, expectations, and deliverables. While these groups would not likely benefit in a financial way from a grant that might be secured, they would want access to their research data. Their participation would be crucial, and the authors would need a thoughtful framework to guide their collaborations and later to share data. They focused on faculty from the School of Education in addition to partners at University College (the college that provides instruction and support for entering IUPUI students). Community partners included members from the IUPUI library board, the Indiana Department of Education, Ivy Tech Community College, and both public and private high school media specialists. There are advantages in involving a cross-section of people with vast interests, talents, perspectives, and investment. Sharing data with partners may seem like an obvious step with benefits for all the players, but it can be fraught with political and legal considerations (Ruskin and Achilles 1995). They had to approach their potential partners with respect for the difficult and important work they do, recognizing what worked well in their systems, rather than trying to point to problems. Also, they could not be sure what story the data would tell once it had been gathered and collated. They hoped it would be perceived as valuable to partners, but they knew it might just as well reveal problems and create more work for already underfunded, stressed school systems. A strong partnership plan would be critical to managing partnerships, as well as to the viability of any proposal they might submit.

As their next step, they decided to hold a stakeholders meeting where they could share their developing research plan and get feedback and observations from those they thought might benefit from the outcomes of our project. They invited stakeholders from the group of partners identified above. They identified individuals from various contacts and networking efforts and reached out to them via email with a description of the needs that led to the research project and a request for their input. They envisioned that going forward, these stakeholders would coalesce into a working group and eventually formal partners who would facilitate access to the students and media specialists needed for the project. In addition to face-to-face meetings and updates via email, they planned to continue the group dialogue via web-based meetings and an online project site where they could post mid-project discoveries and updates. Sixteen people attended the first meeting, all of whom saw value in the emerging research plan and potential benefits for their organizations via the data the project hoped to gather.

By broadening the scope of their project to a wider local community, they hoped to approach the scalable model research project that large national funders are looking for. These conversations and collaborations would also enhance campus engagement with the local community. And this wider web of stakeholders would also help them to disseminate their findings when the project was over, sharing the results and making it more likely that they might impact policy—again, a result that funders were seeking.

OWNERSHIP AND MANAGEMENT

Establishing trust with project partners can be uncertain when gathering data about particular institutions (especially something similar to standardized testing through the *TRAILS* site). There is a fine line between meeting the goals and the requirements of the grant and maintaining the buy-in of partners, when the data, reports, and progress could indicate problems for specific schools. The intent is not to shed light on what might not be working, but to improve and better prepare students to make successful transitions. Therefore, it is important to consider all parties' intent, willingness for transparency, and willingness to maintain open lines of communication throughout the process.

In addition to carefully observing the guidelines of the funding organizations that the authors considered approaching for support, they were also obliged to respect the processes and protocols of the large public university environment in which they work. To submit a letter of inquiry for funding, they had to gain the approval of university leadership via the institutional foundation that oversees fundraising for IUPUI. The possibility of competition from other projects within the university system first requires making a strong internal case before investing time in shaping a case for external funders.

Once they had permission to submit a letter of inquiry for *College Ready, College Bound*, the next step was to contact the university research administration. In addition to foundation boards, academic institutions often have offices that process and submit all grant applications for individual organizations or departments, and that office's staff can be a valuable resource. In particular, the people who work there are able to clarify budget questions about indirect costs, when allowable; any financial matches required by the funder; and the value of in-kind contributions of project inputs such as staff time and facilities. When a grant is awarded, this office administers the funds and monitors reporting. It demands thorough recordkeeping and holds grantees accountable for deadlines and deliverables. The function of this office is emblematic of the fact that once a grant is awarded, the proposal itself becomes a part of a contract agreement (Ruskin and Achilles 1995).

Essential elements of a proposal include:

- Meticulously followed funder guidelines, using the funder's own wording where possible
- A clear explanation of the project and its goals, with a substantive description of need using pertinent, current metrics
- An explanation of why the requesting institution is uniquely positioned to lead the project
- An introduction to key personnel and partners, as well as their individual roles
- A description of the mission that puts the research in context
- A description of expected outcomes
- A detailed, and if possible annotated, budget that clearly tells the story of the research activities, what inputs the library/university will be responsible for (such as staff time and benefits), and the communications plan, which demonstrates to the funder the intent to share findings widely in a way that supports its own goals

A timeline that shows that the project can be executed in a manner that aligns with the foundation's funding cycle:

- A plan for assessment and evaluation
- An explanation of support already committed for the project, as well as how we might broaden and continue our funding base to sustain the project through multiple phases (Ruskin and Achilles 1995)

The authors' timeline for proposals, meetings (cancelled twice due to ice and snow), and implementation had to be flexible. Academic time is a snail's pace—glacial in some cases—and the more parties that are involved, the more bodies to coordinate. Funding takes time; release of funds takes time. Institutional review board activities take time. Hiring support takes time. Implementation takes the most time, but once the process starts, it seems like there is never enough, and results have to be calculated at lightning speed. Constituents both inside and outside of the organization want to know when decisions will be made; when funds will be dedicated, released, and applied; and what types of follow-up will take place. Assessing impact and sustainability are crucial to closing the loop by showing evidence of discovery and change; these are key not only to report to the funding organization, but to all bodies involved in the process.

FURTHER DISCUSSION AND FUTURE PLANS

The nature of this project poses some particular challenges for pursing foundation support. Over the 15 years, foundations have changed their giving strategies to focus on K-12 initiatives and notably reduced their funding for higher education (Schneider 2007), pointing to shortfalls of innovation and measurable results (Marcy 2003). In addition, many external constituents do not realize that librarians are teachers, presenting an additional obstacle for creating a compelling rationale for the IUPUI project. Over the course of the last year (going on two), the authors were forced to rethink the questions they were answering . . . or asking, as well as how best to gather data, demonstrate that what they set out to find is what they expected, and how to change course when research, funding, or partnerships required revision. It was and continues to be an important question for them about what the role of library instruction is and could be, and not about what they can "fix." Library professionals often meet with students about their research questions and help finding resources, and the process of seeking grant funding is just like any other research project. Librarians, in the same way they advise their students, should not be afraid to refine their questions and look for new resources. Currently, the authors have engaged in the TRAILS assessment with 14 public and private high schools in the Marion county area, and over 1,200 students have participated in the project. Further follow-up will include focus groups consisting of K-12 librarians, faculty and administrators, and additional opportunities for assessment and professional development.

College Ready, College Bound will have implications and significant potential benefits for high school educators and students, as well as for higher education constituents. As the authors continue to raise funds for the next phase of the project, they hope their activities will help the wider community better understand the role of library instruction in student success. Like other teachers across the country, librarians are working to prepare students for the 21st-century workplace—some for jobs that do not even exist yet, as well as for their future roles as informed and engaged citizens of a global society.

BIBLIOGRAPHY

ACT. *The Forgotten Middle: Ensuring that All Students are on Target for College and Career Readiness before High School.* Iowa City, IA: ACT, 2008. http://www.act.org/research/policymakers/pdf/ForgottenMiddle.pdf (accessed October 28, 2012).

ACT. *2009 ACT National Curriculum Survey.* Iowa City, IA: ACT, 2009. http://www.act.org/research-policy/national-curriculum-survey/#.UI08msXR6So (accessed October 28, 2012).

American Library Association (ALA). "State of America's Libraries: A Report from the American Library Association." Chicago: American Library Association, 2010.

Barton, Paul E. and Richard J. Coley. *Parsing the Achievement Gap II.* Princeton, NJ: Educational Testing Service, 2009.

Beere, Carole A., James C. Votruba, and Gail W. Wells. *Becoming an Engaged Campus: A Practical Guide for Institutionalizing Public Engagement.* San Francisco: Jossey-Bass, 2011.

Davis, Denise M. *The Condidtion of U.S. Libraries: School Library Trends, 1999-2009.* Chicago: American Library Association, 2009.

Gibson, Craig, and Christopher Dixon. "New Metrics for Academic Library Engagement." Association of College & Research Libraries (ACRL) 2011 Annual Conference, Philadelphia, Pennsylvania. http://www.ala.org/ala/mgrps/divs/acrl/events/national/2011/papers/new_metrics.pdf.

Kent State University Libraries. "TRAILS: Tool for Real-Time Assessment of Information Literacy Skills." http://www.trails-9.org/ (accessed October 28, 2012).

Kienzl, Gregory S., Brian A. Sponsler, Alexis J. Wesaw, Amal Kumar, and Jill Jones. "Smart Money: Informing Higher Education Philanthropy." Washington, D.C.: Institute for Higher Education Policy, 2011.

Kresge Foundation. "Higher Education Productivity." Troy MI: Kresge Foundation, 2012. http://www.kresge.org/programs/education/higher-education-productivity (accessed October 28, 2012).

Lumina Foundation. "Results and Reflections: An Evaluation Report/Making the Numbers Add Up: A Guide for Using Data in College Access and Success Programs." http://www.luminafoundation.org/publications/Results_and_Reflections-Making_the_numbers_add_up.pdf (accessed October 28 2012).

Marcy, Mary B. "Why Foundations Have Cut Back in Higher Education." *Chronicle of Higher Education* 49, no. 46 (2003): B16.

National Center for Educational Statistics. "Fast Facts - SAT Scores." Washington, DC: U.S. Department of Education, 2012. http://nces.ed.gov/fastfacts/display.asp?id=171 (accessed November 4, 2012).

Ruskin, Karen B., and Charles M. Achilles. *Grantwriting, Fundraising and Partnerships: Strategies that Work!* Thousand Oaks, CA: Corwin Press, 1995.

Schneider, John C. "Foundations and Higher Education: Whose Agenda?" *Connection: The Journal of the New England Board of Higher Education* 21, no. 5 (Spring 2007): 28–31.

Section III: Programs and Resources

11

Supporting the High School to College Transition on a Shoestring

Kate Zoellner

Librarians across the educational continuum share a common goal of helping students develop information literacy skills that are critical to academic success and lifelong learning. The need for these librarians to work together was formally expressed in the *Blueprint for Collaboration*, which stated: "All educators—teachers, faculty, and librarians—share roles in helping students acquire information literacy skills effectively. Collaborative efforts that enhance the ability of these groups to fulfill their mission are imperative" (AASL/ACRL 2000, Background). Lack of funding and resources is often seen as an obstacle for librarians wishing to fully engage in these mission-critical collaborations. Librarians are challenged by shrinking budgets that result in the loss of staff positions and the need to do more with less; many K-12 schools are without certified school media specialists or librarians, too. Yet there are low-cost or free resources and approaches available to librarians with the time and determination to make use of them. This chapter will identify and explore several of these cost-free options and tools that can aid collaboration and support preparing students for successful transitions.

There are many ways in which high school and college librarians can collaborate to foster students' transitions to college and in turn student academic success, including low and no-cost options. As a first step, librarians need to understand what colleges expect of their students. Librarians can then utilize this knowledge and other resources to offer students research activities and experiences to facilitate their academic transition.

To understand student needs in higher education and offer learning activities that meet those needs, librarians can share knowledge and collaborate across grade levels, and can design and utilize learning activities that both engage students and prepare them for college-level research. Sharing and collaborating need not be resource intensive. Some approaches high school librarians can take to learn about college-level educational expectations include networking with librarians at pipeline institutions, participating in professional development initiatives, and investigating relevant educational standards. Developing learning activities and engaging students can then occur through the alignment of information literacy curricula, on-campus site visits, access to college library collections, and/or the use or modification of free web materials and tools.

PROFESSIONAL DEVELOPMENT

Librarians have several resources available to help them learn about supporting student transitions and the role information literacy education plays. These include talking with other librarians, pursuing continuing education, exploring pertinent online resources and learning about information literacy and the role they play.

Colleagues as Resources

To understand what is expected of students when they enter college, librarians working in secondary education must communicate with individuals working in higher education (Burhanna 2007). One of the most efficient ways to do this is by networking with librarians at pipeline institutions. Librarians at these institutions can explain what services the college or university offers to students that are different than or similar to those offered at their high school and public library. Librarians can also share information on the expectations faculty members have for first-year students such as example assignments.

Continuing Education Resources

Fostering and participating in professional development is another key way to make connections with librarians across what often seem like separate educational systems, lacking common goals and communication pathways. High school or college librarians can invite one another to provide a guest lecture for their students at the other's institution. Presenting one's experiences with students and instructors provides a beginning conversation from which collaborations can grow. If travel is a constraint, Skype or other web calling or conferencing software can be used to mitigate the barrier. Local and regional meetings also provide learning opportunities. For example, an academic librarian can ask if high school librarians in the local school district meet regularly and then seek an invitation to attend the meetings. Similarly, a high school librarian can ask to participate in the local university library's continuing education sessions. Participating in meetings and education in these ways enables librarians to see the bigger educational picture and to potentially learn from one another based on organic conversations in addition to asking specific questions.

Online Resources

In addition to face-to-face networking and professional development, no-cost options to expand contacts and knowledge include blogs as well as open access journals, listservs, and webinars. Local, state, and national professional associations, and the educational opportunities they organize and afford, such as member listservs, conferences, and online trainings, are a low-cost means of meeting potential collabora-tors and learning new strategies and information to support work with students.

Standards Resources

Whether or not a librarian chooses to be a formal member of a professional associa-tion, he or she still has free access to many association resources. Librarians can inves-tigate and access the academic standards that associations write or endorse that are relevant to high school and college research. For example, both the Association of College and Research Libraries' (ACRL) *Information Literacy Competency Standards for Higher Education* and the American Association of School Librarians' (AASL) *Standards for the 21st-Century Learner* are freely available in full text online. One of the main goals of educators working across the education continuum (e.g., P-20 initia-tives) is streamlining and scaffolding educational standards through alignment. For this reason, librarians must be aware of the ways in which such alignment is already occur-ring within the profession, in their state, and at the local level.

Creating collaborative partnerships, developing professionally, and investigating the use of educational standards requires time, not funding. Continually taking advantage of these networking and learning opportunities is time well spent, leading librarians to a better understanding of the research needs of high school students once they enter higher education. This knowledge can then be applied in your teaching practice, to the design of bridging learning activities, or the use of activities already available, that both engage students and prepare them for college-level research. There are several low- and no-cost approaches librarians can use towards these ends, too.

STUDENT DEVELOPMENT

A number of free or low-cost resources also exist for librarians to use in engaging students in learning and to help prepare them for successful transitions. Resources include physical library spaces and collections, research-based learning activities and assignments and open educational resources, most freely available online.

Physical Resources

One way to engage students is through the physical university library. This can occur via site visits and offering access to collections. Since most high school library collec-tions cannot provide the depth and range of materials available at an academic library, academic librarians can facilitate the borrowing of physical items from their libraries by high school teachers and students. Students using the materials will then begin to understand the types and depth of resources that will be accessible to them when they enter college or university, such as historical newspapers and specialized databases. The students can also begin to learn about the ways in which finding and using the sources may require different information seeking and evaluation skills. Visits to aca-demic libraries are another, though potentially high cost, way to engage high school students. Visits may be a stand-alone program, such as the program at Wayne State University, or they may be built into currently existing on campus programs, such as the Summer Bridge Program at California State University (Nichols, Spang, and Padron 2005/2006; Haras and McEvoy 2007).

Research Resources

Learning activities that take place in high schools or online can be co-developed, or sought and repurposed. For example, librarians at a high school's pipeline institution can share the instructional activities they use with students, and together the librarians can design scaffolded and corollary assignments. Research projects can also be developed by school and college librarians that involve the analysis of first-year syllabi to identify the information literacy skills required during students' first year (Oakleaf and Owen 2010). If a formal study is too time intensive, high school librarians can explore university web sites to find first-year course syllabi, and can look to library web sites for handouts and pathfinders.

Open Educational Resources

Web sites that aggregate materials for librarians and educators, such as lessons plans and assessment measures, are another no-cost resource to consult in designing research activities. These sites are developed and maintained by both nonprofit and for-profit entities. Key professional association web sites to consult include:

- American Association of School Librarians (AASL) (www.ala.org/ala/mgrps/divs/aasl/)
- ACRL Information Literacy Resources (www.ala.org/ala/mgrps/divs/acrl/issues/infolit/)
- ACRL Instruction Section (IS) (www.ala.org/ala/mgrps/divs/acrl/about/sections/is/)
- AASL/ACRL Interdivisional Committee on Information Literacy (www.ala.org/ala/mgrps/divs/aasl/aboutaasl/aaslgovernance/aaslcommittees/informationliteracy.cfm)
- Library Instruction Round Table (LIRT) (www.ala.org/ala/mgrps/rts/lirt/)

The AASL web site connects librarians with the Standards for the 21st Century Learner Lesson Plan Database and the Best Websites for Teaching and Learning, among other resources. The searchable Lesson Plan Database includes plans that support school librarians in teaching the *AASL Standards* and that have been vetted by AASL reviewers. The database has been slowly growing since it was initiated in December 2010; it can be browsed by grade level and content area. AASL began the Top 25 Websites for Teaching and Learning award in 2008. In addition to their teaching and learning focus, web sites are selected for inclusion in the list if they are free, easy to use, and connect to the *AASL Standards*. Among other resources, the Information Literacy Resources web site of ACRL offers a Standards Toolkit to walk librarians through the *Information Literacy Competency Standards for Higher Education*, and the ways to use and adapt them. The ACRL-IS web site connects you to the Peer-Reviewed Instructional Materials Online (PRIMO) Database, among other resources. PRIMO materials can be used to teach information literacy concepts and skills. For example, there are sites on generating keywords, understanding databases and peer review, plagiarism, and more.

In addition to professional association online resources, myriad other web sites provide guidance on learning activities and aggregate lesson plans. Select sites are described in Table 11.1. Note that there is some overlap between the content on these sites.

In addition to sites that offer lesson plans and guides, one unique site exists that specifically addresses for students the high school to college transition as it relates to

Table 11.1.

Select Open Educational Resources Web Sites

Web Site and Address	Description
Gateway to 21st Century Skills http://www.thegateway.org	Lesson plans, learning activities, and online projects for grades PreK-12 that are already available on various Internet sites. Search by keyword, subject, grade, P21 student outcome (Partnership for the 21st Century 2011), teaching method, assessment methods, and more. Materials are provided by public, government, and non- and for-profit groups such as the Library of Congress, National Education Association, PBS, and ReadWriteThink.
OpenCourseWareConsortium http://www.ocwconsortium.org	Focuses solely on university-level open courseware materials. For each course, the syllabus, student readings and assignments, as well as lectures and notes are usually included. Browse by language and source; search by topic. Materials are provided by higher education institutions and related organizations worldwide, such as Massachusetts Institute of Technology (MIT) and United Nations University.
Open Educational Resources (OER) Commons http://www.oercommons.org	Online textbooks, videos, lesson plans, activities, readings, university courses, and other educational materials. Browse by subject area, grade level, material type, and provider. Search by keywords and conditions of use (e.g., Creative Commons Attribution). Materials are provided by public, government, non- and for-profit groups such as Connexions of Rice University, Internet Archive, National Park Service, SciVee, and individual authors.
S.O.S. for Information Literacy http://www.informationliteracy.org	Lesson plans, handouts, podcasts, videos, teaching ideas, and a platform to create web-based lessons to support the teaching of information literacy skills for K-16. Search by keyword, subject, author, grade level, or content type; search by AASL, ACRL, national, or state standard. Materials are submitted by individual authors or collaborators and are reviewed by two independent peers before being posted to the site.

research and libraries, Transitioning to College: Helping You Succeed (www .transitioning2college.org). The site offers high school students streaming modules to teach them about the key differences between work and libraries in high school and in college. Additionally, the site provides a glossary of new terms for students (e.g., government documents, electronic reserves) and points to additional resources for students and educators alike (e.g., Purdue University Online Writing Lab). The site was developed by Kent State University and funded by the Institute for Library and Information Literacy Education and a Library Services Technology Act grant.

Table 11.2.

Assessment Resources Web Sites

Web Site and Address	Description
TRAILS: Tool for Real-Time Assessment of Information Literacy Skills http://www.trails-9.org	Online knowledge assessment tool designed for teachers and school librarians to use with students in grades 3, 6, 9, and 12. The multiple-choice items are based on standards from AASL and Ohio Academic Content Standards. All cover five areas: develop topic; identify potential sources; develop, use, and revise search strategies; evaluate sources and information; recognize how to use information responsibly, ethically, and legally. The tool enables teachers to identify students' information-seeking skills so that they can then modify or target their instruction to improve student performance.
RAILS: Rubric Assessment of Information Literacy Skills http://railsontrack.info	A research project designed to explore and help academic librarians assess information literacy outcomes through the use of analytic rubrics. The site and project, begun in 2010, aim to offer rubrics for academic librarians to use, as well as training materials on the ways to use and score the rubrics. Browse rubrics by topic and/or by creator.

There are far fewer online no-cost resources, perhaps only two, that focus solely on measuring information literacy skills so that librarians can determine if students are learning from the activities they design. The two resources are described in Table 11.2.

Utilizing materials already available to educate and engage students in research activities is an efficient and low-cost endeavor. Online educational resources can be used as they exist, modified to address local needs, or viewed as models from which to design lessons, activities, and assignments. Finding out what materials are available and what assignments are given to first-year students at pipeline institutions is another approach to designing research experiences students can apply in college. Site visits may be an option for libraries with some funds, too, as a way to give students a visceral experience of conducting research at the college level. Having students view the Transitioning to College videos or open courseware materials can also give them a sense of what is to come.

MOVING FORWARD WITH YOUR SUPPORT

Supporting students in their high school to college transition does not require funding; rather, it requires that librarians dedicated to preparing students for successful academic transitions invest the time to learn what students need to be able to do once they graduate from high school and to use that understanding to design learning activities that bridge educational gaps. High school and college librarians, through collaboration and utilizing no- and low-cost existing resources, can create learning activities that support and guide students through the high school to higher education transition.

BIBLIOGRAPHY

American Association of School Libraries (AASL)/Association of College & Research Libraries (ACRL) Task Force on the Educational Role of Libraries. *Blueprint for Collaboration.* Chicago: Association of College and Research Libraries, American Library Association, 2000. http://www.ala.org/acrl/publications/whitepapers/acrlaaslblueprint (accessed October 29, 2012).

Bruch, Courtney, and Katherine Frank. "Sustainable Collaborations: Libraries Link Dual-Credit Programs to P-20 Initiatives." *Collaborative Librarianship* 3, no. 2 (2011): 90–97.

Burhanna, Kenneth J. "Instructional Outreach to High Schools: Should You Be Doing It?" *Communications in Information Literacy* 1, no. 2 (2007): 74–88.

Dobie, Dawn, Nancy T. Guidry, and Jan Hartsell. "Navigating to Information Literacy: A Collaboration between California High School and College Librarians." California School Library Association (*CSLA*) *Journal* 34, no. 2 (2010): 6–9.

Haras, Catherine, and Suzanne L. McEvoy. "Making the Bridge: Testing a Library Workshop for a Summer Bridge Learning Community." *Research Strategies* 20, no. 4 (2007): 257–270.

Hayden, K. Alix. "Together We Are Stronger: K-16 Information Literacy Collaborations." Presentation at the Treasure Mountain Canada National Research Symposium Transforming Canadian School Libraries to Meet the Needs of 21st Century Learners, Edmonton, Canada, June 2–3, 2010. http://tmcanada.pbworks.com/f/ Together+We+are+Strongersz+-+Hayden.pdf.

Nichols, Janet W., Lothar Spang, and Kristy Padron. "Building a Foundation for Collaboration: K-20 Partnerships in Information Literacy." *Resource Sharing & Information Networks* 18, nos. 1–2 (2005/2006): 5–12.

Oakleaf, Megan, and Patricia L. Owen. "Closing the 12-13 Gap Together: School and College Librarians Supporting 21st Century Learners." *Teacher Librarian* 37, no. 4 (2010): 52–58.

Partnership for 21st Century Skills. *Framework for 21st Century Learning.* Washington, D.C.: Author, 2011. http://www.p21.org/overview/skills-framework (accessed October 29, 2011).

12

Information Literacy and 21st-Century Skills: Training the Teachers

Ann Walker Smalley and LeAnn Suchy

INTRODUCTION

Teachers are unprepared to integrate information literacy and 21st-century skills into their curriculum for K-12 students. Quite often, these skills are not discussed in teacher education programs in higher education, leaving teachers ill prepared to foster this knowledge that their students need in an information society (Loomis et al. 2008, 1). "Educators need extensive professional development to learn how to help students master 21st-century literacy skills" (Fahser-Herro and Steinkuehler 2010, 59).

Library media specialists can assist in the information literacy and 21st-century skills development of students in K-12 classrooms, but many teachers do not recognize what students can learn from library media specialists. A complaint from media specialists "is that many teachers are either not interested in, or are resistant to" collaboration (Roux 2008, 58). However, when teachers do collaborate, they see that media specialists can help their students evaluate and find reliable resources and can contribute to student learning (Roux 2008). If teachers can see this value when they are willing to collaborate, why are more teachers not doing this?

The need to develop these valuable collaborations is the reason that the Metronet Information Literacy Initiative (MILI) is a beneficial program for teachers, media specialists, and ultimately students. MILI is a collaborative project between Metronet and individual school districts within its region. Metronet is a multicounty library system in the Minneapolis–St. Paul, Minnesota, metropolitan area that serves all types of libraries—school, public, academic and special libraries. Designed for library media specialists and teachers, MILI is a training program that advocates teaching information literacy and 21st-century skills in the classroom and the collaboration between teachers and media specialists to better prepare students for higher education and the world they will encounter upon graduation. MILI is funded out of the state appropriation that Metronet receives as one of seven multicounty multitype library systems in Minnesota. MILI has the complete support of Metronet's governing board because it meets Metronet's vision of connecting librarians from all types of libraries to extend the reach of resources.

Metronet provides all of the training and support for MILI participants. It also provides supplies needed for MILI. The largest expense is personnel, with minor investments in the wiki and the blog site on Ning that participants use. There is one full-time employee for MILI training and coordination, the MILI program manager. The director of Metronet spends approximately 10 percent of her time on MILI. In addition, the school districts that are part of MILI provide meeting space, teacher time off and substitutes as needed, continuing education or board credits, and any additional incentives they wish to provide.

MILI GOALS AND BEGINNINGS

MILI's goal is to help teachers integrate the *Minnesota Educational Media Organization (MEMO) Recommended Standards for Information and Technology Literacy* (Minnesota Educational Media Organization 2009) into their teaching. These standards were developed in 2004 to describe the processes and specific skills a learner must understand and practice in order to meet a minimum level of information literacy. The standards are divided into four general areas: the research process, technology use, reading and media literacy, and responsible use of technology and information.

After a lobbying effort by MEMO and the Minnesota Library Association, the standards were designated as an information source in the refresh of Minnesota Content standards. Minnesota law states, "The commissioner of education must revise and appropriately embed technology and information literacy standards consistent with recommendations from school media specialists . . . " (Office of Revisor of Statutes 2012, 120B.023, Subd. 2).

This successful effort was well received by librarians in all types of libraries but raised the question of how teachers and media specialists would learn about the standards and incorporate them into their teaching. In 2006, Metronet began developing MILI as a model for professional development that can be used in any district to train teachers and library media specialists on the concepts in the standards.

The focus of the MILI curriculum is about teaching the research process rather than on teaching specific tools or resources. For instance, when using databases, the focus is to teach how to choose one, evaluate content, and manage the data and resources found rather than teaching how to search a specific database. The teaching of the research process is woven throughout the MILI curriculum in the form of three Rs:

1. **Research:** Improve the ability of participating students to conduct research by teaching their instructors a research process focused on the five steps of the Research Project Calculator (RPC). The RPC is an interactive online tool that provides a research process model for students, teacher and media specialists.
2. **Reliable resources:** Help teachers and students identify and use available, reliable resources in the research process to produce accurate, authentic research products.
3. **Responsible use:** Increase teachers' and students' understanding of the legal and ethical issues related to information and technology use, including plagiarism and copyright.

Since the MILI curriculum revolves around the three Rs, for the program to be most effective, teacher participants must have a research project in their curriculum. The end product of the research project is not defined by MILI, but the teachers must be willing to incorporate the three Rs into their research assignments. MILI helps teachers do this by designing each MILI session to address one or more of the Rs. Web 2.0 tools—blogs, wikis, online collaboration tools, and more—are included in the instruction in context of one or more of the three Rs and where using these tools enhances teaching and student learning.

Another important MILI goal is to raise awareness of the impact of library media programs on students and on teachers. As a library organization, Metronet knows the value of well-funded, professionally staffed library media programs; thus a goal of MILI is to encourage collaboration between media specialists and classroom teachers.

METRONET AND SCHOOL DISTRICT RESPONSIBILITIES

MILI began in the St. Paul public high schools in the 2006–2007 academic year. The first year held steep learning curves for all parties involved and highlighted a need to clearly define party responsibilities. Since the 2007–2008 school year, a written agreement between Metronet and school districts has been used. The agreement states that all participating school buildings must have a full-time certified media specialist who is participating (or has participated) in the MILI program. Other responsibilities are defined in the following lists.

Metronet will:

- Develop and present a two-day orientation, 30-minute monthly webinars, and up to nine after-school trainings for media specialists and teachers to include:
    - Documentation and implementation of the curriculum
    - Participation tracking by media specialists and teachers via blogs and attendance at sessions, and transmitting this to the district for participant credit
    - Working with school liaisons to ensure teachers participate as agreed
    - Meeting logistics (food, supplies, handouts, wiki, trainer fees, etc.)
- Work with each school district to establish a rubric for the training so that teachers, library media specialists, district administrators, and participants all understand the expectations and requirements to receive credit for participation
- Conduct evaluation of MILI program participants and other evaluation as determined

School districts will:

- Provide payment or other incentives for district staff participating in MILI; payments or other incentives are determined by the individual school district but may include tangibles (e.g., computer hardware) or appropriate credit
- Track and apply any credit for licensure, continuing education (CE) credits, merit pay, or related awards
- Designate a liaison to work with Metronet and be the contact person for district participants who may have questions about credits, participation, or incentives
- Recruit media specialists and teachers to participate
- Obtain commitment from participants that they will attend all training/meeting sessions and complete all requirements of the MILI program

- Provide meeting space for all training sessions; training spaces must have adequate technology to accommodate all participants
- The willingness and ability to unblock Web 2.0 tools used for educational purposes

Teacher and library media specialist participants sign a contract verifying their understanding of their responsibilities, including that they will:

- Attend the full two-day orientation session
- Attend all after-school sessions
- Arrive on time and stay through the entirety of meetings
- Attend all monthly webinars
- Commit to the time involved in participating in the program, which is estimated to be approximately 70 hours over the 10 months, not including the two-day orientation; it includes attending all meetings from September to May and about an hour a week outside of class completing the required assignments and blogging regularly to document progress
- Complete all activities to meet the minimum requirements of the MILI program according to schedule, including any assignments
- Document achievement of personal and professional goals related to the training by posting to individual blogs
- Share their expertise and experience in after-school trainings and other venues
- Complete project evaluations according to the schedule provided

MILI TRAINING

The MILI program is 10 months long. It begins in August, before the start of school, with an intensive two-day introduction to information literacy, MILI goals and expectations, and sessions on the tools participants need, including navigating the MILI wiki and participation in the MILI Ning. During the academic year, teacher and media specialist participants meet twice a month. The first session is a 30-minute webinar where that month's foundation content is delivered. The second session is a two-hour, in-person meeting after school. In this second session, participants hear more about the topic and receive hands-on training in the concept or tool. All of the MILI training is delivered by librarians with experience in academic, public, and/or school libraries.

A new topic relevant to one of the three Rs is discussed each month. Topics vary and can include collaboration, research databases, productivity, web searching, copyright, plagiarism, capturing the social media backchannel conversation, note taking, social bookmarking, and presentations. Every session includes how the concept or tool is being used in education and how using it with students can improve their information literacy and 21st-century skills. No tool or concept is taught merely for its own sake. Web 2.0 tools in particular are put into the context of classroom teaching. While some of the "how" is included in the session, the real value to teachers and media specialists is the "why" of using a tool and the outcomes they may experience when using the tool with students.

Research

MILI begins by highlighting the research process and asks participants to evaluate previous assignments using the ART Evaluation of Assignments, a tool designed for the MILI program. With this tool, participants analyze whether a previous assignment was authentic, incorporated the research process, and was supported by the teacher and media specialist. Participants answer questions about their assignment, including:

- Does the project encourage students to think critically, solve problems, and be creative?
- Are students guided to locate, gather, and evaluate information from a variety of reliable resources?
- Are students encouraged to use the media center or another library?
- How does the assignment help students avoid plagiarism and create original work?
- Does the teacher give tools to help students through the steps of the research process?
- Do the teacher and students evaluate the research process and how the process affected the product? Do they discuss how to improve the process?

Using these questions, participants brainstorm better ways to incorporate research into their assignments and collaborate with media specialists in identifying where students may find difficulty with the research and where media specialists could help.

After analyzing their assignments, participants then use the Research Project Calculator, a tool that helps break down the research process into five steps: question, gather, conclude, communicate, and evaluate. This calculator is designed to help students work through assignments by breaking down the research process and giving tips and tools they can use to complete each step. Teachers can log into the calculator to add their own information in each step; therefore, while the calculator is designed to help students work through assignments, it also helps teachers analyze research skills included in their assignments.

Since many students begin and end their research online, where it is easy to copy and paste, plagiarism issues are part of the MILI curriculum. Rather than devote time to tools that detect plagiarism, participants learn about creating low-probability-of-plagiarism projects (Johnson 2007). The idea of designing assignments that give students choices, demand critical thinking skills, are hands-on, and answer real questions is new to many participants (Johnson 2007). Participants are encouraged to work with each other to incorporate low-probability-of-plagiarism pieces into their assignments.

Reliable Resources

After participants have analyzed their assignments and incorporated more research skills, the next step in the MILI program is encouraging them to engage their students with reliable resources. It is no secret that students typically search Google before using the library, but they have misconceptions that Google is easy, reliable, and saves them time (Corbett 2010). Quality information can be found using Google, but the types of things students usually find and use are far from academic and often unreliable. MILI participants are taught how to "think like a librarian" and consider how information is created, organized, retrieved, and applied. Participants learn better search techniques so that they find more useful and reliable Internet results. Participants are introduced to advanced search tips for Google as well as given information on other search engines they could use, including the Internet Public Library and Google Scholar.

The discussion of Google searching and the Internet serves as an introduction to searching the subscription databases available through the participants' school, public, and academic libraries. These databases are discussed in depth, particularly those in the Electronic Library for Minnesota (ELM), a suite of databases available to every resident of the state. Participants analyze the databases using the Database Exploration

Checklist, a tool designed for the MILI program. The checklist is a list of questions about the databases that helps determine which ones might work best for students or for a particular topic. Some of the checklist questions include:

- What subject areas does this database cover? Is the database useful for a particular type of project?
- Is there a student population that would find this database and its content useful?
- How many publications does the database include? Which years of publication are covered? How frequently is it updated?
- Are there convenient guides for moving through the database? Tutorials? Where is the "Help" button?
- Are there useful special features? Lexile levels, image search, primary resources, multimedia, or other features?

Advanced database features such as citations tools, content and journal alerts, organizing resources, and sharing content are also introduced.

Once teachers find the databases that will be useful for their students, they are encouraged to meet with their media specialists to discuss search strategies. Teachers are urged to plan time in their research curriculum for their students to meet with the media specialists for training using library resources.

Responsible Use

Once students find reliable resources, they need to understand how to use the resources responsibly within copyright and fair use guidelines. MILI participants are given tools and information so that they can help their students understand how to ethically use the information that they find.

The copyright webinar introduces what it means to be a content creator in the 21st century. It then offers a basic overview of what copyright is and is not, a review of what is in the public domain, and an overview of fair use. It also introduces participants to the Creative Commons, a new concept to most of them. It ends with an assignment to review the MILI Copyright wiki, read some of the copyright scenarios posted there, and comment on them. The Copyright wiki is a supplemental source created for the program that includes scenarios, resources for teaching about copyright, and lists of copyright-friendly resources for photographs, images, music, and more.

The webinar and assignment result in many detailed questions that the participants bring to their next in-person session. Rather than trying to answer long, involved questions on individual situations, the after-school session uses a game show format with questions on the webinar content. The competition is not only to answer the questions, but also explain the concept or situation. This helps keep the discussion on broader copyright concepts, applying fair use factors, content creation, resources, and ways to teach copyright concepts to students. While some participants still want specific answers (they are directed to their district copyright policies and resources), most leave with a greater understanding of fair use, public domain, and copyright, as well as new knowledge about Creative Commons.

Web 2.0 Tools

While creating research-based assignments, finding reliable resources, and using them responsibly are the key factors in the MILI program, participants are also introduced to Web 2.0 tools that help organize, evaluate, and use information. Since many of these tools can streamline staying informed or can help organize information and research, the MILI program addresses how these tools work, how they can be used in education, and how they help students engage with their classmates and the greater world.

For instance, when discussing productivity, MILI training focuses on RSS feeds and the ability to organize information in an RSS reader. Participants are told how information is organized, what RSS feeds are, where to locate RSS feeds (including in library databases), and how to manage RSS feeds in a reader. Most participants are new to this concept and unaware that tools like this exist to aid in the location and organization of information.

More tools and concepts are introduced throughout the program, with participants creating Google Documents, Diigo social bookmarking accounts, Screencast-O-Matic or Jing videos, and presentations with tools like Animoto and Storybird.

MILI EVALUATION

It is important to the success of MILI that the program be evaluated each year. There are several methods used to evaluate participation and the content of the program, including participants' blogs, observation of participant progress, and surveys.

Blogging

Every MILI participant joins the MILI Ning. Throughout the 10 months of the program, participants are required to blog in the Ning at least once a week. Participants have flexibility about what they blog, but they are encouraged to write about what they are learning, share how they have used what they have learned in MILI in their classroom or personally, explain new tools they have discovered, or discuss other MILI-related topics. If they miss the live version of the webinar, they must watch the archived version and answer questions about it on their blog. Participants are also encouraged to comment on others' posts. Because every MILI participant joins the same Ning, this is where interdistrict communication is seen.

Through the blog posts, MILI instructors and district staff can see that participants are engaged and almost immediately start using concepts and tools with their students. It is not uncommon for participants to share library databases and tools like blogs and wikis with their students the day after they learn about them. This is not expected of participants, but year after year, they are enthusiastic to try new concepts quickly in their classrooms.

In their blogs, participants often give thoughtful analysis of how they use these new concepts or tools with their students. Almost all participants have reported that after learning about library databases and better ways to search the Internet, they see their students begin to find and use higher quality resources in their assignments. Participants also regularly report an increase in the level of engagement they see online from their introverted students when they incorporate blogs, wikis, or the use of backchannel tools like TodaysMeet during discussions.

Another trend in teacher blog posts is their analysis of the collaboration with their media specialists or their plans to do so in the future. Teachers and media specialists who already collaborate are able to expand their teaching to include new tools and resources that both have learned in MILI. Participants also report an increase in the amount of technology students use to report their findings. Students move beyond traditional reports and begin to use online or district tools to create podcasts and video presentations.

Observation of Monthly Progress

It is easy to see participants' progress month-to-month. Some participants enter the program stating that they are technologically savvy, but they quickly learn that being technologically savvy and having 21st-century skills means much more than being able to search Google. These participants may know about blogs and wikis, but not how to effectively use them in classrooms. Most do not understand the depth of library databases, tools like Google Docs for collaboration, ways to organize information through RSS feeds, or copyright concepts. Many participants can quickly pick up new tools and at the end of the program, they are the ones that most highly report usage of multiple tools with their students.

Participants with low technology skills have a difficult time in the MILI program because this training is fast-paced and designed on the assumption that participants have solid computer skills. While lower-skilled participants may learn much throughout the program, they are slower to adopt concepts and tools with their students. Most of them report that they will use tools and concepts with their students in the school year following the MILI program.

Survey

Participants receive an extensive survey at the completion of the program. The questions focus on the course evaluation, MILI content and teaching, their learning, and the demographics of how many students they teach that could potentially receive MILI content in the classroom.

The MILI course receives high marks. Eighty-five percent of participants report that MILI has expanded their knowledge and experience with Web 2.0 tools and information literacy concepts to a great extent. Sixty-five percent of participants report that if MILI were offered in their district again, they would go through the program one more time, and 90 percent of participants would recommend the MILI program to their colleagues.

MILI content and teaching also receives high praise from participants. More than 80 percent of participants state that MILI has either moderately or greatly increased their collaboration with media specialists, ability to teach the research process, students' use of reliable resources, and use of 21st-century tools and concepts in their classroom.

When it comes to their own learning, dramatic growth is seen in MILI participants. When asked how often they had used tools or concepts taught in MILI in their classroom before the program and how often they used those tools or concepts after MILI, almost all participants report a rise. Before MILI, for most tools or concepts, 10 to 20 percent of participants reported using them. After MILI, depending upon the tool, 70 to 90 percent of participants reported using them regularly in their classrooms.

More than 6,000 students have been taught concepts or learned about tools their teachers or media specialists learned in the MILI program. MILI has helped teachers in many disciplines incorporate information literacy and 21st-century skills in their teaching. Participants from many different subject areas, including history, English, mathematics, chemistry, physics, special education, and physical education, have gone through the program.

CONCLUSION

The effects of the MILI program are immediate. Teachers report teaching more research skills, expanding the use of technology, and collaborating more with media specialists in their classrooms. They report that their students become more proficient in identifying reliable resources and using them responsibly. Collaboration between media specialists and teachers shows students the value of asking a librarian for help.

MILI has proven successful in all of the districts where it has been taught. This success is due to a variety of reasons:

- **All tools and concepts are taught in context:** Participants are given not only the mechanics of a tool or concept, but also how it can work in a classroom, why it can help increase information literacy, and what outcomes can be expected when they use the tool or concept with students.
- **The gift of their time and instructors' time:** This adds a lot of value to participant success. Participants make a significant commitment of time to their own learning and see the result quickly when they fully participate in the webinars and after school sessions. They also have access via chat, email, and in person to the Metronet librarians who understand the tools, the concepts, and their application.
- **The ripple effect has enabled MILI to reach far beyond participants who have been in MILI:** MILI participants have reached out to their colleagues to share what they have learned through formal and informal staff development sessions in buildings and districts. Word of mouth about the value of MILI has meant that every session in every district is full the second year it is offered. The ripple effect has statewide implications, too. After the MILI program is introduced into a district, that district's usage of the statewide ELM databases rises noticeably. At least half of the top 10 users of ELM databases are MILI schools.

All MILI training materials are available online and licensed under a Creative Commons license: http://metronetmili.pbworks.com. This program can be adapted in any school district across the country, and Metronet encourages the use and adaptation of training materials.

BIBLIOGRAPHY

Corbett, Patrick. "What about the 'Google Effect'? Improving the Library Research Habits of First-Year Composition Students." *Teaching English in the Two-Year College* 37, no. 3 (2010): 265–277.

Fahser-Herro, Danielle, and Constance Steinkuehler. "Web 2.0 Literacy and Secondary Teacher Education." *Journal of Computing in Teacher Education* 26, no. 2 (2010): 55–62.

Johnson, Doug. "Plagiarism-Proofing Assignments." Last modified June 15, 2007. http://www.doug-johnson.com/dougwri/plagiarism-proofing-assignments.html (accessed October 29, 2012).

Loomis, Steven, Jacob Rodriguez, Rachel Tillman, and John Gunderson. "The Logic of Convergence and Uniformity in Teacher Production." *Teaching Education* 19, no. 1 (2008): 1–10.

Minnesota Educational Media Organization. "MEMO Information and Technology Literacy Standards." Last modified December 12, 2009. http://api.ning.com/files/wfKa-V7N9BWkTn3hMa2aRb-UnCMuL4m*lyp-RwUGMCI_/infotechlitstandards04.pdf.

Office of Revisor of Statutes, State of Minnesota. "120B.023, Minnesota Statutes 2012, Subd. 2." St. Paul, MN: Author, 2012 https://www.revisor.mn.gov/statutes/?id=120B.023&year=2012#stat.120B.023.2 (accessed October 29, 2012).

Roux, Yvonne R. "Interview with a Vampire, I Mean, a Librarian: When Pre-Service Teachers Meet Practicing School Librarians." *Knowledge Quest* 37, no. 2 (2008): 58–62.

13

Libraries and the Early College: Notes from the Field

Meghann Suzanne Walk, Brian L. Mikesell, Matthew Harrick,
and Teresa Tartaglione

Those who follow public education are aware that for a decade now, the great debate has centered on No Child Left Behind and the use or misuse of accountability measures and standardized tests. However, this decade has also seen the rise of the early college movement, an alternative approach to the perceived shortcomings in American high school education.

Many colleges, especially community, have long had programs that allow individual high school students to enroll in courses prior to high school graduation. What distinguishes the early college movement from these dual enrollment programs is that early college programs enable cohorts, rather than individual students, to attend college at a younger than usual age. This often happens through institutional partnerships between high schools, known as early college schools, and associated colleges (though in the case of the Bard College affiliates, the early college is a self-contained college that enrolls students full-time before they finish high school).

The explosion of early college can be directly attributed to the Bill & Melinda Gates Foundation Early College High School Initiative (ECHSI). Since 2002, this initiative has grown to include over 200 early college schools on the model of the Middle College High School at LaGuardia Community College in New York City. In these programs, a high school, most frequently operating on a college campus, offers successful students the opportunity to take courses in the partner college tuition-free. ECHSI schools target students underrepresented at traditional colleges, such as low-income students, English-language learners, minority students, and those who would be the first in their family to attend a postsecondary institution (Berger, Adelman, and Cole 2010).

The Gates Foundation's interest in early college was inspired by the opening of Bard High School Early College (BHSEC) in 2001 (Berger, Adelman, and Cole 2010). The BHSEC campuses are formed through a partnership between public school systems

(New York City and Newark, New Jersey, at present) and Bard College, but the result is a unified institution that is both a high school and an accredited college serving students ages 13 to 18.

Bard High School Early College, in turn, drew directly from Bard College's long-standing innovation in early college education, Bard College at Simon's Rock. Simon's Rock, founded in 1966, does not have an affiliated high school. Instead, it is a four-year liberal arts college that accepts students after tenth or eleventh grade. Simon's Rock was founded on the belief that not only are some students ready for college at a younger than usual age, but that they are in fact ripe for the intellectual explorations that are the hallmark of liberal arts education (Sharpe 2006).

This chapter will share the experiences of librarians from across the spectrum of early college. Brian Mikesell is the director of the Alumni Library at Bard College at Simon's Rock; Meghann Walk is the library director at Bard High School Early College–Manhattan; Teresa Tartaglione is the school librarian for Manhattan/Hunter Science High School; and Matthew Harrick is adjunct assistant professor/reference librarian at Brooklyn College. Each of these librarians will describe their experiences, as well as unique aspects of their programs.

BARD COLLEGE AT SIMON'S ROCK, ALUMNI LIBRARY

Simon's Rock is a four-year, liberal arts college that admits students after tenth or eleventh grade. The transition to college for Simon's Rock students is not gradual and is more abrupt even than the usual student's path because students elect to leave high school before finishing and start college early. Inevitably, this means that students miss out on some experiences traditionally associated with high school.

Most freshmen have never been in an academic library; most have yet to experience the bewildering array of print and electronic resources academic libraries provide; most have not confronted a major research project; and most do not want to admit it when they are struggling. This may be especially true for early college students, whose self-image is often bound up in being ahead of the curve. Adding to this lack of orientation is the fact that they are skipping over some high school assignments and classroom activities that would help them learn to find and evaluate information, synthesize information for use in academic projects, cite sources properly to avoid plagiarizing, and understand the multitude of media formats in which information is now packaged. How, then, does the Alumni Library support the Simon's Rock students' transition from high school to college given these challenges?

Information fluency instruction is a key part of the strategy. All students at Simon's Rock take a sequence of seminars over their first three semesters, and a required part of each seminar is information fluency labs taught by librarians. Similar in concept to science labs—the classes supplement and support the curriculum of a full academic course. The labs meet three times per semester to fill in the blanks for students transitioning from high school to college. They include writing assignments, discussion, and hands-on practice. Each lab session builds on previous ones and expects that students are becoming more sophisticated information consumers. By the third semester, there is less "how to" and more discussion and debate, based on the notion that well-educated college graduates should have a sophisticated understanding of their information environment and information ethics.

Another way that the library supports the transition to college is through its mission to provide individualized, in-depth service. This is primarily possible through the advantages of the small size of the student body. The advantageous ratio of library staff to students allows staff to engage with students in a way that is impossible at most colleges. Not only are librarians able to spend more time working with a student on a project or assignment, but they are able to get to know most students personally, which helps break down students' resistance to asking for help.

Finally, the Alumni Library as place is an essential component. For many students, the library plays an important role in their life as a "third place," a concept developed by Ramon Oldenburg and Dennis Brissett (Oldenburg and Brissett 1982; Oldenburg 1999)—somewhere other than "home" (dorm) and "work" (classroom) that engages them in the community and provides something essential that is otherwise lacking. It is one of the most popular places on campus, providing a unique mix of social and academic space. As such, the library provides spaces that are a flexible fit with students' changing needs rather than the needs of previous generations. Students visit the library for a wide range of activities, and the space accommodates different noise levels, varying study habits, assorted computing needs, and a mixture of comfortable furniture options. The library, then, becomes a crossroads with endless possibilities for interaction, ensuring that students not only have a superb academic experience of which the library is a central part, but also providing them with meaningful, safe places where they can grow into their adult selves as part of a community.

BARD HIGH SCHOOL EARLY COLLEGE

Bard High School Early College (BHSEC) radically tests the philosophy that guides Simon's Rock, operating on the principle that young adult education can and should be transformed to inspire the intellectual awakening too often reserved for the postsecondary years (Botstein 1997). The result is a set of public high schools that obliterate the transition from high school to college.

Not only an early college, not a high school linked to a college, BHSEC is literally an institutional hybrid—a high school early college. Professors teach in both ninth and tenth grades (the high school) and eleventh and twelfth grades (the accredited college program, known at BHSEC as Year 1 and Year 2), while students earn both a high school diploma and an associate's degree. This means that BHSEC must maintain the scholarly quality integral to its status as a liberal arts college while ceaselessly improving its teaching to meet the universal commitment to educating students from diverse backgrounds that is the hallmark of K-12 public school. At the BHSEC–Manhattan campus, this has entailed an expansion of the library mission from service to teaching.

At BHSEC–Manhattan, the library inhabits the same physical space as subject faculty, allowing for informal interactions that can lead to more formal collaborations. Therefore, library instruction is a natural part of the pedagogical landscape. Most exciting, feedback from students, parents, and faculty (especially social studies, science, and college seminar professors) has generated the momentum for the integration of information literacy instruction from ninth grade through Year 2. Though assignment-aligned access strategies remain the domain of librarian-led workshops, the librarian is working with departments to develop professor-led information literacy instruction. In this context, information literacy is broadly understood as "learning how to learn"—especially how to learn at a liberal arts college. This means 13- to 18-year-olds read texts written for academic or well-educated audiences (in Common Core language, complex texts). They must learn to read strategically, and to read for both the what and the why. In other words, they have to start transitioning from understanding nonfiction texts as either information in the colloquial sense (objective, discrete, factual) or "just" opinion to the more complicated world of knowledge and its construction. Instruction (formal or informal during every possible teachable moment) that aids students in this development enables adolescent students to successfully make the high school to college transition.

Of course, a commitment to teaching does not diminish the function of the library as resource provider. Collection size is one major traditional difference between high school and college. At BHSEC, patrons access academic journals through subscriptions to full-text databases such as JSTOR, but the print collection is limited. Like the school, the print collection is young and therefore is relatively small. Furthermore, the BHSEC campus libraries are the size of two or three classrooms, which means on-site print access will likely remain limited. Using regional connections, BHSEC has taken multiple routes to overcome this gap and maintain its integrity as a college. Students are taught to appreciate and navigate the vast resources of the New York Public Library. Also, unlike other New York City public high schools, the BHSEC campuses are independent members of the Metropolitan New York City Library Council (METRO) library consortium, and therefore interlibrary loan is a regular part of library services.

Finally, BHSEC–Manhattan has discovered that students are one resource the library has in abundance. At any given time, approximately 10 percent of students are in the library, and each year, the library becomes more effective at taking advantage of this. College students can volunteer at the Math Center, provide general homework help at the Year 2 tutoring table, or earn general education credits as Writing Center tutors or library interns. Together, student ownership, access to college-quality collections, and an evolving learning how to learn information literacy curriculum help the BHSEC library erase the gap between high school and college.

MANHATTAN/HUNTER SCIENCE HIGH SCHOOL

The Manhattan/Hunter Science High School (MHSHS) was founded in 2003 in partnership with Hunter College and is an early college high school located on Manhattan's Upper West Side. MHSHS aims to enroll students who have not necessarily excelled in middle school, but who have a great interest in science and learning and have the potential to succeed, provided they receive adequate support and guidance. Upon acceptance into MHSHS, students work under the expectation that they will complete the majority of their high school requirements during ninth, tenth, and eleventh grades, combining New York State and Hunter College curricular requirements. These courses are taught with college-level critical thinking skills in mind, in partnership with MHSHS and Hunter College faculty members, with some classes offering both high school and college credit. Seniors in good standing spend their senior year on the Hunter College campus, completing high school courses taught in the college style and taking an undergraduate science course of their choice. Students with a qualifying grade point average are met with an acceptance to Hunter College upon their high school graduation, should they wish to attend. Regardless of their choice of college, all graduating seniors should leave MHSHS with college credits.

MHSHS is part of a unique situation—the school resides within the Martin Luther King (MLK), Jr. Educational Campus and is one of six high schools located within one large building. As a campus, the six schools maintain their own identities but share certain facilities, including the campus's newly established school library media center. Having opened in September of 2009, the campus library is located in a neutral space with easy access from the cafeterias. It is hard to say how a school that relies so much on questioning and research existed without the resources of a library, but MHSHS's principal, Susan Kreisman, fought to bring the library into existence.

Still, the challenge becomes how one library can adequately serve the unique needs of an early college high school, when the needs of five other schools also have to be addressed. Collection development has been particularly challenging. All six schools share the library space and materials; therefore, the collection must reflect the New York State general curriculum as well as each school's special focuses (arts, law, theatre, etc.). The reading levels between all six schools vary greatly, adding another challenge to collection development. After three years, the library has developed a solid fiction and graphic novel collection, which attracts student attention and gets them in the door, as well as a broad range of nonfiction and reference materials. The average number of books per student in New York City is around 7. The MLK, Jr. campus library has roughly 2.9 books per student; this is not enough to meet the students' needs.

Collaboration is also a challenge. Because of the divisive nature of a Campus setting, the position of librarian can be isolating. While the librarian works for each school, they are not formally part of the staffs of any of the schools and it can be particularly challenging to connect with teachers. Scheduling classes for six different schools with differing bell schedules means that many needs cannot be addressed. Having one class in researching for a week closes the library to the rest of the building for that period—it is not fair to the other schools. It is a difficult balancing act, and it often means saying "no" more than anyone would like to. Despite the scheduling challenges, in the three years that the library has been open, the MHSHS teachers, specifically in the humanities department, have made a great use of the space. Collaboration between classroom teacher and librarian helps to ensure that students are receiving information literacy instruction in a way that enhances and supports their classroom instruction and assignments.

Recently, the MLK, Jr. campus has received monies from the Manhattan Borough President and the City Council's Office to begin the construction of a new library space. The planned library is located in the same neutral and easily accessible space, but will be twice the size of the existing library and house a computer lab, separate teaching space and seating to accommodate the school's large population. The allocation of these funds demonstrates the importance of the library program's contribution to the MLK, Jr. campus and the impact the library has had on the entire school community.

STAR EARLY COLLEGE HIGH SCHOOL

The STAR (Science Technology and Research) Early College High School program is a collaboration between Erasmus Hall High School in Brooklyn, the Gateway Institute, and Brooklyn College, with support from the New York City Department of Education. Brooklyn College is part of the City University of New York system, and offers undergraduate and graduate degrees to over 16,000 students. Begun in 2003, the program pairs Brooklyn College faculty with high school students to prepare them for college-level science academics and research, while also reinforcing Regents curriculum and study. Receiving partial funding from the Woodrow Wilson Early College and Gates Education Foundations, STAR enrolls over 400 students "who have achieved a 98 percent promotion rate and an attendance rate of 94 percent" Brooklyn College

2012, under STAR). Students are enrolled in the program based on interviews, test scores, and an interest in and willingness to challenge themselves to achieve beyond traditional high school curricula. When students begin the program, they take classes with other STAR peers; upon reaching their junior and senior years, they take college-level classes with Brooklyn College students, and they have the potential to earn a maximum of 30 college credits.

The faculty librarians at Brooklyn College provide the important connection between the students and their research, and between the STAR liaison and the School of Education. Because enrolled high school students likely miss out on library instruction at their home school, it is contingent upon the faculty librarians at Brooklyn College to expose enrolled students to the myriad ways that academic librarians assist in the navigation of scholarly materials. Also, since there are multiple sections of STAR freshmen that come to the library throughout the semester, each for one library session only, instruction must be compressed and concise.

The principle collaboration between STAR and the library is the two-hour instructional session and tour for all STAR freshmen early in the program. Even though these sessions are not topic oriented, there is heavy emphasis on the technology that is available at the library, since one of the main foci of the STAR program is technology itself. Typical bibliographic instruction classes for incoming freshman at Brooklyn College start at a baseline that assumes no prior knowledge of, or experience with, college-level research; the STAR bibliographic instruction sessions address students at a similar level. Because these instruction sessions take place at a college level, they cover more substantively the library's resources, complementing the level of research the students are doing. Brooklyn College Library is in prime position not only to focus student research and provide the skills to turn their research into quality projects, but also to offer access to the library's resources: subscription databases and print journals—the scope, quantity, and depth of which might not be available at their high school library; circulating and reference texts; government documents; and special collections materials. However, the library does not explicitly collect resources for the STAR program or its curriculum.

The librarian structures each STAR class as a micro version of the research process: detailed catalog searching, sophisticated use of general and advanced databases, and evaluating books and articles for currency and content, all take center stage. Recognizing and avoiding plagiarism is highlighted and used as an introduction to the different types of citation style guides. Students then perform a quick search of their own and cite the article or book they have found to immediately apply the skills taught in the session. And even though Millennials are assumed to have an innate familiarity with Internet searching, the profusion of sources on the web demands that the librarian spend time defining information literacy as well, engaging the students to evaluate web sources on their own. The goal for freshman instruction is to instill good research skills and habits so that, by the time they are juniors and seniors, they will be more than capable to succeed and meet the requirements to earn college credit, as well as to promote return visits to the library.

INSIGHTS AND ADVICE

Library involvement is crucial due to the inherent tensions and opportunities stemming from the situations and the missions of early colleges and early college schools, and non-librarian stakeholders are starting to take notice (see, e.g., Rosenbaum and

Becker 2011; Cunningham and Matthews 2011). As for us, a common theme among the diverse experiences of the four early college libraries is the challenge posed by condensed education. Early college situations are certainly not the only time an information literacy or research knowledge gap (or at least a gap in ideal practice) has been noted. Early college, however, presents a situation in which the expectation that students should be taught these skills somewhere else at some other time becomes untenable.

How librarian-educators can respond to this need is influenced by the specific early college programs and partnerships. At Simon's Rock and BHSEC, the library's sole mission is to support the early college, enabling the librarians to steadily make inroads into integrating sophisticated information fluency instruction across all four years of the curriculum. At MHSHS and Brooklyn College, the early college school is one of many programs served by the library. However, as these two programs have evolved, the perceived value of libraries, library resources, and library instruction to administrators and content educators has increased. In the case of MHSHS, this involved the creation of a new school library where none had previously existed. In the case of the STAR program at Brooklyn College, a precollege orientation seminar grew into a ninth grade university library–based research project (Newton and Vogt 2008).

Not surprisingly, the collections gap is another area of concern. Again, it is a concern shared with the traditional high school to college transition, but one made glaringly obvious by the mission of early college schools when combined with the limits placed on collections by youth, space, and differences of funding.

However, at a time when so much focus is on reaching "digital natives" where they are online, it is somewhat surprising that each early college program included an emphasis on the library as space and place. At Brooklyn College, a visit to the physical library precedes even an assignment requiring resources. At MHSHS, the library literally bridges the campus schools and uses acquisitions aimed at reading for pleasure to draw students in. At Simon's Rock and BHSEC, the libraries have clearly established themselves as the "third place" for an eclectic social and academic community. This seems reflective of one of the hallmarks of adolescence—a desire for intense personal connections with others, a desire that can create strong attachments to the place where these connections occur. In this case, that place is the library. Thus the authors' collective advice is to encourage this desire. Make the library into students' "third place." Ask students (and teachers) what materials they want to see in the library. Above all, actively convey to students that the library is their library, and every librarian a guide in this endeavor that is early college.

BIBLIOGRAPHY

Berger, Andrea, Nancy Adelman, and Susan Cole. "The Early College High School Initiative: An Overview of Five Evaluation Years." *Peabody Journal of Education* 85 (2010): 333–347.

Botstein, Leon. *Jefferson's Children: Education and the Promise of American Culture*. New York: Doubleday, 1997.

Brooklyn College. "High School Programs." Brooklyn,NY: Author, 2012. http://www.brooklyn.cuny.edu/web/academics/honors/highschool.php (accessed October 29, 2012).

Cunningham, Cecilia L., and Roberta S. Matthews. "POV: Five Lessons on College Retention from Early Colleges." *Community College Week*, April 18, 2011. http://www.ccweek.com/ news/templates/template.aspx?articleid=2492&zoneid=7.

Newton, Anne, and Kristen Vogt. *Ensuring College Success: Scaffolding Experiences for Students and Faculty in an Early College School.* Boston, MA: Early College High School Initiative, 2008. http://www.earlycolleges.org/Downloads/ STARcasestudy.7.pdf (accessed October 29, 2012).

Oldenburg, Ramon, and Dennis Brissett. "The Third Place." *Qualitative Sociology* 5, no. 4 (1981): 265–284.

Oldenburg, Ray. *The Great Good Place: Cafes, Coffee Shops, Bookstores, Bars, Hair Salons, and Other Hangouts at the Heart of a Community.* New York: Marlowe, 1999.

Rosenbaum, James E., and Kelly Iwanaga Becker. "The Early College Challenge: Navigating Disadvantaged Students' Transition to College." *American Educator* 35, no. 3 (Fall 2011): 14–20, 39.

Sharpe, Patricia. "Early College: What and Why?" In Robert W. Smith, ed., *Time for Change: New Visions for High School*, pp. 121–134. Cresskill, NJ: Hampton Press, 2006.

14

21st-Century Skills and Preservice Teacher Education

Jillian Brandt Maruskin

The phrase "21st-century skills" has been a buzzword among librarians for some time now, but it is now working its way into the vocabulary of some educators and education administrators. Twenty-first-century skills (critical thinking, problem solving, collaboration, creativity, communication, and innovation) are an integral part of ensuring a successful transition into college. New technologies emerge constantly and demand swift adaptation. As such, 21st-century skills are dynamic. The phrase itself will likely morph into something new as technologies and educational standards evolve. Out of these skills has emerged the "21st-century student." No longer satisfied to sit in a chair and be lectured, 21st-century students require learning experiences replete with collaboration and engaging activities.

It has become clear that efforts to ease this transition require collaboration among librarians, educators, and administrators. Academic librarians in particular hold great responsibility because well-prepared college freshman increase the likelihood of retention and student success. In addition, they are in a position to share the expectations faculty will have for students when they arrive at college. Communication between academic and school librarians is essential, and the practice is becoming more common, but there is yet another area where academic librarians can ease the transition to college and the workplace for high school students; namely, by working with preservice teachers.

Targeting preservice teachers is a logical step in the effort to impart and promote 21st-century skills (teaching the teacher). Although the current population of preservice teachers is primarily composed of "digital natives," there is a need for 21st-century skills education. Lei (2009) discovered that growing up in the digital age does not necessarily mean that every child had equal access to the digital technologies. Further, although digital native preservice teachers believe that technology is an indispensible part of their lives, they have conservative attitudes about how it should be used in the classroom. Preservice teachers also harbor concerns over whether technology is a distraction and even where its use is appropriate (Lei 2009).

BACKGROUND

Ohio Wesleyan University (OWU) is a small liberal arts college located in Delaware, Ohio, with a full-time enrollment of approximately 2,000. There are six librarians to support 31 departments on campus. As part of their service, librarians are expected to identify opportunities for instruction.

Ohio Wesleyan University's teacher education program provides students with a solid theoretical base coupled with practical experience. During the 2011–2012 school year, there were 20 students with a declared major of education. Preservice teachers are required to take a teaching workshop (EDUC 377: Teaching Workshop: Supporting and Extending the Learning) in conjunction with completing their student teaching. The teaching workshop focuses on applied instructional technology as well as reading and writing in the content area (the subject area of choice).

A major component of EDUC 377 is the technology assignment (see Figure 14.1). The technology assignment was created to help students complete their Technology Competence Form (see Figure 14.2), a required element for their program portfolio. As outlined in the form, technology competency includes the following: using software applications, information literacy skills, integrating technology into teaching, and collecting data for teaching and learning.

The technology assignment seeks to help students skillfully draw on technology in order to strengthen instructional practices, thus augmenting the ways teachers can and should present concepts and material to learners. The assignment also seeks to emphasize the responsibility teachers have to familiarize learners with the processes of accessing and using information from the various genres of new technology. Finally, it provides the experience of producing information using technological skills.

The context and goal of the technology assignment naturally lent itself to collaboration between liaison librarian to education and a faculty member. This assignment is meant to help students meet an information literacy skills requirement, as well as a requirement to integrate technology into teaching competency. To help students complete this assignment, the librarian created a presentation during which she not only introduces students to Web 2.0 applications (and the responsible use thereof), but also to 21st-century skills, the benefit of collaborating with school librarians, and the various resources available from INFOhio, Ohio's virtual K-12 library.

This chapter will discuss how the content of the library workshop addresses the technology competency requirement form and the technology assignment. There will also be a discussion of student work, as well as student reaction, via the workshop's exit survey.

WORKSHOP INTRODUCTION

Both instances of this workshop took place in the classroom instead of the library. The librarian uses a LibGuide (http://libguides.owu.edu/21stcenturyskills) to supplement the session. Instruction begins with personal reflection. The students are asked the following:

Do you remember what it felt like to be a freshman in college? Were you scared? Did you feel prepared?

Figure 14.1. EDUC 377 Teaching Workshop Technology Application Learning Task

CONTEXT AND GOAL:

The accessibility and plethora of technological resources available to educators seems to necessitate units of instruction that skillfully draw on technology to strengthen instructional practices, augmenting the ways teachers can and should present concepts and material to learners, creatively and effectively engaging them in opportunities to actively interact with core content. Technology also frees the ways in which learners can demonstrate what they know and can do. Teachers not only have a responsibility to familiarize learners with the processes of accessing and using information from various new technologies, in essence how to be a discerning consumer, but also they have a responsibility to provide opportunities for learners to develop skills and experiences as producers using such technological skills, genres, and mediums.

For this learning task you will explore both of these responsibilities that you will assume as a teacher.

PART 1:

Construct a blog, wiki, or podcast for a class, a unit, or a lesson that would be appropriate for your current placement site or teaching assignment. Though you do not have to actually implement it, the use of technology should be something intellectually, contextually, developmentally, psychologically appropriate for your targeted class and unit of instruction.

Some things to keep in mind:

- Content is important – research and make the content meaningful for learners, refer to texts, traditional and non-traditional sources.
- Be creative in how content is displayed, conveyed, used.
- Refer often to Richardson text and notes from J. Brandt Maruskin.

PART 2:

Option 1:

Construct a learning task (assignment) for learners in which they will be asked to create a blog, wiki, or podcast as part of a unit of instruction. Think through carefully what you would like them to produce, what you would like them to accomplish (both in terms of their learning process and product, and what they can share with their peer colleagues via their product), and what you would like them to learn about your content and about technology. This should be for the *same context* as for Part 1.

You should include a rubric or scoring guide for assessing this learning task.

PART 2

Option 2

Develop a lesson plan that uses *technology in integral ways to implement instruction and to enhance student learning of content: skills, material, concepts, dispositions.* Think carefully about your content as well as your standards and learning goals/objectives for the lesson. Consider the information you received in podcasts, wikis, blogs as well as what you know about effective Power Points in addition to the information from today's session. How can you as the instructor use technology to more effectively instruct all learners and how can you develop learning tasks that help students engage with the material in interactive and engaging ways using technology to consider the content, perhaps in new, different, or extended ways. *The lesson should include opportunities for both instruction and student engagement with technology.*

Some things to keep in mind for Part 2:

• Both instruction and the student learning task must incorporate technology.
• Use of technology must be meaningful to support student learning – not just engaging.
• Refer often to Richardson text and notes from Maruskin.
• This does not need to be implemented during student teaching.

General Notes:

• Note date of Workshop Session on your syllabus
• Consult with Jillian Brandt Maruskin: make an appointment at the session, either during the break or via email.
• Technology Competence Form should be completed.
• Due Date: One week after the workshop session. You will be asked to share your work.

The librarian shares a list adapted from Patricia Owen's 2010 article "A Transition Checklist for High School Seniors" of skills college faculty say freshman lack. The class discusses the implications of this perceived gap in knowledge and the role of the high school library and librarian. This discussion emphasizes the relevance of the workshop.

Before proceeding, the librarian shows the students an agenda for the workshop. The agenda is as follows:

• Introduction to 21st-century skills
• INFOhio resources
• Web 2.0 applications
• Practical examples
• Discussion of the assignment

INTRODUCTION TO 21ST-CENTURY SKILLS

Beyond the aforementioned definition of 21st-century skills (critical thinking, problem solving, collaboration, creativity, communication, and innovation), it should be emphasized that these skills transcend research. These are skills that students will use

Figure 14.2. Preparing Competent, Committed, Professional Teachers for a Diverse, Democratic Society

Candidate Name _____

Licensure Program _____

Anticipated Graduation Date _____

Technology Competence Form

I. Using Software Applications

Software	Assignment(s) or Information Systems Workshop(s) Demonstrating Competence (Brief title and one sentence description sufficient).	Department, Course Number, Faculty Signature and Date
• Word Processing		
• Email		
• Presentation (Ex: Powerpoint)		
• Presentation (Ex: Publisher, Podcasts, blogs)		
• Spreadsheets (Ex: Excel)		
• Web Authoring (Ex: Front Page, Wikis) [Recommended but not required].		

II. Information Literacy Skills (completed in EDIC 251 or higher)

Skill	Assignment(s) Demonstrating Competence (Brief title and one sentence description sufficient).	Department, Course Number, Faculty Signature and Date
• Using Research Databases		
• Analyzing Websites		

III. Integrating Technology into Teaching (completed through Student Teaching)

Skill: All of above, including Smart boards	Assignment(s) Demonstrating Competence (Brief title and one sentence description sufficient).	Department, Course Number, Faculty Signature and Date
• Creating lesson plans that use technology meaningfully and effectively with PK-12 students Or • Creating lesson plans that require PK-12 students to use technology meaningfully to extend their learning		

IV. DATA FOR TEACHING & LEARNING (complete through Student Teaching)

Skill	Instructional Unit	Signature and Date
• Uses technology to collect, manage, and analyze data to impact PreK-12 student learning.		

You are responsible for maintaining and updating this form. Complete form must be submitted before program completion.

daily in the classroom, in group work, in test preparation, and in the completion of assignments. To further convey the importance of these skills, the librarian mentions that Ohio is part of the Partnership for 21st Century Skills. P21 is a national organization that advocates for 21st century student readiness. P21 focuses on helping educators integrate 21st century skill into the educational experiences of students. The organization advocates for governmental policies that support this aim (Partnership for 21st Century Skills 2011, "About").

To fulfill one of the most important aspects of the P21 mission, Ohio is on an aggressive timeline to revise and implement its educational standards. The new standards will allow students to be prepared for college and the workplace by developing 21st-century skills and promoting communication, leadership, and collaboration (Partnership for 21st Century Skills 2011, "Ohio"). Ohio has adopted Common Core Standards in English language arts, mathematics, science, and social studies (Common Core State Standards Initiative 2011). Since the main components of these standards are skills like critical thinking, problem solving, and information literacy, educating preservice teachers to impart these skills on their future students is an absolute necessity.

INFOHIO RESOURCES

Since the majority of OWU's preservice teachers go on to teach in the state of Ohio, the librarian devotes a good portion of the workshop to introducing INFOhio resources. INFOhio is a collection of state-funded resources available freely (via username and password) to all of Ohio's K-12 students, teachers, parents, and librarians. In addition, INFOhio provides electronic resources for schools and instructional development for teachers while promoting information and media literacy through the use of technology (INFOhio 2011, "About").

The librarian begins at the INFOhio homepage (http://infohio.org) with a tour of the resources available for each of the grade groups (K-5, 6-8, and 9-12). She points out that many of the resources available through INFOhio are the same as or very similar to OWU resources. This portion of the workshop usually results in questions from students regarding their individual content areas.

It is important to spend some time on the Educator portion of the INFOhio web site, as this should serve as a home base for Ohio teachers. It includes information about Ohio's standards, citation guides, Internet2 (an organization that negotiates on behalf of schools to secure cost-effective network and technology solutions), sample lesson plans, and more. A particularly important part of INFOhio's Educator site, the 21st Century Learning Commons, is discussed in the next section of this chapter.

Although the majority of OWU's students go on to teach in the state of Ohio, assistance is offered to help out-of-state students find comparable resources to use in their classrooms.

INFOhio's 21st Century Learning Commons/21 Essential Things

INFOhio's 21st Century Learning Commons is a place where educators can learn to enhance 21st-century learning for their students by utilizing various technologies and learning methods. Teachers who complete the 21 Essential Things tutorials are eligible for continuing education credits. The tutorials are self-guided, interactive sessions that last anywhere from five to 20 minutes. The sessions cover topics such as effective search engine use, professional development, use of research databases such as EBSCO, and much more. The Commons also hosts forums where teachers can share success stories and provide support for one another.

INFOhio Research Project Calculator

INFOhio's Research Project Calculator (adapted, with permission, from the University of Minnesota's Research Project Calendar) is a simple, interactive way for students to engage in the research process. Students enter information about their assignment (due date, type of assignment, etc.) and are given a timeline to complete the following steps:

- Question
- Gather
- Conclude
- Communicate
- Evaluate

Each step of the research process includes a series of questions and/or tasks as well as an explanation of how each step contributes to the research process as a whole. Students receive email reminders before each step is due.

Teachers have access to support materials to use in conjunction with the Research Project Calculator. Numerous PDF guides are available, including graphics to help students narrow their topics, hints on how to generate research questions, student research planning guides, and much more.

The research project calculator is an important part of INFOhio's resources and, as such, the librarian spends some time demonstrating how it works and showing the supporting materials available to teachers. During both sessions of this workshop, the librarian has had students mention that they wished they had known about the calculator during their time at OWU.

WEB 2.0 APPLICATIONS

Web 2.0 applications (and the appropriate use thereof) play a large role in my workshop. Before launching into a description of Web 2.0 applications, the librarian refers to the technology assignment so that the students understand the context. The opportunities to use such freely available applications in the classroom are endless. The web is bursting with sites to create wikis, blogs, videos, podcasts, picture books, collages, and more. The key for teachers is knowing when and how to use them.

The librarian introduces students to Go2web20.net, an index of web applications organized by purpose (e-learning, collaboration, design, etc.). Students are asked to use this site to keep up with emerging technologies and to determine which technology best suits their students' needs. It is important to emphasize that teachers must be cautious about which applications they use in the classroom. They cannot use a tool just because it seems cutting edge or exciting. It must add value to the learning experience and be age appropriate. Preservice teachers are encouraged to experiment with Web 2.0 applications on their own well in advance of actually using them with students.

PRACTICAL EXAMPLES

Examples are a necessary component of this workshop. For the first installment of the workshop, the librarian created examples of a blog, Wordle, podcast, and Bubblesnaps. Her examples are simple and, as such, did not require a large time commitment. The second installment included work from previous students. Linking to previous student projects is a practice she will continue.

Students are asked to submit links or copies of their work to the librarian but the librarian has been less than successful in compiling an arsenal of student work. Once the assignment is over, students tend to be uncommunicative. In the future, the librarian will compile links on the day of the presentations. By compiling student work and combining it with her own examples, the librarian can represent a variety of content areas and gain familiarity with the large number of available web applications.

One of the ongoing tasks related to this workshop is creating examples using new web applications. To save time and creative energy, librarians should consider keeping a running theme through examples. The OWU librarian, for example, uses Shakespeare's *Hamlet*. A common theme allows students to compare and contrast the usefulness of various web applications without being distracted by widely varying content.

DISCUSSION OF ASSIGNMENT AND WORKSHOP CONCLUSION

After the course instructor leads a discussion of the technology assignment, the workshop concludes with a brief survey (see Figure 14.3). Students are asked to rate the value of various aspects of the session and are given the opportunity to freely comment. According to survey results, all of the students think the workshop will help them complete the technology assignment. They all feel it is their responsibility to prepare their students for college and/or the workforce. They are not sure they will be able to keep up with Web 2.0 applications on their own, but they are also not sure whether they will partner with their school librarian (this disconnect indicates there may be a need for school librarians to more effectively promote their services to faculty). The majority of students feel uncomfortable trying to explain 21st-century skills to someone else. One student wrote, "I would love to see even more types of technology to use in the classroom. It would be really helpful to include a hard copy list of the resources." Another said, "Just learning where to start was really helpful. Also, being reminded that technology can be useful in every discipline is important. Learning more about specific apps would be helpful."

Only students in the second installment of the workshop were surveyed. The librarian plans to review and revise the exit survey before each installment of the workshop.

COMMENTARY

For the past two years, the technology assignment has been given toward the end of the semester. After a discussion with the course instructor, they decided that the assignment will be given earlier, as it can be useful for other coursework. This workshop is always evolving. The librarian and the instructor plan to work closely to determine where else the librarian might be able to insert instruction into this course.

Figure 14.3. Incorporating 21st Century Skills Into The Curriculum: Workshop Exit Survey

Jillian Brandt Maruskin
Public Services Librarian

Please take a moment to provide feedback about the workshop. Note: Your responses may be used in my forthcoming chapter in the book *Informed Transitions: Libraries Supporting the High School to College Transition.*

1. Will this workshop help you complete your Technology Assignment?
   ☐ Yes
   ☐ Not Sure
   ☐ No

2. Do you understand the concept of 21st Century Skills (enough that you could explain them to someone else)?
   ☐ Yes
   ☐ Not Sure
   ☐ No

3. How likely are you to partner with your school librarian?
   ☐ Likely
   ☐ Unsure
   ☐ Not likely

4. Do you think Web 2.0 technologies are an effective way to engage students in the curriculum?
   ☐ Yes
   ☐ Not Sure
   ☐ No

5. Do you feel it is your responsibility to prepare your students for college and/or the workforce?
   ☐ Yes
   ☐ Not Sure
   ☐ No

6. If yes, do you expect to be supported in this effort by your administration?
   ☐ Yes
   ☐ Not Sure
   ☐ No

7. Do you think you will easily be able to keep up with new Web 2.0 technologies to use in your classroom?
   ☐ Yes
   ☐ Not Sure
   ☐ No

8. In your future position, would you be interested in recurring workshops introducing you to new Web 2.0 technologies to use in your classroom?
   ☐ Yes
   ☐ No

Additional Comments (Be Candid!)

_____
_____
_____
_____
_____

About You
Name _____ E-mail _____
Address _____ Phone _____
City, State, Zip _____

Thank you for your participation!

CONCLUSION

Although there is little doubt that 21st-century skills are a vital part of preparing our students for the workforce and college, the challenge remains: How do we make these skills seem important, exciting, and necessary to our teachers? Another challenge lies in the terminology. In some arenas, the phrase "21st-century skills" has been replaced with the term "transliteracy." With workshops such as this one, academic librarians can keep preservice teachers informed and continue the conversation. Thankfully, the curriculum and standards line up with our mission. The evidence for the value of these skills is readily available; our responsibility is to collect and share it with our students and faculty.

BIBLIOGRAPHY

Bubblesnaps. http://bubblesnaps.com (accessed October 27, 2011).

Common Core State Standards Initiative. "Common Core State Standards." Washington, DC: Author, 2011. http://www.corestandards.org/the-standards (accessed October 27, 2011).

Go2Web20. http://www.go2web20.net/ (accessed October 27, 2011).

INFOhio. "21st Century Learning Commons." http://learningcommons.infohio.org/ (accessed October 27, 2011).

INFOhio. "About INFOhio." http://www.infohio.org/ABOUT/about.html (accessed October 27, 2011).

INFOhio. "Research Project Calculator." http://www2.infohio.org/rpc/ (accessed October 27, 2011).

Lei, Jing. "Digital Natives as Preservice Teachers: What Technology Preparation Is Needed?" *Journal of Computing in Teacher Education* 25, no. 3 (March 1, 2009): 87–97.

Maruskin, Jillian. "Incorporating 21st Century Skills into the Curriculum." Ohio Wesleyan University Libraries. http://libguides.owu.edu/21stcenturyskills (accessed October 27, 2011).

Owen, Patricia. "A Transition Checklist for High School Seniors." *School Library Monthly* 26, no. 8 (April 2010): 20–23.

Partnership for 21st Century Skills. "About Us." http://www.p21.org (accessed October 27, 2011).

Partnership for 21st Century Skills. "Ohio Standards." http://www.p21.org/route21 (accessed October 27, 2011).

Prezi. http://prezi.com/ (accessed October 27, 2011).

Wordle. http://www.wordle.net/ (accessed October 27, 2011).

15

SPOT on Transitions: Enhancing 21st-Century Academic Literacies in High School Science Students

Dale Lackeyram, Peggy A. Pritchard, Kim Garwood, and Clarke Mathany

The first year of postsecondary education is a period of tremendous social and emotional development for learners. Compounding this are the increased cognitive demands of university-level courses, including the use of peer-reviewed journal articles as a key source of information. Entering students are expected to know how to find and critically analyze scholarly literature, write clearly, and become independent learners for the first time. For many freshmen, these expectations, in combination with the pace of the academic semester, present a formidable academic transition challenge.

One approach to helping students through this transition is to offer supplementary academic support and training in the freshman year. Most colleges and universities do this, including the University of Guelph (Guelph, Ontario, Canada). From the learner's perspective, however, participation in these activities increases the burden on individuals who are already feeling overwhelmed. An alternate approach is to introduce academic transition training to students in the terminal years of high school, when they are considering and preparing for postsecondary education. This strategy has the added advantage of introducing new academic skills in a familiar context where students can apply them and experience their immediate relevance.

In this chapter, four members of the University of Guelph Library's Learning and Curriculum Support Team describe the Science Portal for Ontario Teachers (SPOT), a web-based toolbox consisting of a variety of ready-made and customizable resources for high school science teachers and their students. SPOT can be viewed online at http://www.lib.uoguelph.ca (enter "SPOT for teachers" in the search bar). Hosted on the University of Guelph Library's web site, SPOT provides free access to customized lesson plans, academic skills support modules, and links to other resources. It also features a template that allows teachers to create their own assignments. All these resources are designed to be integrated into the existing Ontario high school curriculum.

In "Information Literacy in the Educational Process," Lenox and Walker rightly observe that teachers must be prepared to "teach students to become critical thinkers, intellectually curious observers, creators, and users of information" (1993, 315). The University of Guelph Library team reflects a concern for each of these areas of development; in creating SPOT, they drew upon their respective knowledge and expertise as science learning specialist, academic librarian, writing specialist, and accredited high school teacher. They also recognized the importance of engaging directly with their target audiences, so they conducted focus groups with university students who had recently made the transition from high school, with high school science teachers, and with instructors of first-year science courses.

FEEDBACK FROM STUDENTS

The students interviewed fell into two groups: those who had some experience with scholarly literature, including journal articles, and those who did not. Students in the former group reported that they were much more at ease when asked to do assignments using journal articles in their first year, whereas students in the latter group found the tasks much more challenging.

FEEDBACK FROM HIGH SCHOOL TEACHERS

The teachers were eager to help their students prepare for the transition to university through assignments that involved reading, critical thinking, and academic writing. They identified three specific concerns, which subsequently informed the design of SPOT. They needed:

1. Free access to peer-reviewed, scientific journals. But they believed this was not possible because they are not associated with institutions of higher learning.
2. An understanding of how to select appropriate journal articles that could be used in their science curricula.
3. Information and resources to help scaffold students' development of university-level skills in critical reading and writing.

It is interesting to note that the teachers identified their own need to search for, access, and evaluate journal articles, but they did not identify information literacy as one of the important transitions skills their students should develop. Instead, they focused on their students' ability to write at a college level as the major need.

FEEDBACK FROM FIRST-YEAR INSTRUCTORS

The feedback the authors received from faculty reinforced what they had heard from students and high school teachers. They emphasized the importance of journal articles as a source of information for university science students, and pointed to the lack of experience with the journal literature as an important academic skill transition gap for their students.

The sections that follow describe the SPOT components (Table 15.1) in detail and emphasize how they are designed to help students develop their ability to read, understand, analyze, and draw meaning from scientific journal articles. They include a

Table 15.1.

Description of SPOT Components

Component	Description	Learning Activities
Lesson Plans	Downloadable lesson plans to be used in specific upper year science curricula (e.g., chemistry, chromatography) Include step-by-step instructions for an in-class activity involving a scientific journal article	• Access scientific journal database and select articles • Gain familiarity with scientific journal article format, structure, and style • Practice critical reading and analysis of journal articles • Synthesize understanding through writing
Academic Skills Support Resources	Downloadable modules and links to related resources, organized by academic skill area:	
	Researching "Searching for Scientific Journal Articles" module; link to open access scientific journal database	*Research* • Identify the need for information • Access a database of relevant, scholarly literature • Efficiently search for and retrieve relevant articles
	Writing "Paraphrasing" module; link to template for students to use in writing assignment; "Academic Integrity" tutorial	*Writing* • Understand and recognize plagiarism • Recognize a proper paraphrase and how to write one
	Learning Links to additional resources (e.g. "Guide for University Learning" tutorial)	*Learning* • Explore and learn more about academic skills development in higher education
Additional Resources for Teachers	1. Solution sets to ready-made lesson plans 2. "Create Your Own Assignment" template; template and instructions for teachers to create their own journal article assignment	1. Self-assess (or participate in group assessment) and identify areas for improvement 2. Same as for Lesson Plans (A, earlier in the table), but with content and objectives determined by instructor

discussion of the benefits of this suite of teaching aids to high school teachers and students, and to information literacy, writing, and learning specialists in higher education; offer suggestions for how this model can be adapted for use in other educational contexts; and identify key collaborations that have contributed to the success of this model. Finally, future directions for SPOT are outlined.

LESSON PLANS

High school science teachers wanted their students to be introduced to journal articles and how to read and write about them. Supporting the development of these skills is the objective of the Lesson Plans component of SPOT. Each lesson plan corresponds to one of four Ontario Secondary School science subjects: biology, chemistry, earth and space science, or physics.

Gaining Familiarity with Scientific Literature

To make the conventions of scientific writing less mysterious, the lessons provide a preview of what these texts look and "sound" like. They introduce disciplinary ways of thinking and doing by asking students to practice identifying the hypothesis, methods, and findings of the articles. Using these structured prompts, the University of Guelph Library team aimed to make the components of scientific writing more visible. They also aimed to move students from being passive readers to active participants in the process of understanding and analyzing scientific journal articles.

Analyzing and Evaluating Academic Sources

Each of the lesson plans requires students to read and analyze a scientific journal article using a student template sheet that guides this process by prompting them to examine the journal article systematically. For example, step 1 of the template asks, "What is the hypothesis/aim/objective of the paper?" and then goes on to direct students to "Write down the hypothesis that the authors are testing." This is followed by questions about the methods, results, and significance of the authors' findings.

Synthesizing Information and Developing Arguments

In addition to analyzing academic sources, students must be able to synthesize information from sources and use information from sources to support their own arguments. While many students at the first-year level are able to effectively express ideas in writing, they frequently struggle to move from descriptive to critical forms of writing. Being able to go beyond reporting information to taking a position in relation to that information is vital to students' progress in their academic careers. To help students develop an awareness of the difference between reporting and critiquing, the template asks students, "Why should we believe the authors?" and then provides direct questions about the kinds of evidence to look for to support their answers to this question. Students are then asked to synthesize these points with the question: "Based on your analysis, are the claims of this journal article accurate?"

ACADEMIC SKILLS SUPPORT RESOURCES

Each lesson plan presumes that students have two key skills: the ability to search for and retrieve scientific journal articles, and the ability to paraphrase content. For many high school students, however, these skills are not fully developed. Through SPOT's Academic Skills Support Resources component, students have access to (1) downloadable modules that introduce these skills in a succinct way so that they can grasp basic concepts and immediately apply them to the activities in the lessons and (2) links to related resources. The modules and links are grouped by academic skill set: information research, writing, and learning.

"Searching for Scientific Journal Articles" Module

One set of skills that is often overlooked by science teachers, college instructors, and university professors who are designing support for writing assignments is information literacy. It is often taken for granted that students know how to effectively find, access, and critically evaluate relevant sources, and that they can do so with minimal instruction or guidance. A growing body of research suggests that this assumption is not correct (Burhanna and Jensen 2006; Julien and Barker 2009). In SPOT, the University of Guelph Library team created the "Searching for Scientific Journal Articles" module to provide intentional support for the development of information literacy skills based on selected standards defined by the American Association of School Librarians (AASL) (2007), and by the Association of College and Research Libraries (ACRL; 2000). These relate to:

- Identifying the need for information
- Accessing a database of relevant, scholarly literature
- Efficiently searching for and retrieving relevant articles

Two other aspects of information literacy—the critical evaluation of the article and the development of a well-written review of the article—are addressed by the activities in SPOT's Lesson Plans component.

Identifying the Need for Information and Accessing a Relevant Database

The teachers who were interviewed recognized their own lack of familiarity with the scientific literature and relevant databases, and they generally held the mistaken belief that they and their students did not have access to *any* scholarly literature because their school libraries did not subscribe to the same scholarly journals and databases that are available through colleges and universities. In SPOT, the authors simplified access to peer-reviewed scientific and scholarly literature by directing teachers and students to DOAJ, the Directory of Open Access Journals (http://www.doaj.org).

Efficiently Searching for and Retrieving Relevant Articles

Teachers have two options when using SPOT's teaching aids. They may (1) assign one of the lesson plans, which specifies the article students are to retrieve and analyze or (2) create their own journal article assignments in which students must search for, retrieve, and analyze an article of their own choosing. In the first scenario, the information research module, "Searching for Scientific Journal Articles," guides students through the process of performing a title search on DOAJ.

The second scenario provides students with a far greater appreciation of, and experience with, the real-life information-seeking behaviors of students in higher education. In a series of clear steps accompanied by appropriate screen shots, the information research module guides students through the basics of:

- Keyword searching
- Breaking their topic into concepts and brainstorming the concepts to come up with additional keywords

- Truncation, phrase, and Boolean searching
- Conducting a search in DOAJ
- Critically evaluating their results and refining their search to yield best results

These information literacy skills are equally important for *teachers* to understand and master so that they can provide appropriate support for their students' learning. More practically, to create new journal article assignments teachers need to know how to search DOAJ.

"Paraphrasing" Module

Essential to writing effectively about sources is paraphrasing and citing ideas correctly. This task is not always as straightforward as it might seem. As the Council of Writing Program Administrators (WPA) notes, students are often unfamiliar with the concept of academic integrity and may not have well-developed strategies for incorporating and citing sources (2003). It is not uncommon for students to unwittingly misuse sources by failing to paraphrase thoroughly or provide proper documentation. To help students learn these skills, the council recommends that teachers provide explicit instruction on paraphrasing and citing, and opportunities for students to ask questions, practice these skills, and receive feedback. With this in mind, the "Paraphrasing" module was developed. It introduces students to the basic skills of paraphrasing, including tips on how to adopt new language and structure, and how to check paraphrases for thoroughness and accuracy. The module provides side-by-side examples of good and poor paraphrases to emphasize the importance of going beyond simply changing a few words here and there when encapsulating ideas.

Links to Related Resources

In addition to providing access to downloadable modules, the Academic Skills Support Resources component of SPOT includes links to academic resources on information research, writing, and learning that offer students additional opportunities to develop and enhance their skills. Students can navigate directly to the Directory of Open Access Journals, as well as to interactive learning objects on academic integrity, university learning, and time management that were developed by specialists at the University of Guelph.

The "Academic Integrity" tutorial provides information about how the university views academic integrity and plagiarism, includes illustrations and exercises to help students avoid key pitfalls associated with academic misconduct and writing, and encourages the development of positive behaviors, rather than the avoidance of misconduct.

The "Guide for University Learning" and "Time Management" tutorials contain text, video, and interactive exercises that highlight a broad range of topics and issues most students face when making the transition from high school to postsecondary education. Examples include using textbooks and lectures effectively, and dealing with perfectionism and procrastination. Like the other resources, these are designed to be used independently by high school students or in conjunction with classroom instruction.

ADDITIONAL RESOURCES FOR TEACHERS

SPOT provides some additional resources for teachers. These include solution sets for the lesson plans, an assignment template, and links for feedback and support.

Solution Sets

Solution sets for the downloadable lesson plans are available to teachers upon request. A link to the University of Guelph's Learning Services team is available through the SPOT website.

Create Your Own Journal Article Assignment Template

The Create Your Own Journal Article Assignment template allows teachers to determine their *own* subject content and develop new lesson plans that are built upon the same framework for learning and academic skills development that underlies each of the ready-made lesson plans.

Opportunity for Feedback and Support

A link on the web site enables users to offer feedback and seek support. Both provide invaluable information that contributes to the continued improvement and development of the site and its content.

BENEFITS OF SPOT

SPOT offers many benefits to teachers, students, and learning and curriculum support specialists.

Benefits to Teachers

For teachers, the most obvious benefit of SPOT is having free access to resources and teaching aids that are immediately relevant and can be practically implemented in the classroom. Teachers are mandated by the Ontario high school science curriculum to "help students achieve the curriculum expectations" and "provide numerous hands-on opportunities for students to develop and refine their investigation skills, including their problem-solving skills, critical and creative thinking skills, and communication skills, while discovering fundamental concepts through inquiry, exploration, observation, and research" (Ontario Ministry of Education 2008, 8).

With this in mind, the authors designed lesson plans that contain a sequence of short, manageable tasks that directly address curriculum needs, and they supported these activities with academic skills support modules. Each lesson plan outlines in detail the specific high school curriculum expectations being met so that teachers can integrate the materials seamlessly into their course content.

Another benefit to teachers is having easy and free access to peer-reviewed scientific journal articles (through the link to DOAJ), and strategies for efficiently searching for and retrieving resources. In addition, the "Create Your Own Journal Article Assignment" module, when paired with the "Searching for Scientific Journal Articles" module, provides teachers with a reliable, guided, and sustainable mechanism for adapting to changes in curriculum objectives.

Benefits to Students Transitioning to Postsecondary Institutions

By introducing high school students to the research and writing skills outlined in the lesson plans, these learning activities make some of the expectations of higher education more explicit to learners. This exposure to the cognitive skills required for postsecondary success in the sciences prior to entry into university could reduce the learning curve students experience during the first year of postsecondary education. The use of these resources has not been limited to the high school setting; members of our team have used them in first-year science courses to help students master these academic skills in their first few months of higher education. In a variety of contexts, the stepwise lesson plans and modules help reduce some of the mystery that might otherwise surround these academic tasks.

Benefits to Learning and Curriculum Support Specialists in Higher Education

It is important not only for high school teachers to understand and prepare their students for the expectations of higher education, but also for university and college educators to learn more about the challenges that teachers and students face in the high school setting. The University of Guelph Library team gained invaluable knowledge from speaking to high school teachers and to current university students who had recently completed the transition to tertiary-level education. Though many of their comments echoed what the authors had learned from the literature (e.g., Morosanu, Handley and O'Donovan 2010), these meetings gave them something they could not have gathered from the pages of a journal: the opportunity to ask questions and clarify information, and to hear teachers and students from different contexts interact and debate with one another about the issues and challenges as they see them. As learning and curriculum support specialists, the authors were able to gain a deeper appreciation of the learning curve that students experience when transitioning to tertiary education, and this knowledge will continue to influence them as they design learning support programs.

HOW TO CUSTOMIZE FOR OTHER CONTEXTS

One of the central aims in creating the SPOT web site was to provide tools that could be easily customized to meet the needs of diverse classroom settings. For example, the lesson plans and templates can be modified by changing the language to reflect specific learning objectives and aims as educational contexts change. Similar models of outreach can be used by other academic libraries, taking into consideration the support resources they have to offer and the local high school context. Other institutions are welcome to link to the academic skills support resources created at the University of Guelph Library, or they can adapt these materials for their own resources.

COLLABORATION: THE KEY TO SUCCESS

The collaboration of specialists from library, learning, and writing backgrounds was essential to developing a comprehensive site for teachers and students; and the colocation of these specialists in the library was a great advantage in this process. Most college and university campuses will have access to such expertise, even if the people are not located within the same administrative unit. The authors recommend reaching beyond the walls of the library to form such partnerships, if necessary.

Seeking direct input from their target audiences helped them focus their efforts. For example, talking with high school teachers and recent high school graduates revealed the great diversity of high school experiences. Collaborating with these groups helped them to prioritize the learning objectives that SPOT highlights. In addition, gathering feedback from discipline-specific university instructors enriched the development of SPOT by allowing them to better understand the level of disciplinary skill required of an entering science student.

Members of the library's web development team were also key partners in this project. They created the web presence for the portal and provided a mechanism that allows for the updating of content in a timely and efficient manner.

FUTURE DIRECTIONS

For SPOT to be successful, it must continue to incorporate content that is relevant and engaging; it must advance and change, just as scientific research continues to. Therefore, one ongoing priority will be to update SPOT with current science topics and lesson plans. In the longer term, the authors would like to replace the static "Academic Skills Support Resources" modules with interactive learning objects that include self-assessment. Naturally, funding is an issue with their more ambitious aims; in collaboration with an academic department at their institution, they have secured funding that they hope will allow them to pursue these directions.

CONCLUSION

This work demonstrates the central role that libraries can play in bringing together high schools, postsecondary institutions, and the learners who are making the transition between the two. At the core of this role is a communication process that brings together *all* perspectives: university science instructors, academic support specialists (which, in our context, includes professional librarians), high school teachers, *and* the learners themselves. As academic support specialists and facilitators of these discussions, the University of Guelph Library team was better able to identify and understand the core skills, knowledge, and values that learners needed in order to make the transition to university-level learning. In summary, they offer SPOT—and in particular the process they used to develop it—as a model of the leadership role academic libraries and academic support specialists can play when responding to the needs of high schools and universities. A distinguishing feature of this model is that it provides an opportunity to establish greater continuity between high school and university classrooms, and allows all to participate in the process of supporting the transition to university learning.

BIBLIOGRAPHY

American Association of School Librarians (AASL). *AASL Standards for the 21st-Century Learner*. Chicago: American Library Association, 2007.

Association of College and Research Libraries (ACRL). *Information Literacy Competency Standards for Higher Education*. Chicago: American Library Association, 2000.

Burhanna, Kenneth J., and Mary Lee Jensen. "Collaborations for Success: High School to College Transitions." *Reference Services Review* 34, no. 4 (2006): 509–519.

Council of Writing Program Administrators (WPA). *Defining and Avoiding Plagiarism: The WPA Statement on Best Practices*. Author, 2003. http://wpacouncil.org/node/9 (accessed February 25, 2012).

Julien, Heidi, and Susan Barker. "How High-School Students Find and Evaluate Scientific Information: A Basis for Information Literacy Skills Development." *Library & Information Science Research* 31 (2009): 12–17.

Lenox, Mary F., and Michael L. Walker. "Information Literacy in the Educational Process." *Educational Forum* 57, no. 3 (1993): 312–324.

Morosanu, Laura, Karen Handley, and Berry O'Donovan. "Seeking Support: Researching First-Year Students' Experiences of Coping with Academic Life." *Higher Education Research & Development* 29, no. 6 (2010): 665–678.

Ontario Ministry of Education. *Science: The Ontario Curriculum Grades 11 and 12 (Revised)*. Toronto, Ontario: Queen's Printer for Ontario, 2008.http://www.edu.gov.on.ca/eng/curriculum/secondary/2009science11_12.pdf (accessed October 29, 2012).

16

Nebraska Students in Transition: The Evolution of a Partnership

Toni Anaya and Charlene Maxey-Harris

INTRODUCTION

Since 2010, the University of Nebraska–Lincoln (UNL) libraries have been collaborating with the Office of Admissions on an innovative program working with high school seniors through the Nebraska College Preparatory Academy (NCPA). Over the past 10 years, Nebraska has been affected by Nebraska's dramatic changes in racial and ethnic diversity. Despite a rapid rise in ethnic diversity over the past 10 years, the state was still 90 percent white at the time of the 2010 census. Over the past decade, UNL has been interested in actively recruiting students and faculty from ethnically diverse backgrounds. This initiative centers on recruitment strategies within the state that tap into the cultural richness of Nebraska's residents.

In 2006, Harvey Perlman, chancellor at University of Nebraska–Lincoln, created an innovative program to recruit first-generation, low-income high school seniors through the Nebraska College Preparatory Academy (http://go.unl.edu/s0c). The aim of this program is to promote the benefits of higher education among Nebraska's underserved populations and to provide academic and financial resources for first-generation, low-income high school students to pursue postsecondary education. NCPA is a unique collaboration between the University Libraries and the Office of Admissions and is funded solely through private donors and grants, unlike similar initiatives focused on supporting first-generation, low-income students, like the nationally recognized and federally funded Upward Bound and the Ronald McNair Scholars program. In November 2008, voters in Nebraska approved a ban on affirmative action, Nebraska Civil Rights Initiative 424 (Ballotpedia 2012), which prohibits discriminating against or granting preferential treatment to individuals or groups based on race, gender, or national origin. This bill has hindered the University of Nebraska's ability to recruit students from diverse populations. The university has altered its approach to attracting students who are first-generation college attendees with low income and experiences living or working in diverse communities. In 2009, despite these challenges, the university celebrated the most ethnically and racially diverse freshman class in its 140-year history (UNL 2009).

LITERATURE REVIEW

The review of the literature centers on libraries providing programming and services to high school students or first year freshman college students from these special populations: underrepresented groups, first-generation college attendees, Generation 1.5 students, and economically disadvantaged students. The term Generation 1.5 has been used in the literature to describe immigrant students who move to the United States at the age of 12 or older and enroll in school in the United States (Rumbaut and Ima 1988). Emily Love (2009) explored the ways libraries support underrepresented students. She provides a thorough review of the various ways libraries have worked with students of color over the years. The majority of the activities focused on the library's role in supporting the Upward Bound and Ronald McNair Scholars programs, and student peer-to-peer mentoring programs. In addition, relationships cultivated with cultural centers, multicultural services, and other academic support departments yield a growth of library programs and instruction to students.

As colleges and universities strive to increase the number students of color on campus, several studies focus on library usage and information literacy for this group. Ethelene Whitmire's (2003, 2004) studies on library usage are pivotal for other growing research in this area. Based on her research, she determines differences between Asian American, African American, Latino, Native American and white undergraduates. She found that "students of color are using the library at higher rates than White undergraduates" (2003, 160). According to Haras and colleagues "Generation 1.5 are neither international students nor do they see themselves as ESL learners. They are somewhere in between first-generation, adult immigrants who are foreign-educated and second generation, U.S. born, English speaking children of immigrants. Generation 1.5 students often grow up without academic skills in their first language; they may not experience growth in their first language skills; they may be English-dominant yet not identify with English; or, they may be English-dominant without experiencing its full linguistic range" (2008, 426).

Many generation 1.5 population studies focus on U.S. Latino high school and first-year students in urban settings and their attitudes toward libraries and research skills. Some of the studies link information literacy to academic performance (Adkins and Hussey 2006; Asher, Case and Zhong 2009; Haras, Lopez and Ferry 2008; Haras 2011. Shoge (2003) surveyed African American undergraduate and graduate professional students in Delaware and Maryland on their perceptions of library activities and its impact on their academic performance.

Overall, there is the perception that just being in the library improves academic performance; however, this perception does not translate into academic success. To impact academic performance, students need to know about academic libraries' services and the resources as well as how to use these services and resources effectively. Central themes in the studies suggest first-year students of color do not associate academic libraries with the development of research and critical thinking skills. Academic libraries need to direct their attention to finding out what the needs of underrepresented students are and then develop a plan to begin meeting their needs and make their academic spaces (physical and online) inviting to these students. Libraries continue to need to edge their way into existing academic support services and admissions programs to offer tours, instruction, and programming. Establishing these partnerships opens the pathway to building collaborative learning projects and developing ways to impact student retention.

BACKGROUND

NCPA targets students from two high schools, one rural and one urban, with similar demographics. There have been 294 scholars involved in the program at Grand Island Senior High School (GISH) and Omaha North Magnet High School (ONMHS), with 38 seniors active in the program during the 2011–2012 academic year. The Grand Island school district serves 8,350 students, of whom more than 69 percent are Hispanic. GISH, which is located in Grand Island, Nebraska, is the only public high school in the Grand Island public district, and enrollment is 2,114. The ethnic and racial makeup of students is predominantly white (53 percent) and Hispanic (42 percent). See Table 16.1 for a complete breakdown by race and ethnicity. This high school is considered to be in a rural area of Nebraska (NCES 2010, GISH). In contrast, the Omaha public school district serves 48,690 students. Omaha North Magnet High School is one of seven public high schools and resides in the largest city in Nebraska. The student enrollment is 1,940. The ethnicity and race of these students is predominantly African American (47 percent) and white (44 percent). Table 16.1 provides a complete overview of ONMHS student ethnicity and race (NCES 2010, ONMHS).

The selection process for NCPA is competitive and is handled through the University of Nebraska–Lincoln Office of Admissions. Admissions officers select high achieving promising ninth grade students to join a cohort of their peers (NCPA scholars) and complete a 9-12 curriculum focused on science and math to prepare them for the rigors of college coursework. NCPA scholars and their parents also participate in a community-based college access counseling program to learn about college admission and the financial aid application process. Of the scholars involved in the program,

Table 16.1.

Nebraska College Preparatory School (NCPA) student ethnicity and race

NCPA High Schools	Enrollment (2009–2010)	Ethnic and Racial Breakdown of High School Students (%)	
Grand Island Senior High (GISH) (rural)	2,114	White	53
		Hispanic	42
		African American	2
		Asian/Pacific Islander	2
		American Indian/Alaskan Native	1
Omaha North Magnet High School (ONMHS) (urban)	1,940	African American	47
		White	44
		Hispanic	5
		Asian/Pacific Islander	2
		American Indian/Alaskan Native	1

83 percent belong to a racial or ethnic minority, and 100 percent are low-income, first-generation students. The scholars' average high school grade point average (GPA) is currently 3.39 (on a 4.0 scale), which is an impressive indicator of the program's potential.

Following high school graduation, NCPA scholars who complete their senior capstone research poster, who maintain the required GPA, and whose parents have sufficiently engaged in the college access program are guaranteed a full scholarship to UNL (3.0 or higher GPA) or Metro Community College (2.5–2.99 GPA). Once students accept the scholarship to UNL and transition from high school to college, they become members of the Institute of Excellence (IOE), a retention program for NCPA scholars. The library's collaborative goal with the IOE is to support and teach these scholars information and research skills needed to be successful in their first two years at the university.

EVOLUTION OF A PARTNERSHIP

Opportunity often knocks on doors yet to be opened. A prime example of this is the evolution of the collaborative partnership between the UNL libraries and the UNL Office of Admissions.

Initially, the diversity and multicultural studies librarians approached the Office of Admissions because they wanted to provide outreach services to prospective students involved recruitment programs. These services included exhibits and library tours highlighting services, resources, and student employment opportunities. Librarians also attended and led workshops at campus diversity symposiums. Soon these services began to include one-time instruction sessions for related groups such as Upward Bound summer visits and students on academic probation. These one-shot, or single meeting, instruction sessions included interactive group projects and scavenger hunts to connect students with the various library collections and services.

In 2008, new opportunities to collaborate with UNL admissions officers developed when the diversity and multicultural studies librarians were invited to create a pilot library program designed to prepare Summer Institute for Promising Scholars (SIPS), a group of incoming minority and first-generation students, with research skills to succeed in college. This transitional program, SIPS, provided academic credit and a book scholarship for students who successfully complete the five-week program. Librarians redesigned the five-week Introduction to Library Research online course in partnership with the UNL English department so that the research class supported coursework research in the English 151 course. Students worked in small groups on their final project for the English course. Each group created a poster presentation, which served as the final summer capstone research project and was presented at the final program celebration. After the successful outcome of the final project, this model was then incorporated into the new chancellor's initiative, Nebraska College Preparatory Academy.

NEBRASKA COLLEGE PREPARATORY ACADEMY

Librarians initially met with the NCPA assistant admissions director regarding the NCPA program in late 2008. At that time, the Office of Admissions was unsure how to move forward with the requirements of the program. The following fall, due to the libraries' involvement with SIPS and the successful creation of the capstone research component with that program, the Office of Admissions invited the diversity and multi-cultural studies librarians to create and coordinate the research component for a small pilot group of nine Omaha North High School students in the first NCPA 2010 senior graduating class. The Grand Island Senior High School senior class was not required to complete a research capstone due to differences in the initial program creation.

Active work in the pilot group of the first cohort of NCPA scholars began in the fall of 2009, with library instruction provided by UNL librarians in collaboration with high school teachers. Librarians worked with the group throughout the school year rather than providing one-time instruction sessions. Library instruction embedded into the school year allows students to build upon skills learned and provides support to high school teachers.

In 2010, a three-day summer library research boot camp was developed for the incoming NCPA 2011 senior graduating class, the second cohort. This boot camp allows students to focus on research skills and working in teams without the pressure of being in school. Librarians engage students in critical thinking activities, discuss characteristics of the academic environment, and teach about using library resources. The concepts introduced at the boot camp are also reinforced with exercises throughout students' senior year to support their English research project. These exercises include the use of research logs, one-minute feedback papers, checklists for scholarly information, and citing sources. Assessments are built into the exercises as well. NCPA goals align with some of the Association of College & Research Libraries (ACRL) *Standards for Information Literacy*. At the end of the year it is expected that students will be able to:

1. Describe different types of information resources in order to identify the forms needed to complete their project
2. Construct an effective search statement in order to locate and select appropriate information resources
3. Evaluate the quality of information found in their search in order to determine validity (ACRL 2000)

In addition to these goals, librarians help students develop presentation skills and knowledge about academic culture and expectations of college classes. In the spring, students complete their posters for the final capstone project and proudly display them to their teachers, school administrators, and University of Nebraska administrators.

The library component has grown considerably since the first senior graduating class of nine students in 2010. The senior capstone research project is now a required component of the program for both participating schools.

In 2010 and 2011, librarians worked with the second cohort, which consisted of 26 seniors from GISH. ONMHS did not have a senior NCPA scholar class. For the 2011–2012 school year, UNL librarians worked with a group of 38 students from both high schools in the third cohort. Program completion rates for NCPA seniors have improved in just two years. In 2010, the first year librarians worked with NCPA, 77 percent of seniors completed their projects and agreed to attend UNL. As of August 2011, 85 percent of NCPA seniors matriculated at UNL, while the remaining 15 percent are attending other area colleges (NCPA 2011). See Table 16.2 for complete college matriculation data for NCPA scholars by cohort.

The impact of this collaboration has far-reaching implications; the UNL Office of Admissions has committed to supporting this program through 2020 and wishes to

Table 16.2.

NCPA/IOE Scholars

	Grand Island (GISH)	Omaha North (OMNSH)	Total Enrollment at Community College	Total Enrollment at UNL
First Cohort 2010 Senior Class	24	9*	0	33
Second Cohort 2011 Senior Class	26*	0	3	23
Third Cohort 2012 Senior Class	31*	7*	0	38

maintain libraries' role in coordinating the capstone research project. The opportunity to provide support and instruction to over 1,000 students over the course of the NCPA program is exciting and will allow the libraries to directly impact the recruitment and retention of first-generation, low-income students at UNL, which is a priority goal of the university, as stated in Chancellor Perlman's 2011 State of the University address (UNL 2011). The interpersonal relationships developed with students will also impact student persistence, retention, and confidence as well as encourage leadership development on campus.

STUDENTS IN TRANSITION

The Institute of Excellence, the college group for the NCPA students, is in its second year of development. UNL libraries now support 33 students as they transition from their homes in rural and urban areas to matriculate at UNL. The collaborative goal is to support and teach these scholars information and research skills needed to be successful during their first two years in college. The library is currently incorporating this program librarywide as the program grows to recruit and retain over 100 NCPA/IOE scholars per year over the next 10 years.

INITIAL RESULTS

Efforts by the library include providing services such as mini library "boot camps" where students receive short, intense instruction sessions based upon topics previously covered in other programs. This integrated method of providing instruction, according to recent research by Wong and Cmor (2011), is a key way to impact student learning and academic performance. The instruction offered throughout the semester changes based on students' point of need and covers issues such as the virtual library, proper citation, and research basics.

Retention rates for the first cohort of the group, a total of 33 students, was approximately 88 percent, with slightly over 50 percent meeting the NCPA scholarship qualifications with a 2.78 GPA. In comparison, overall retention rates for first-time, full-time freshman at UNL was 83.6 percent (University of Nebraska–Lincoln 2012). Overall, NCPA students have been successful transitioning to the university when compared to other first-year students. In 2011, UNL enrolled 23 freshman scholars in the second cohort of IOE, all of whom are still attending classes.

Much is being done to encourage NCPA and IOE scholars to succeed; however, there are some challenges. While each participating high school has different obstacles to overcome, there are some common issues students face, including preparation in math, reading comprehension, and writing; social integration and personal (family) struggles; and issues with emotional and mental wellness due to the harsh conditions of poverty (NCPA 2011). These challenges are consistent with those identified by Barry and colleagues (2009). While student and family commitment is strong at the rural school (GISH), it creates challenges for those students once they move into residential housing; being the first to leave the family home to go off to college causes stress for not only the student, but also for family members. These challenges leave students with concerned parents who lack the knowledge to help them navigate the university's bureaucratic system.

Students at the urban school (ONMHS) face similar familial circumstances; however, the level of commitment from their parents continues to evolve. Scholar and parental participation contrasts sharply between the two high schools. While GISH has a large cohort each year, ONMHS continues to have small groups enrolled and active in NCPA. One possible reason for this disparity is the number of competing programs and/or opportunities for students in Omaha. With the varied requirements of the program, parents may fail to participate, assuming their child will receive aid from other programs that do not require such a high level of parental participation. GISH has many fewer recruitment programs, and school administrators are empowered to accommodate the program's special academic needs.

CONCLUSION

Not only are the UNL libraries helping these students to transition, the services provided by the libraries are also in transition as they develop this new program. More individuals are being integrated into the NCPA/IOE work team, and efforts are being made to create collaborative relationships with the school librarians as well as teachers at participating schools. As research projects are developed over the course of the year, the multicultural studies and diversity librarian program coordinators plan to incorporate more subject specialists to aid students in the research and development of their projects as a way to build early connections to areas of research.

These efforts will allow the library staff to play a more holistic role in recruitment and retention of these students. Future goals include developing curriculum for younger students in NCPA to begin teaching information literacy in their first three years of involvement as well as creating assessment tools to aide in evaluating impact. Research opportunities are also developing to create a research study to investigate the impact of library bibliographic instruction and the development of information literacy on first-generation students from high school through college graduation. Based on the library usage studies reviewed in the literature, we are also interested in studying the attitudes and library experiences of Generation 1.5 students from rural settings. As larger numbers of students join the Institute of Excellence as university students, it will be interesting to explore which skills need to be revisited, their academic performance, and retention of these scholars compared to peers of similar background not involved in the program. As we continue to develop the program, assessment of the assignments and exercises will inform us of the quality of the end product and new directions for instruction.

These preparatory and transition programs are important not only to libraries, but also to retention efforts. This model allows the library to be directly involved with preparing first-generation students to succeed in college and giving them the skills they need to be successful. Students need to understand how to use reference materials, find books, evaluate scholarly articles, and properly cite their sources. Research has shown that students do not understand the benefits of using an academic library instead of the public library (Adkins and Hussey 2006; Haras 2011). By reinforcing the advantages of using an academic library and increasing student exposure to a large variety of library staff, we are ensuring our library is a welcoming place for students and encouraging them to discover opportunities to explore the library profession. The coordinating librarians provide a multiethnic perspective, have firsthand experience as first-generation college attendees, and are familiar with many of the barriers and challenges faced by this group of students. They serve as role models for the profession, thus opening the pipeline to introduce these students to library and information careers. Students gain the self-confidence to understand how to use these resources to share with their colleagues as they develop as leaders. They will also know how to work with faculty and know their perspective and experience are valued through other learning communities on campus.

As institutes of higher education begin to focus on providing access to students from low- income, first-generation families, libraries must be ready to provide appropriate services to this population. They must recognize the level of need, understand the challenges, and be willing to answer the door when nontraditional opportunities come knocking.

BIBLIOGRAPHY

Adkins, Denice, and Lisa Hussey. "The Library in the Lives of Latino College Students." *Library Quarterly* 76, no. 4 (2006): 456–480.

Association of College & Research Libraries (ACRL). *Information Literacy Competency Standards for Higher Education*. Chicago: American Library Association, 2000. Asher, Curt, and Emerson Case. "A Generation in Transition: A Study of the Usage and Attitudes toward Public Libraries by Generation 1.5 Composition Students." *Reference & User Services Quarterly* 47, no. 3 (2008): 274–279.

Asher, Curt, Emerson Case, and Ying Zhong. "Serving Generation 1.5: Academic Library Use and Students from Non-English-Speaking Households." *College & Research Libraries* 70, no. 3 (2009): 258–272.

Ballotpedia. "Nebraska Civil Rights Initiative, 424 (2008)." 2012. http://ballotpedia.org/wiki/index.php/Nebraska_Civil_Rights_Initiative,_424_(2008) (accessed October 29, 2012).

Barry, Leasha M., Cynthia Hudley, Melissa Kelly, and Su-Je Cho. "Differences in Self-Reported Disclosure of College Experiences by First-Generation College Student Status." *Adolescence* 44, no. 173 (2009): 55–68.

Haras, Catherine. "Information Behaviors of Latinos Attending High School in East Los Angeles." *Library & Information Science Research* 33, no. 1 (2011): 34–40.

Haras, Catherine, Edward A. Lopez, and Kristine Ferry. "(Generation 1.5) Latino Students and the Library: A Case Study." *Journal of Academic Librarianship* 34, no. 5 (2008): 425–433.

Love, Emily. "A Simple Step: Integrating Library Reference and Instruction into Previously Established Academic Programs for Minority Students." *Reference Librarian* 50, no. 1 (2009): 4–13.

National Center for Education Statistics (NCES). *Common Core Data*. Grand Island Senior High School (GISHS) 2009–2010. http://tinyurl.com/7kcyqmk (accessed October 20, 2011).

National Center for Education Statistics (NCES). *Common Core Data*. Omaha North Magnet High School (ONMHS) 2009–2010. http://tinyurl.com/788vgsa (accessed October 20, 2011).

Nebraska College Preparatory Academy. Annual Report 2010-2011. University of Nebraska-Lincoln, 2011. http://admissions.unl.edu/files/pdfs/college_prep_academy/360-12NCPA annualreportFINAL070711.pdf (accessed November 2, 2012).

Rumbaut, Ruben G., and Kenji Ima. *The adaptation of Southeast Asian refugee youth. A comparative study. Final report to the Office of Resettlement*. San Diego,CA: San Diego State University, 1988.

Shoge, Ruth C. "Library as Place in the Lives of African Americans." In *Learning to Make a Difference: Proceedings of the Eleventh National Conference of the Association of College and Research Libraries, April 10–13, 2003, Charlotte, North Carolina*. Chicago: Association of College and Research Libraries, 2003.

University of Nebraska–Lincoln (UNL). "Fact Book 2011–2012." UNL, 2012. http://irp.unl.edu/factbooks.html (accessed November 2, 2012).

University of Nebraska–Lincoln (UNL). *Nebraska College Preparatory Academy 2010–2011 Annual Report*. Lincoln: University of Nebraska–Lincoln, 2011.

University of Nebraska–Lincoln (UNL). "State of the University Address 2009." http://0-www.unl.edu.library.unl.edu/ucomm/chancllr/sua2009/ (accessed October 29, 2011).

University of Nebraska–Lincoln (UNL). "State of the University Address 2011: Undergraduate Education and Enrollment." http://0-www.unl.edu.library.unl.edu/ucomm/chancllr/sua2011/sua2011_2.shtml (accessed October 31, 2011).

Whitmire, Ethelene. "Cultural Diversity and Undergraduates' Academic Library Use." *Journal of Academic Librarianship* 29, no. 3 (2003): 148–161.

Whitmire, Ethelene. "The Campus Racial Climate and Undergraduates' Perceptions of the Academic Library." *portal: Libraries and the Academy* 4, no. 3 (2004): 363–378.

Wong, Shun Han Rebekah, and Dianne Cmor. "Measuring Association between Library Instruction and Graduation GPA." *College Research Libraries* 72, no. 5 (2011): 464–473.

17

College Student for a Day: Facilitating Successful Field Trips to an Academic Library

Ann Marie Smeraldi

The professional literature offers abundant evidence that high school librarians strive to provide meaningful learning experiences that require students to learn and practice key information literacy skills that align with state educational standards and the American Association of School Librarians' (AASL) *Standards for the 21st Century Learner.* Patricia Owen's (2010) transition checklist of skills and Michael O'Sullivan and Kim Dallas's (2010) case study of their high school's research paper class offer excellent examples. Research suggests that students who attend high schools with librarians and active information literacy instruction programs graduate with a better understanding of the research process than peers enrolled in schools without a librarian or program (Smalley 2004). Despite the evidence that high school librarians are proactive and effective, academic librarians consistently observe that first-year college students arrive on campus unprepared for the intellectual tasks that await them. Recent research verifies these observations; high school seniors transitioning to the status of first-year college students lack the higher order thinking skills essential to successfully completing sophisticated research that requires complex problem solving and advanced information literacy competency (Daniel 1997; Fitzgerald 2004; Katz 2007; Salisbury and Karasmanis 2011).

The interplay of various factors contributes to these knowledge and skill deficiencies among first-year college students, making it difficult for educators to tease out the exact causes and identify viable solutions. David Conley (2008, 24) offers a model that measures college readiness against four facets: cognitive strategies, content knowledge, academic behaviors, and contextual skills and knowledge; when viewed through this multifaceted lens, many students appear not college ready. Although not explicitly labeled as information literacy skills, many of the cognitive skills Conley (2003) identifies as fundamental to college readiness closely match the outcomes outlined in the Association for College & Research Libraries' (ACRL) *Information Literacy*

Competency Standards for Higher Education. The growing divide between high school preparation and college expectations emphasizes the need to align high school curriculum with higher education's standards to create a comprehensive continuum of learning both in the classroom and the library.

FOUNDATIONS FOR COLLABORATION

AASL and ACRL information literacy standards provide a framework for creating a continuum that supports the development of information literacy competency from high school to college. Librarians working in secondary and higher education are uniquely poised to assist in bridging the knowledge gap by aligning what happens in high school libraries with college research expectations. Since the introduction of the AASL/ACRL special task force's *Blueprint for Collaboration*, a report that encourages collaborations between school and academic librarians, librarians on both sides of the information gap have been experimenting with creative ways to fit these two pieces of the college readiness puzzle together. Recognizing the need to play a more active role in assisting high school students with the transition to college, the Michael Schwartz Library at Cleveland State University (CSU), an urban research university located in Ohio, moved forward with its commitment to education across all grade levels and hired a first-year experience librarian (FYE librarian) to work with the freshmen population and to serve as a high school liaison.

Prior to hiring the FYE librarian, the high school outreach program at CSU received a small number of visitor requests; participants received a library tour and temporary borrowing privileges. Over the course of three years, the FYE librarian enhanced the program to include a tour, discussion of college expectations and plagiarism, specialized information literacy instruction, use of a computer lab, on-campus database access, and borrowing privileges if desired. Visit requests from high schools continue to grow. Best practices for facilitating field trips to an academic library and creating meaningful learning experiences for participants have gradually emerged through trial and error, but the most significant factor identified is the formation of effective partnerships between the high school and academic librarians interested in closing the gap between secondary and postsecondary education.

Through strong partnerships, academic and high school librarians can build the scaffolding that will support students as they journey through their first college semester. Librarians on both sides of the knowledge gap must make efforts to form these alliances. Academic librarians can begin by contacting their admissions office to determine the top feeder high schools for their institutions. Knowing this information provides a focus for concentrating outreach efforts; sending introductory letters or emails that outline the services offered to high schools opens the lines of communication.

School librarians do not have to wait for these invitations; they can make the first move and contact academic libraries within a reasonable proximity to their schools. Because community service is a part of their mission, public universities may already have established programs. A quick search of the library's web site will be useful for identifying the correct individual to contact. The contact us or directory pages can be checked for titles such as a first-year experience librarian, high school outreach coordinator, or head of instruction. An inquiry by phone is also an effective way to obtain information.

Joining one another's professional associations, regional organizations, and consortia presents opportunities for making connections. Contributing to the work of the High School to College Transition Task Force of the Information Network for Ohio Schools (INFOhio) and the Ohio Educational Library Media Association (OELMA) proved to be invaluable experiences for the FYE librarian at CSU. Through active membership, the FYE librarian quickly learned about the issues affecting school librarians, better understood similarities and differences, and forged important relationships within the preschool through high school community. Joining listservs and attending conferences hosted by these organizations makes it easier for the FYE librarian to remain current on the issues affecting secondary school education. As a result of participating in these organizations, she has gained valuable insights that have allowed her to create programming that targets the specific needs of high school and first-year college students. By taking similar actions, high school librarians also develop a better sense of college expectations and academic demands. Mutual understanding and respect provide fertile ground for blossoming partnerships.

PLANNING THE ACADEMIC LIBRARY VISIT

Once a viable high school–academic librarian partnership has been established, the work of planning a visit to the academic library can begin. Successful field trips necessitate a significant amount of planning for both librarians. High school librarians benefit from using a checklist during the planning process (see Table 17.1). Before contacting the academic librarian, the school librarian should work with a teacher to determine students' needs and identify specific goals for the visit. English teachers are often the most receptive to planning an excursion to an academic library, but they may need convincing to give up precious class time. An enthusiastic history, art, or science teacher

Table 17.1.
Planning the Visit: A Checklist for High School Librarians

• Identify a nearby academic library with a high school outreach program.
• Inquire about the academic library's program.
• Partner with a teacher to create a research assignment and plan the fieldtrip.
• Develop an assignment for the visit.
• Select multiple dates for the visit.
• Secure permission from the high school's administration.
• Contact the academic librarian to schedule the visit and work out the visit details.
• Share the assignment with the academic librarian and ask for feedback.
• Make transportation arrangements.
• Acquire parental consent.
• Enlist volunteer chaperones.
• Prepare students for the visit.
• During the visit, be prepared to assist when needed.
• After the visit, assess the visit, compile data, and share with others.
• Send a thank you note to the hosting librarian or a letter to his or her supervisor.
Consult http://researchguides.csuohio.edu/fytransition_educators for additional details.

who assigns a substantial research paper or project may also be willing to collaborate. Sharing the scholarly work of researcher's such as Katz (2007), Conley (2006), and Fitzgerald (2004) (whose articles illustrates the information literacy deficiencies prominent in first-year college students) or VanScoy and Oakleaf (2008) (whose research delineates the expectations of college professors) will help make a convincing case.

The key to a productive visit involves a paper, senior capstone, or other major project with clearly defined research needs that require the use of scholarly sources beyond the scope of the high school library media center's collection. To meet college expectations, these assignments should incorporate higher order thinking skills that require students to solve ambiguous problems through the collection, evaluation, and synthesis of information from a variety of high-quality sources (O'Sullivan and Dallas 2010; Conley 2006; Salisbury and Karasmanis 2011). The typical high school research assignment involves a report requiring students to produce an only factual summary of information found during research. This type of research keeps students within the domain of lower order thinking. Students are not challenged to apply the critical thinking skills crucial for achievement in college (Gordon 2002).

When creating or revising an assignment, use the AASL and ACRL information literacy standards as a guide. Consider how the AASL and ACRL standards intersect and complement each other. When viewed together, these standards create a complete picture of the skills needed to be an effective information user, critical thinker, and lifelong learner (Cahoy 2002). The Partnership for 21st Century Skills recently introduced the "Framework for 21st Century Learning." This framework presents a fresh perspective on how to integrate 21st-century skills such as information and media literacy into core subjects to help students master the knowledge, skills, expertise, and literacies needed to be successful in work and life. The school librarian and teacher should use the AASL and ACRL standards and 21st-century skills framework to select appropriate learning outcomes for the assignment.

After developing the learning outcomes, the high school librarian can contact the academic librarian and share the assignment. Contact should be made at least two weeks in advance, preferably sooner to allow ample time for planning. The school librarian will want to determine several possible dates for the visit and be prepared to be flexible. During the discussion, key questions need to be answered: the best time to visit, length of the visit, services offered, available resources such as the print and electronic collections and computers, group size limits, student to adult ratios, and restrictions on borrowing privileges. Parking, printing, lunch, and other details may also be addressed at this time.

Academic libraries that offer outreach programs to high schools need formal guidelines for planning the visits. The Michael Schwartz Library at Cleveland State University makes this document accessible on its website at http://library.csuohio.edu/information/visits.html. Placing this information on the institution's web site facilitates the scheduling process. The guidelines should reflect any limitations and include statements about the services, resources, borrowing privileges, printing accommodations, and electronic database privileges offered to high school groups. It is important to explicitly state that the university's students, faculty, and staff are given priority over other groups. The FYE librarian uses the guidelines during the planning process to make decisions that ensure a positive experience for both the guests and the library staff. Academic librarians that coordinate high school visits will find that a simple checklist will help facilitate the planning process (see Table 17.2).

Table 17.2.

Hosting a Visit: A Checklist for Academic Librarians

• Establish formal, published guidelines for the high school outreach program.
• Create an email template to use for inquiries about the program.
• Prepare a simple attitudinal assessment to gather feedback.
• Design generic lesson plans and supporting materials in advance that can be easily modified.
• Enlist and train staff and student workers who are able to assist.
• Clarify the expectations, student needs, and learning outcomes for the visit.
• Ask for a copy of the research assignment from the high school librarian.
• Browse the high school's library web site to gain familiarity with resources.
• Create or modify a lesson plan for the visit.
• Identify appropriate resources and search tools to introduce.
• Develop a schedule for the day that includes short breaks.
• Notify staff who will be affected by the visit.
• Ask the high school librarian for a copy of the assessment data.
• Evaluate the visit, noting what worked and what needs improvement.

Open communication and continuous collaboration are essential throughout the planning process. Asking the academic librarian for his or her input on the assignment and learning outcomes fosters a positive relationship. The academic librarian can offer feedback on how to enhance the assignment to better reflect the research skills college students need during their first year. The school librarian will want to review his or her students' current level of information literacy competency with the academic librarian. Focusing on the information literacy skills students possess serves as a better benchmark than stressing their deficiencies. This positive assessment of abilities allows the librarians to design an instruction session that reinforces current knowledge and uses students' strengths to introduce new concepts (Salisbury and Karasmanis 2011).

With the assignment in hand and the learning outcomes, needs, and expectations understood, the academic librarian can begin to prepare the session. Groups visiting Cleveland State work with the FYE librarian to customize their learning experiences to meet their objectives, but the instructional session and independent research time are always the focal point. The instruction session lasts approximately 45 minutes, and a minimum of one hour is recommended for independent research. The FYE librarian uses the assignment to determine the appropriate resources. He or she selects relevant titles to create a mobile reference collection to bring to the instruction room. When selecting the databases, he or she focuses on introducing databases the students will not have access to at the high school or public library.

The FYE librarian concentrates on teaching skills that support the learning outcomes identified during his or her consultations with the school librarian. If they are not already included in the learning outcomes, he or she will recommend the following topics: constructing search statements, identifying subject terms, distinguishing source types, evaluating sources, and avoiding plagiarism. Because each group has different assignments and needs, designing the instruction session demands the most time and attention.

Fortunately, the other learning experiences offered to high schools during their visit apply to all students. Inspired by the work of VanScoy and Oakleaf (2008) and Owen (2010), the FYE librarian at CSU created a lesson that incorporates active learning and introduces the expectations of college professors; this lesson identifies key differences between high school and college. Another lesson uses an audience response system to tests students' understanding of plagiarism. This activity defines plagiarism and describes the consequences as stated in CSU's Student Code of Conduct. Each lesson is about 30 minutes. Both lessons present crucial information for future college students, and the only preparation needed is a quick review and update of the lessons before delivery.

Most groups opt to include the library tour because the library's size makes a lasting impression. Students have the opportunity to safely explore a new and often overwhelming environment during the tour. Research indicates that this experience may help alleviate students' anxieties about the library (Onwuegbuzie, Jiao, and Bostick 2004). The tour demands minimal preparation and can be conducted by any willing library staff. The FYE librarian at CSU recommends using student library workers to lead the tours. Student workers familiar with the library's physical space can quickly learn the tour stops and the details to share about each area. The high school guests respond positively to having a college student lead the tour. They participate more and ask questions about their guide's college experiences. The information given on the tour highlights the differences between academic libraries and high school or public libraries. Differences stressed on the tour include the Library of Congress classification system; the arrangement of fiction, bound periodicals, microforms, and readers; and collection development practices. To add interest, the group visits specialized areas such as Archives, Special Collections, and Multi Media Services. The full tour lasts 45 minutes, but it can be shortened as needed by omitting specialized areas.

The available time and group size determine the flow of the visit. A typical schedule for a group of 25 staying the entire school day (approximately 9:00 a.m. to 2:00 p.m.) includes a tour, short break, college expectations or plagiarism lesson, lunch, information literacy instruction, and individual work time. This full schedule of changing events keeps students engaged; too much down time leads to students quickly getting off task. Groups with less time typically ask for the tour, instruction session, and individual research time. During the instruction, the FYE librarian incorporates information about college expectations and plagiarism.

Although a group of about 25 is preferred, the FYE librarian is keenly aware that high schools often need to bring larger groups to make the expense of the bus transportation and the commitment of time and staff worthwhile. CSU facilities can accommodate no more than 54 students. Schools are asked to bring at least one adult per 14 students. Larger groups place additional stress on the library staff and facilities because they require more staff and space. Any groups larger than 30 are divided into smaller groups so that one group attends the tour while the other receives instruction. Groups then switch places and meet later in the day for common a work time. Facilitating the visits requires a high degree of organization and flexibility. Smart librarians will have an alternate plan in case the unexpected happens.

Prior to the field trip, the FYE librarian prefers that the students receive introductory lessons, including university policies and behavioral expectations, about academic libraries from their high school librarian. Students who arrive well prepared and cognizant of expectations accomplish more during their visit to the university library.

In addition to a thorough review of the assignment and purpose for the field trip, an exhaustive search of the school library's collection for potential sources needs to be conducted. Beginning the search process in the school library gives students time to get to know their topics and practice important information literacy skills.

The school librarian should introduce the Library of Congress classification system and guide students through a search of the university's online catalog. Students can create a list of specific books or items to review when they arrive at CSU. Lessons that address brainstorming search terms, creating Boolean statements, and identifying scholarly sources are also useful. The FYE librarian recommends that students, under the guidance of their teacher and librarian, set specific goals to accomplish during the visit. Students should also be instructed to bring their assignments, notebooks, pens, USB drives, copier change, and any other materials they may need to complete their work.

Prior to the visit, the school librarian may wish to gather assessment data that gives a clear picture of students' current skill levels. This data can be used to determine specific skills for the academic librarian to teach. Kent State University Libraries' Tool for Real-Time Assessment of Information Literacy Skills (TRAILS) is an excellent online assessment that can be used as a pre- and posttest to document student learning. Oakleaf and Owen (2010) provide an assessment model for collecting evidence from college course syllabi that can be used to inform information literacy instruction at both educational levels. This model also nurtures supportive partnerships between academic and school librarians. Assessment data, both anecdotal and statistical, has the potential to provide substantial evidence to guide program development and substantiate both the school and academic library's validity as a place of teaching and learning within the context of the educational system.

All this preparation involves a great deal of work for the school librarian, but the effort is worth the results. The lessons taught prior to the visit provide context for the students and allow the academic librarian to construct learning experiences that build on prior knowledge to teach new concepts. Linking what is taught in the school library with what is taught during the academic library visit increases student learning. Step by step, students develop the cognitive skills that will facilitate their transition from high school report writing to sophisticated scholarly inquiries that demand critical thinking and complex problem solving. It is easy to see how such experiences help narrow the knowledge gap and improve college readiness.

Professional articles dating as far back as the 1980s explain the advantages high school students receive from visiting a university library and working with an academic librarian (Burhanna and Jensen 2006; Islam and Murno 2006; Pearson and McNeil 2002; Cosgrove 2001). In addition to valuable learning experiences, students get a glimpse of college life and an opportunity to test the waters. Lonsdale and Armstrong (2006) note that high school students who receive instruction from an academic librarian in the university setting receive a preliminary orientation to college life and its academic expectations. More specifically, collaborative partnerships between secondary and postsecondary educators have the potential to improve school performance, familiarize students with college teaching practices, expose students to scholarly sources available in the university's vast collection, encourage college attendance, relieve anxieties associated with the transition to college, and equalize student opportunities (Lonsdale and Armstrong 2006).

Additionally, carefully crafted research assignments assist students in acquiring other skills fundamental to college success such as time management, organization, personal responsibility, and academic integrity. Successfully completing an assignment that necessitates the use of an academic library and its scholarly sources builds confidence in high school students. Arranging the field trip reinforces the value of the library and demonstrates its vital role in education. Students also learn that the librarians are friendly, helpful, and supportive.

OVERCOMING OBSTACLES

The student learning outcomes outlined earlier in this chapter make a strong case for collaborations between librarians working in secondary and in postsecondary education. However, numerous obstacles often stand in the way of these partnerships. Both school and academic libraries have suffered serious budget cuts that make it difficult to find the time, staff, resources, and funding needed to support such excursions. Many school librarians work alone or are the only certified librarian for the district, making it difficult to convince principals to approve and fund field trips. School librarians, like academic librarians, frequently encounter faculty who resist giving up class time or redesigning an assignment. Without supportive colleagues on both sides, librarians' progress in closing the gap will be slow.

Academic libraries are running on leaner staffs, making it harder to support outreach programs. The FYE librarian at CSU plans, organizes, and facilitates the entire visit with each group of high school students, but cooperation from other areas that are affected—for example, circulation, technical services, student employment, and systems—is vital. Although coworkers are willing to assist, they may be unable to put aside their immediate priorities. Community service is a part of the CSU library's mission, but outreach activities must be carefully managed to avoid disrupting services to college students and faculty, monopolizing space and other resources, and placing extra burdens on the staff. The FYE librarian uses the following strategies to avoid having a negative impact on the library's daily operations: scheduling high school groups during nonpeak times, avoiding dates with library events already scheduled, soliciting help far in advance, recruiting student workers, checking dates and times with staff members, and communicating plans via email.

Asking high school groups to give serious thought to the actual need for borrowing privileges has reduced staff workloads and stress levels. Because high school students rarely use the library privileges granted by the university library, creating user records, checking out materials, and recovering borrowed items generates a great deal of unnecessary work. The FYE librarian encourages guests to photocopy and use electronic databases. Because both Cleveland State and Cuyahoga County Public Library (CCPL) are part of the Ohio Library and Information Network (OhioLINK), students who have an account at CCPL are able to check out books from CSU and request books from OhioLINK members. The FYE librarian advises school librarians to help their students sign up for a CCPL account several weeks before visiting. With a little creative thinking and willingness to be flexible, there are solutions for most of the issues that arise when managing an outreach program.

Because high school outreach programs require tremendous support from the library administration, school librarians may encounter difficulties when attempting to locate a college or university libraries in their area able to host their students. Academic libraries thinking about starting a high school outreach program should consider the institutional benefits. Implementing an outreach program can be a powerful recruitment tool.

High school outreach promotes college readiness and higher education, and offers the opportunity to achieve the community service goals that are a part of institutional mission statements. Fortunately for area high schools, the library administration at CSU supports the high school outreach program and the FYE librarian's efforts to create a smoother transition for college bound students. Both the administration and the FYE librarian recognize the tremendous benefits of aligning high school and college information literacy standards and instruction program.

Students and institutions are not the only ones benefiting from high school–academic librarian partnerships. Librarians profit both professionally and personally from these partnerships. School and academic librarians who work together quickly realize they have the same goal—preparing 21st-century learners to be information literate—and that their greatest difference may be the size of their libraries. They discover the barriers each must face when trying to implement comprehensive information literacy programs, and they can offer one another support in overcoming these obstacles. School librarians discover the cognitive skills their students will need for college success, and academic librarians gain insight into the competency levels of incoming freshmen. Through collaborative relationships, librarians increase their understanding of each other's roles and can begin to visualize how to coordinate their work to improve the educational experiences of current and future college students. Together they can address deficiencies in students' abilities to efficiently and effectively use information to solve problems. As school and academic librarians work together, a solution to the college readiness puzzle becomes more apparent.

BIBLIOGRAPHY

Ameika, Martha. "Introducing College Research at the High School Level: A Jump Start on Success." *Voice of Youth Advocates* 31, no. 5 (December 2008): 408–409.

American Association of School Libraries (AASL). *Standards for the 21st-Century Learner.* http://www.ala.org/ala/mgrps/divs/aasl/guidelinesandstandards/learningstandards/ standards.cfm (accessed October 20, 2011).

American Association of School Libraries (AASL) / Association of College & Research Libraries (ACRL) Task Force on the Educational Role of Libraries. *Blueprint for Collaboration.* Chicago, IL: American Library Association, 2002. http://www.ala.org/ala/mgrps/divs/acrl/publications/whitepapers/acrlaaslblueprint.cfm (accessed October 20, 2011).

Association of College and Research Libraries (ACRL). *Information Literacy Competency Standards for Higher Education.* http://www.ala.org/ala/mgrps/divs/acrl/standards/informationliteracy competency.cfm (accessed October 20, 2011).

Barefoot, Betsy. "Bridging the Chasm: First-Year Students and the Library." *Chronicle of Higher Education* 52, no. 20 (January 20, 2006): B16.

Burhanna, Kenneth J. "Instructional Outreach to High Schools." *Communications in Information Literacy* 1, no. 2 (September 2007): 74–88.

Burhanna, Kenneth J., and Mary Lee Jensen. "Collaborations for Success: High School to College Transitions." *Reference Services Review* 34, no. 4 (2006): 509–519.

Cahoy, Ellysa Stern. "Will Your Students Be Ready for College? Connecting K-12 and College Standards for Information Literacy." *Knowledge Quest* 30, no. 4 (2002): 12–15.

Cleveland State University Michael Schwartz Library. "High School Group Visits." http://library.csuohio.edu/information/visits.html (accessed November 1, 2012).

Conley, David T. "Rethinking College Readiness." *New England Journal of Higher Education* 22, no. 5 (2008): 24–26.

Conley, David T. *Understanding University Success: A Report from Standards for Success: A Project of the Association of American Universities and the Pew Charitable Trust.* Eugene, OR: Center for Educational Policy Research, 2003.

Cosgrove, John A. "Promoting Higher Education: (Yet) Another Goal of Bibliographic Instruction of High School Students by College Librarians." *College & Undergraduate Libraries* 8, no. 2 (2001): 17.

Daniel, Eileen. "High School to University: What Skills Do Students Need?", in *Information Rich but Knowledge Poor? Emerging Issues for Schools and Libraries Worldwide, Research and Professional Papers Presented at the Annual Conference of the International Association of School Librarianship Held in Conjunction with the Association for Teacher-Librarianship in Canada,* ed. Lynne Lighthall and Ken Haycock. Seattle: International Association of School Librarianship, 1997. ERIC, ED412942.

Fitzgerald, Mary Ann. "Making the Leap from High School to College." *Knowledge Quest* 32, no. 4 (2004): 19–24.

Gordon, Carol A. "A Room with a View: Looking at School Library Instruction from a Higher Education Perspective." *Knowledge Quest* 30, no. 4 (2002): 16–21.

Islam, Ramona L., and Lisa Anne Murno. "From Perceptions to Connections: Informing Information Literacy Program Planning in Academic Libraries through Examination of High School Library Media Center Curricula." *College & Research Libraries* 67, no. 6 (2006): 492–514.

Katz, Irvin R. "Testing Information Literacy in Digital Environments: ETS's iSkills Assessment." *Information Technology & Libraries* 26, no. 3 (2007): 3–12.

Kent State University Libraries. "TRAILS: Tool for Real-Time Assessment of Information Literacy Skills." http://www.trails-9.org/ (accessed October 18, 2011).

Latham, Don, and Melissa Gross. "Broken Links: Undergraduates Look Back on Their Experiences with Information Literacy in K-12 Education." *School Library Media Research* 11, (January 2008): 2.

Lonsdale, Ray, and Chris Armstrong. "The Role of the University Library in Supporting Information Literacy in UK Secondary Schools." *Aslib Proceedings* 58, no. 6 (2006): 553–569.

Nutefall, Jennifer E. "Information Literacy." *Research Strategies* 18, no. 4 (2001): 311–318.

Oakleaf, Megan, and Patricia L. Owen. "Closing the 12-13 Gap Together: School and College Librarians Supporting 21st Century Learners." *Teacher Librarian* 37, no. 4 (2010): 52–58.

Onwuegbuzie, Anthony J., Qun G. Jiao, and Sharon L. Bostick. *Library Anxiety: Theory, Research and Applications.* Lanham, MD: Scarecrow Press, 2004.

O'Sullivan, Michael K., and Kim B. Dallas. "A Collaborative Approach to Implementing 21st Century Skills in a High School Senior Research Class." *Education Libraries* 33, no. 1 (2010): 3–9.

Owen, Patricia. "A Transition Checklist for High School Seniors." *School Library Monthly* 26, no. 8 (2010): 20–23.

Partnership for 21st Century Skills. "A Framework for 21st Century Learning." http://www.p21.org/index.php (accessed November 1, 2011).

Pearson, Debra, and Beth McNeil. "From High School Users College Students Grow: Providing Academic Library Research Opportunities to High School Students." *Knowledge Quest* 30, no. 4 (2002): 24–28.

Salisbury, Fiona, and Sharon Karasmanis. "Are They Ready? Exploring Student Information Literacy Skills in the Transition from Secondary to Tertiary Education." *Australian Academic & Research Libraries* 42, no. 1 (2011): 43–58.

Schroeder, Robert. "Both Sides Now: Librarians Looking at Information Literacy from High School and College: Tips." *Educators' Spotlight Digest* 4, no. 1 (March 1, 2009): 5. ERIC, EJ899891.

Smalley, Topsy N. "College Success: High School Librarians Make the Difference." *Journal of Academic Librarianship* 30, no. 3 (2004): 193–198.

Smeraldi, Ann Marie. "High School to College Transition: Resources for Librarians and Teachers." http://researchguides.csuohio.edu/fytransition_educators (accessed March 12, 2012).

Smith, Suzanne. "The Top 10 Things High School Seniors Need to Know about College Libraries." *Book Report* 20, no. 5 (March 2002): 42.

Tabar, Margaret. "Rite of Passage: A Visit to a University Library." *Knowledge Quest* 30, no. 4 (March 1, 2002): 29–30.

Ury, Connie J. "Value Added: High School Research Projects in an Academic Library." *Clearing House* 69, no. 5 (May 1996): 313.

VanScoy, Amy, and Megan J. Oakleaf. "Evidence vs. Anecdote: Using Syllabi to Plan Curriculum-Integrated Information Literacy Instruction." *College & Research Libraries* 69, no. 6 (2008): 566–575.

Young, Robyn. "A Collaborative Effort: Importance of the Relationship between School Libraries and the University." *Indiana Libraries* 25, no. 3 (December 15, 2006): 16–17.

18

Dual Enrollment Students: Starting the Library Connection Here

Thomas L. Reinsfelder and Jill E. Thompson

INTRODUCTION

Many school and academic librarians desire to help students successfully transition from high school to college. These librarians from different organizations are often interested in working together but can find it difficult to know where to begin. Any effort to establish partnerships of this nature should consider starting with the students that these librarians already have in common. In trying to find that right opportunity for collaboration, librarians must not forget that many high school students may already be enrolled in colleges and universities through dual enrollment programs or similar initiatives. Both school and academic librarians have a responsibility to contribute to the success of dual enrollment students.

DUAL ENROLLMENT: HISTORY, GROWTH, AND CONTEXT

The idea of exposing high school students to college-level coursework is certainly not new. Over the past half-century, in an effort to help students become more prepared for future success, high schools and colleges experimented with different programs. Educational leaders and policymakers created new initiatives so that students could participate in the college experience while still in high school. One of the most common options is often referred to as dual enrollment, where high school students, most often seniors but sometimes juniors, enroll in one or more college courses before completing high school. In some states, dual enrollment programs may be known by different names such as dual credit, concurrent enrollment, or a postsecondary option. These programs differ from some more recent but less common efforts described as early college, where starting in ninth or tenth grade, students simultaneously earn both high school and college credit (Brewer, Stern, and Ahn 2007). Dual enrollment also differs from

Advanced Placement (AP) and International Baccalaureate (IB) programs by allowing students to earn credits as a traditional college student, rather than being awarded college credit for advanced work completed in high school.

The phrase "dual enrollment," when first used in the 1960s, had a slightly different meaning than it does today. Policymakers initially defined dual enrollment as "an arrangement whereby a child or youth regularly and concurrently attends a public school part time and a nonpublic school part time" (Gibbs et al. 1965, 1). These early programs, also referred to as "shared time," allowed high school students to participate in activities at more than one school and often involved sharing resources between nonpublic and public schools (U.S. Congress 1964). The 1970s saw growth in the number of programs seeking to build partnerships between high schools and colleges (Brossman 1975; DeLuca 1977; Voorheis 1979). By the late 1970s, most states reported options that allowed high school students to earn college credit prior to graduation. In many, a formal statewide program or policy addressed the dual enrollment concept; in other states, initiatives were more locally based (Vernon 1978).

Programs in the United States continued to evolve and by 2003, forty-eight percent of degree-granting institutions eligible for federal student aid under Title IV had students in dual enrollment programs (Kleiner and Lewis 2005). Based on an analysis of this same data, Hoffman, Vargas, and Santos (2009) noted that "98 percent of public two-year institutions had high school students taking courses for college credit, compared to 77 percent of public four-year institutions, 40 percent of private four-year institutions, and 17 percent of private two-year institutions" (44). While most of these dual enrollment courses have been located on a college campus, others are offered within the high school, at another location, or online (Kleiner and Lewis 2005).

Most state governments now formally design or support dual enrollment programs. The details may look different from state to state, but the underlying idea remains the same. By 2005, only 10 states lacked legislation or regulation addressing dual enrollment (Karp et al. 2005). By 2008, all but seven states encouraged dual enrollment programs, and two more were developing such policies (Ewell, Boeke, and Zis 2008). However, a state without a formal policy did not necessarily prevent local schools from establishing their own arrangements with colleges.

POLICY ISSUES AND RECENT GOVERNMENTAL ACTION

Dual enrollment programs have grown in popularity, but policymakers still face challenges, including issues related to equity, standards, articulation of educational standards, public relations, and perhaps most importantly, funding (Krueger 2006). When it comes to tuition, bills may be paid by school districts, state grants, or students (Education Commission 2009). States, universities, and local school districts facing financial difficulties are likely to reduce funds for dual enrollment programs, placing greater responsibility on the students and parents who wish to participate.

So do these programs positively impact students? Research indicates that dual enrollment can effectively increase student performance and success (Karp 2008; Swanson 2010). At the same time, Lewis and Overman (2008) acknowledges that dual enrollment can improve performance but questions if these gains justify the costs. Other reports express the concerns of college and university faculty who question arrangements through which students receive college credit for taking courses taught by high school teachers in high schools (Schwalm 1991). Professors also observe that some students receiving college credit while in high school are not as prepared as more traditional students and often do not adequately understand important introductory content or the context of the material (Reisberg 1998).

In recent years, federal lawmakers attempted to provide greater support for dual enrollment programs. Senator Herb Kohl, Wisconsin Democrat, introduced the Fast Track to College Act in 2009, which would have provided up to $150 million to support dual enrollment and early college programs while requiring matching funds from local schools (U.S. Congress 2009). The bill was not passed in the 111th Congress. Similar legislation was reintroduced by both Senator Kohl and Representative Dale Kildee, Democrat from Michigan, in early 2011, with no further action as of February 2012 (U.S. Congress 2011).

DUAL ENROLLMENT IN PENNSYLVANIA

Prior to 2011, school districts in Pennsylvania could apply for funds under a dual enrollment grant through the state department of education, which covered tuition, books, fees, and transportation. In the 2009–2010 year, only $8 million of the requested $37 million in dual enrollment funds were made available. As a result, each district's grant was reduced (Pennsylvania Department of Education n.d.). When funding is not available from the state or school district, high school students or their parents pay any remaining tuition and fees for college courses. To assist with the cost, some colleges do offer a reduced tuition rate for current high school students. The 2011–2012 Pennsylvania state budget, initially proposed by the governor, stated an interest in expanding dual enrollment opportunities. However, state leaders eliminated all dual enrollment funding for the 2011–2012 academic year, replacing it with a proposal to use a portion of each student's basic education funding to support dual enrollment (Pennsylvania Office of the Budget n.d.).

ESTABLISHING AND STRENGTHENING
A WORKING RELATIONSHIP

Penn State–Mont Alto (PSMA), a branch campus of Pennsylvania State University, serves about 1,200 students and offers several four-year degree programs along with the first two years of many other degrees that can be completed at other campuses within the university. Because many students are from the local area, librarians were interested in learning more about library activities at local high schools.

Over the years, the library at PSMA had limited interaction with high school students and librarians. Interaction would usually occur when students were advised to visit a college library to complete an assignment, or when high school students might briefly visit the library as part of a campus tour. PSMA librarians became interested in getting to know some of the school librarians better to share ideas and perhaps partner on projects to help students become more prepared for the first year of college.

With state funding that was intended to encourage dual enrollment programs, this campus saw a significant number of students who were still enrolled in high school. Area high schools encouraged juniors and seniors to enroll in one or two classes to earn some college credit before graduation. The program at PSMA is known as dual enrollment or early to college. Students from a school district that was awarded dual enrollment funds from the state are called dual enrollment students. High school students from schools not receiving dual enrollment funds are called early to college students and pay their own way (Penn State Mont Alto n.d.). Even though the state government has reduced support for these programs, many high school students still seem to have an interest in completing one or more college courses before graduation.

One of the academic library's interactions with high school students resulted from a high school library club's visit. Later, a PSMA librarian travelled to meet with the school librarian at the school library to learn more about how things work on from the school librarian's point of view. More specifically, the goal was to find out how students use the school library in the years just before they enter college. PSMA librarians began talking about opportunities for collaboration and started looking closely at a grant opportunity. The Library Services and Technology Act (LSTA) grant being administered through the Office of Commonwealth Libraries sought proposals for an Information Access grant. One of the special priorities was "for college libraries and high school libraries whose institutions are cooperating in a dual enrollment program for high school students" (Office of Commonwealth Libraries 2008, 2). This seemed like an excellent opportunity.

Several librarians from other area high schools that had students participating in the Dual Enrollment/Early to College (DE/ETC) program were contacted. They were invited to participate in the grant proposal that could possibly offer some funding to support collaborative efforts. Through visits to high schools and meetings with librarians, PSMA librarians eventually developed a plan of action and established an activity budget. We applied for and received the grant of just over $31,000.

During the 2008–2009 school year, the PSMA library worked with local high school librarians to support DE/ETC students from several area high schools, including Chambersburg, Greencastle, McConnellsburg, and Waynesboro. Approximately 130 high school students from these schools were enrolled in college courses at Penn State–Mont Alto in the fall of 2008.

The collaborative efforts of PSMA librarians and the four high schools were supported by this grant and consisted of five key elements:

1. High school librarians and academic librarians initially met as a group at the PSMA library to discuss issues of common interest, learn about the university library, discuss ways to enhance collaboration, plan library/research-related activities, establish a budget, and finalize plans for student visits to the library.

2. Group visits to PSMA were scheduled so that DE/ETC students could learn more about the library and the campus. Along with their high school librarian, students participated in activities designed to enhance familiarity with a university library. Topics covered included how a college library is different from a high school library (organization, resources, and services), the importance of developing a research topic, using a library catalog to find books, using library databases to find articles, understanding scholarly resources, and avoiding plagiarism and citing sources. Each visit lasted for most of the school day and included a group lunch at the campus dining facilities.

3. Grant funds enabled the purchase of library materials at each high school and PSMA to support the specific educational needs and interests of DE/ETC students.

4. Several school libraries expressed a need for additional computers to support students enrolled in college courses. Grant funds helped to provide a few computers to school libraries. Students enrolled in college courses were given priority on these computers.

5. A PSMA librarian made follow-up visits to participating high schools to meet with school librarians, evaluate the efforts, and discuss future possibilities.

BENEFITS OF THE PARTNERSHIP

This collaborative initiative significantly impacted the programs and services of both the high school and academic libraries. To begin, grant funds allowed significant additions to library collections targeted toward this unique user group. Another significant benefit was the opportunity for DE/ETC students to attend an academic library orientation with a university librarian. These students gained a more authentic understanding of academic library resources and conventions while getting acquainted with college librarians. Surrounded by the research environment of the PSMA library, the dual enrollment students came to better understand research expectations at the college level while developing an appreciation for using a wide variety of tools to access information for a specific need. They learned about the importance of basic research and information technology skills, and why information needs to be evaluated critically and competently. Students also came to understand that professors would expect ethical use of information and personal responsibility in all completed assignments. Additionally, high school librarians obtained a better understanding of how their students would be expected to use academic libraries in the near future. This, along with a greater awareness of common academic library services and resources, can help them better prepare students for future success.

Although many dual enrollment students choose to continue at other colleges or universities after high school, this initial exposure to an academic library can be beneficial regardless of where they pursue their education. Once familiar with the general concepts of library catalogs, research databases, subject libraries, and services such as interlibrary loan and course reserves, students can more comfortably use any academic library. In fact, one of the activities involved looking at various academic library web sites to observe the many similarities. Finally, and perhaps most importantly, this project enabled all librarians, school and college, to learn from one another by sharing information and ideas from our different libraries.

CHALLENGES ALONG THE WAY

Overall, the experience was positive for all involved as evidenced by feedback from students and librarians. However, as with any major project, some unexpected challenges arose. None proved to be a true hardship, but several areas required more time or effort than initially expected.

First, a project like this requires a substantial commitment of time. Any grant project includes the completion of a great deal of paperwork. There was the initial grant application, then the quarterly updates with details of all financial transactions, and the final report to document in detail all completed activities. The university and participating school districts used different procedures for ordering items and processing financial transactions, so these differences had to be resolved. In addition to working with multiple business offices, the grant required letters of support from academic administrators at the university as well as the schools. All of the administrators were supportive, especially since grant funds were involved and would provide additional opportunities and resources for the students. Fortunately, because it is not uncommon for units within the university to apply for and work with grant funding, assistance was available from professionals who are more experienced with navigating the process. At some institutions, as experienced PSMA, there may even be an office dedicated to supporting those who are working with grant applications and related projects to make sure all of the requirements are satisfactorily met.

Another challenge came when trying to accommodate librarian and student schedules to work around school and university events, and arrange for transportation between the schools and the campus. When scheduling an event with more than a few people, it is nearly impossible to find a time that is ideal for all, so PSMA librarians just did the best they could. However, it was somewhat disappointing that the actual student participation in library activities was lower than had been hoped. Many chose not to take the time away from their classes and other activities. But the students who did spend a day on the college campus with their school librarians did seem to enjoy themselves and feel the day was worthwhile. In the future, it may be wise to shorten the length of the student visits to no more than a couple of hours so that more students are able to attend. PSMA librarians also could have done a better job of selling the program to college-bound students, explaining why it would be beneficial to invest some time now to learn about academic libraries and how they work.

GOING BEYOND DUAL ENROLLMENT STUDENTS

A current trend is for high schools to find ways to successfully prepare and transition students to the postsecondary part of their education. Where dual enrollment programs are already in place, a library-to-library connection is a logical component of that process and a good place to start. However, partnerships established to enhance library services for dual enrollment students should not end with this small group of students.

It is likely that after a strong relationship has been formed, high school and college librarians will find additional ways to work together on future projects that will benefit even more students. As programs and relationships are developed, there is an increased likelihood that information and resources will be shared between the libraries. Consequently, a better understanding of academic expectations and what is being taught on both sides will allow library professionals to better assist students with the transition from high school to college.

BIBLIOGRAPHY

Brewer, Dominic J., Stefanie Stern, and June Ahn. "An Introduction to 'Early College.' " *Education Finance and Policy* 2, no. 2 (2007): 175–187.

Brossman, Sidney W. "Concurrent Enrollments in California High Schools and Community Colleges." *High School Journal* 58, no. 4 (1975): 122–130.

DeLuca, James P. *Dual Enrollment: An Opportunity for Highly Motivated High School Seniors to Attend a Community College and High School Concurrently.* Presented at the Third Annual Conference on Urban Education. Norfolk, VA: Old Dominion University, 1977, ERIC, ED 158810.

Education Commission of the States. "Funding Dual Credit Programs: What Do We Know? What Should We Know?" *Progress of Education Reform* 10, no. 1 (February 2009): 1–4. http://www.ecs.org/clearinghouse/79/48/7948.pdf (accessed February 22, 2012).

Ewell, Peter, Marianne Boeke, and Stacey Zis. *State Policies on Student Transitions: Results of a Fifty-State Inventory.* Boulder, CO: National Center for Higher Education Management Systems, 2008, ERIC, ED 512592. http://www.eric.ed.gov/PDFS/ED512592.pdf (accessed February 22, 2012).

Gibbs, James E., Carl J. Sokolowski, August W. Steinhilber, and William C. Strasser. *Dual Enrollment in Public and Nonpublic Schools: Case Studies of Nine Communities.* Washington, D.C.: U.S. Department of Health, Education, and Welfare, Government Printing Office, 1965.

Hoffman, Nancy, Joel Vargas, and Janet Santos. "New Directions for Dual Enrollment: Creating Stronger Pathways from High School through College." *New Directions for Community Colleges* 2009, no. 145: 43–58.

Karp, Melinda M., Thomas R. Bailey, Katherine L. Hughes, and Baranda J. Fermin. "Update to State Dual Enrollment Policies: Addressing Access and Quality." Washington, D.C.: U.S. Department of Education, Office of Vocational and Adult Education, 2005. http://www2.ed.gov/about/offices/list/ovae/pi/cclo/cbtrans/statedualenrollment.pdf (accessed February 22, 2012).

Karp, Melinda M., and Katherine L. Hughes. "Study: Dual Enrollment Can Benefit a Broad Range of Students." *Techniques* 83, no. 7 (2008): 14–17.

Kleiner, Brian, and Bernard Lewis. "Dual Enrollment of High School Students at Postsecondary Institutions: 2002–03," Washington, D.C.: U.S. Department of Education, National Center for Education Statistics, 2005. http://nces.ed.gov/pubs2005/2005008.pdf (accessed February 22, 2012).

Krueger, Carl. *Dual Enrollment: Policy Issues Confronting State Policy Makers.* Denver, CO: Education Commission of the States, March 2006. http://www.ecs.org/clearinghouse/67/87/6787.pdf (accessed February 22, 2012).

Lewis, Morgan V., and Laura Overman. "Dual and Concurrent Enrollment and Transition to Postsecondary Education." *Career and Technical Education Research* 33, no. 3 (2008): 189–202.

Office of Commonwealth Libraries. *Information Access Grant Application Guidelines.* Harrisburg, PA: Department of Education, 2008.

Penn State Mont Alto. "Early to College/Dual Enrollment." http://www.ma.psu.edu/Admissions/30757.htm (accessed February 22, 2012).

Pennsylvania Department of Education. "Dual Enrollment Grant Program: 2010–2011 Program Grant Application Guidelines." http://www.portal.state.pa.us/portal/server.pt/gateway/PTARGS_0_123625_873619_0_0_18/PDE-Dual%20Enrollment%20Guidelines%202010-2011.doc (accessed February 22, 2012).

Pennsylvania Office of the Budget. "2011–12 Governor's Executive Budget." http://www.portal.state.pa.us/portal/server.pt/community/current_and_proposed_commonwealth_budgets/4566 (accessed February 22, 2012).

Reisberg, Leo. "Some Professors Question Programs That Allow High-School Students to Earn College Credits." *Chronicle of Higher Education* 44, no. 42 (1998): 39–40.

Schwalm, David E. "High School/College Dual Enrollment." *WPA: Writing Program Administration* 15 nos. 1–2 (1991): 51–54.

Swanson, Jodi. "Dual Enrollment: The Missing Link to College Readiness." *Principal Leadership* 10, no. 7 (2010): 42–46.

U.S. Congress. House. Committee on Education and Labor. *Shared-Time Education: Hearings before the Ad Hoc Subcommittee on Study of Shared Time Education.* 88th Cong., 2nd Sess., February 24, 1964.

U.S. Congress. Senate. *Fast Track to College Act of 2009*. S 627. 111th Cong., 1st Sess., *Congressional Record* 155, (March 18, 2009): S 3370-3373.

U.S. Congress. House of Representatives. *Fast Track to College Act of 2011*. HR 925 / S 154. 112th Cong., 1st Sess. March 3, 2011.

Vernon, Christie D. *Concurrent Enrollment of High School Students in College: A Status Report*. Paper prepared for the American Association of Community and Junior Colleges Annual Conference, Atlanta, GA. 1978, ERIC, ED 176815.

Voorheis, Greg P. "Concurrent High School–College Enrollments." *Educational Record* 60, no. 3 (1979): 305–311.

19

Using Technology to Provide Support to Remote Students Participating in Dual Enrollment Programs

Louis E. Mays

Academic librarians are always challenged to find new, innovative methods of serving distance learners. This chapter will be an overview of providing library support to dual enrollment high school students at remote locations, sharing experiences learned at Southern State Community College in southwestern Ohio. Students and faculty members at off-campus sites often feel alienated from the campus. Access to library resources may be limited or nonexistent at remote sites due to lack of equipment, lack of financial support, or inadequate access to the Internet. These issues are very much a part of the challenge when serving dual enrollment high school students.

Opportunities in higher education for high school students are at an all-time high. Numerous states have initiated some sort of postsecondary enrollment option (PSEO) for high school students. Enrollment in these PSEO dual enrollment programs is increasing each year. Traditionally, PSEO students leave their high school to take college courses at a local community college or university campus. This "brain drain" from the high schools is of concern to many high school administrators because revenue is also lost when dual enrollment students leave the high school site for campus. High school principals, already facing financial constraints, have collaborated with admissions representatives in higher education, and the result in many states has led to dual enrollment programs. Dual enrollment means the high school student remains at the high school location but can enroll in college courses taught at the high school. Some dual enrollment students may also leave the high school and take college classes on campus. Most states fund dual enrollment programs with local grants and scholarships or reduced tuition rates for students. Few states use state subsidies to fund these programs. Georgia, for example, uses their state lottery system to fund the HOPE grants program that provides help with college tuition, fees and books for citizens 16 and over. The present rate of funding for dual enrollment at Southern State Community College is 80 percent of the tuition bill is invoiced to the student's originating high school and the other 20 percent is paid by the state of Ohio. Ohio is developing a standardized dual enrollment funding model for subsidy distribution. As it stands now, sometimes the student or parent may have to pay a portion of the cost to the college or high school. Funding varies by state, and even within states. In terms of textbooks, the high school, college, or student may purchase the books, depending on local policies and available funding. This type of financial aid incentive is of interest to parents who wish to keep the cost of college attendance down.

Faculty members teaching these courses are usually qualified high school teachers but can sometimes be faculty from the campus. Selection and evaluation of faculty members is usually done by faculty members or administration in the relevant department from the college. Mentoring of dual enrollment faculty often involves review of course syllabi, textbooks, and other items of interest to faculty members. Access to library resources, however, may not necessarily be part of the mentoring or orientation session for the college unless promoted by the academic library.

LIBRARY SUPPORT IN DUAL ENROLLMENT COURSES: GETTING STARTED

Unfortunately, many dual enrollment agreements are made between a high school and a college without the involvement of academic and student support personnel. The academic library is often left out of the process. It is vital that the academic library become an integral part of dual enrollment services, and librarians should take the initiative to become informed and more involved. Here are a few suggestions to start the process:

- Identify your college's dual enrollment coordinator and make a point to meet with him or her regularly. Contact the admissions office, distance education staff, or academic services personnel to identify who is responsible for dual enrollment at the high school.
- Ask to be placed on the agenda of campus workshops and orientation sessions for dual enrollment faculty members. Use this time to disseminate information about library services, set up orientation sessions, and get to know your remote faculty members.
- Ask your dual enrollment coordinator to send you a list each term of all classes being taught, including title, location, faculty member.
- Contact the high school technology coordinator and school librarian to collaborate. If you use technology to communicate with these remote sites, the school librarian or technology coordinator can help facilitate at the local site.
- Create an email list of dual enrollment faculty, especially those that are likely to use library resources, and communicate with them regularly about the library.
- Create web-based template guides, like LibGuides, for remote locations that provide access to resources from the academic library. Make sure the LibGuides provide information about remote authentication.

USING TECHNOLOGY IN DUAL ENROLLMENT

In the past, many schools provided field trips for students to college campuses. These field trips were both informational and revealing to the transitioning high school student. For many students, it was their first experience visiting a college campus. Other field trips were more specific in nature, including visits to the academic library for advanced research and exposure to resources in higher education not available at the school library. For the most part, those days are over for most public schools due to budget constraints. Many field trips are a thing of the past unless funded by grant money.

How can K-12 and higher education collaborate to lessen the gap between school sites and campuses? The one thing we all have in common is technology. Most schools are equipped with broadband Internet connections and computers. If the academic library staff cannot visit the school site, why not use this technology for outreach services?

PLATFORMS

Live synchronous connections between the campus and school are most useful when using technology. There are a variety of options available, including open source and proprietary platforms. Both locations can use headsets with microphones to give every connected individual a voice and identity. Webcams are also useful when putting a face to a name.

Asynchronous learning management systems (LMS) (e.g., Blackboard, Moodle) also provide a great repository of resources helpful to students and faculty members at remote locations. Transitioning students should be introduced to LMS as a part of their overall college experience. Content on the LMS should be provided by the academic library staff, student services, academic support, and other services useful to new college students.

Web-based platforms similar to LibGuides and CampusGuides are also useful for disseminating campus resources to remote users. Many academic libraries already subscribe to these services. If created, they can be more accessible to users as they bypass the LMS, which requires pre-enrollment before access. The real challenge when collaborating is content. What content do you provide? We will explore this by taking a closer look at how a librarian at Southern State Community College has used many of these strategies to support remotely located duel enrollment students.

SOUTHERN STATE COMMUNITY COLLEGE: CASE STUDY

Southern State Community College (www.sscc.edu) is a small community college located in the southern Appalachian region of Ohio. This multicampus college refers to dual enrollment as either PSEO campus or PSEO high school. The college is located in a rural setting and provides PSEO high school dual enrollment courses to over 20 high schools in a seven-county area of southern Ohio. In 2011, PSEO off-campus students in high schools comprised 4.8 percent of Southern State's enrollment. The rate of growth between 2008 and 2011 was 311 percent (Purvis 2011). The college provides instruction in 22 locations, offering a variety of classes, including English, math, social sciences, business, and chemistry. Faculty orientation and informational sessions are provided on campus at least twice a year. No student orientations are provided at the high schools. Students are encouraged to attend orientation on campus, which may be many miles from their homes or the school site.

After learning about Southern State's PSEO program and how it works, the college librarian determined that the college had to come up with a way of disseminating information to all of these high school sites. He selected the Blackboard LMS as a method of communicating with all parties involved in the PSEO high school dual enrollment program. A Blackboard site containing four portals was created (see Figure 19.1).

Acting as overall coordinator, the librarian built the portal for students and created a core portal for the remaining three areas. The librarian is involved in content found in three of these portals (Students, Faculty, and Technology Coordinators). The following list provides details on the purpose and content of each portal:

1. **Student portal:** The student portal is composed of four areas: library resources, student services, a link to the Blackboard Collaborate Suite (Blackboard Collaborate 11 and Blackboard Instant Message synchronous learning systems), and academic support resources to help students succeed. The library resources link provides access to research databases (including instructional video tutorials for using the databases), a link to the library home page and online library catalog, RefWorks (a bibliographic management web site), and a link to other resources including a site to check for plagiarism, a map showing free Wi-Fi hotspots, an interactive map showing locations where broadband is available, and other helpful information about transitioning from high school to college, including resources to help students succeed academically.

Figure 19.1.
Southern State Community College's PSEO Blackboard Portals

2. **Faculty portal:** The faculty portal is similar to the student portal. The only difference is that the faculty portal also provides information about sources of digital media, marketing materials for library resources, information for setting up a plagiarism course site, and a link for what is new in the library, which includes ways of keeping in touch with the library in social media sites (a preferred medium for high school students). Each LMS site is unique per high school location, so faculty at a particular location can easily request additional unique resources for their LMS site.

3. **Technology coordinator portal:** This portal is extremely important to maintain due to the fact that school networks are heavily filtered. Information provided here helps the technology coordinator identify which ports should be opened on the school network in order to access vital higher education resources. Any problems associated with filtering as they relate to chatting, videoconferencing, application sharing, or whiteboard applications are recorded as white papers and posted on the site so that technology coordinators can work closely with faculty members, librarians, and their colleagues at regional Instructional Technology Centers located throughout the state. The academic library staff must collaborate with the college Information Technology (IT) department and the school technology coordinator to ensure that students and faculty members are not blocked from web sites used in college instruction.

4. **Admissions and administration portal:** Information provided here assists administrators and school counselors register and admit dual enrollment students. State and national college guidelines are provided to guide school administrators and counselors in successfully enrolling students. This portal should include local college policies and procedures related to the selection and enrollment of eligible PSEO high school students.

How Does It Work?

Just prior to the beginning of a high school year (not the academic year on campus), the college reviews and updates the LMS master site for PSEO High School Dual Enrollment on Blackboard. The college librarian also keeps a list of all additional resources at specific school sites. A Blackboard course is created for each dual enrollment school site, and the unique resources requested by faculty at that school are added to the Blackboard site.

After the admissions office at the college confirms students in the course sections at a particular high school, those students are enrolled in the Blackboard site for that school, either by the faculty member or by a designated representative from the college. The Blackboard site is not for a specific course; rather, it is for all courses taught at the high school. Instructors, technology coordinators, and selected school administrators are also given access to Blackboard. Students and new faculty members are instructed to register for the synchronous instant messaging system provided (at Southern State Community College, it is Blackboard IM). Once this is done, both the asynchronous and synchronous communication links are established.

Faculty and students at a school site can now make appointments. These appointments can be online class orientation sessions, specific instruction on various library and college resources, or any other type of live communication needed by the school site. Since the school class schedule is usually only about 50 minutes per class session, and college classes are longer sessions with fewer meetings per week, college personnel must adjust their schedules accordingly so that they are available online.

Figure 19.2.
First-day connection at Zane Trace High School, Chillicothe, Ohio

A Typical Remote Classroom Orientation

The college librarian works closely with the adjunct faculty member at the school site and establishes scheduled appointments for virtual class orientation sessions. The facilitator may be the school technology coordinator, school librarian, or a faculty member. Since school block scheduling usually consists of 50 minutes each day, back-to-back virtual class visits are necessary to cover the objectives agreed upon between the faculty member and academic librarian. The following is a typical schedule for orientation.

Day One

On the day of the virtual class visit, the academic librarian connects to the facilitator before class begins to test the audio, chat, video, and whiteboard applications. At our high schools, we use computer classrooms so that each student can sit at a computer. They can see an overhead projector, which has sound (see Figure 19.2). A microphone is used for two-way audio. If a microphone is not available, a phone simulcast can be established.

At the first session, students are introduced to the academic librarian. It is advisable to have the college's LMS administrator sit in on the first class in case any last-minute enrollments need to be made. Students are then instructed to log in to their LMS. The LMS shortcut has already been installed by the technology coordinator using guidelines provided in the course site. After troubleshooting student logins in coordination with the LMS administrator, students are then instructed on how to register and then login to instant messaging. Blackboard IM provides chat, audio and videoconferencing, and whiteboard access. Under the School tab, students can choose Ask a Librarian for individual assistance. All of this is covered in the first session.

Day Two

By this time, the LMS administrator is no longer needed. After a question and answer session, the students log in to the LMS and IM systems. RefWorks is used at

Southern State, so the objective of day two is to get every student registered on RefWorks and to help each student customize his or her account and create a folder for future research papers. If time remains, the academic librarian can provide a demonstration of how to search the online library catalog while exporting a record to RefWorks.

Day Three

It is now time to learn how to utilize selected library resources. Students are referred to their LMS student portal for library resources. Use of the online library catalog and discussion of our state network of libraries called OhioLINK is reviewed. A demonstration on how to request an item is given. At some of our sites, it is not convenient for students to use one of our campus libraries as a pickup location for requested library materials, so we review "pickup anywhere." Requested items can be sent to any OhioLINK library location using the student's library barcode number. Some remote students use their Southern State card to request items as pickup anywhere and have to drive only a few miles to the nearest OhioLINK library in their community.

Day Four

This day is spent on using library resources for research. A demonstration on how to use research databases, how to evaluate resources, and how to export references to RefWorks is provided. Students are introduced to journals and learn the distinction between magazines and journals. By this time, students should be familiar with Blackboard, Ask a Librarian, RefWorks, the research databases, and the online library catalog.

OTHER RESOURCES

Helpful resources provided by the academic library can be utilized for PSEO high school classes. A plagiarism-checking program like Turnitin or Blackboard's SafeAssign can be useful for these classes. Assistance is provided to help adjunct faculty at school sites set up a Turnitin login site on Blackboard so that they can have their students check their own papers. Some prefer to check students' papers themselves after they are submitted for a grade.

Transitioning to College is a good web site to help students transition to using academic libraries. This web site (http://www.transitioning2college.org) is mostly designed for students attending a larger campus out of high school. A link to this site is provided in the student portal of the Southern State Blackboard site.

Many other resources can be included on the Blackboard site, including information about other services provided by the college and the academic library. Links to electronic journals and reference content are often useful to remote users. Links to online technology resources like Atomic Learning can be is beneficial to remote users. Ohioans are fortunate to have access to Learning Express Library and the Job & Career Accelerator. These resources are invaluable to the transitioning student. Digital video resources are also popular with remote faculty members. Many schools do not provide access to digital content found in higher education. It is important to inform both faculty members and students of the availability of these types of resources. Content links to those resources can also be easily added to a specific Blackboard PSEO high school site.

THE ISSUES

There are obvious issues on both the college and high school sites. In other words, school filtering is not the only obstacle facing academic librarians and faculty members involved in PSEO high school programs.

On the campus side, here are some of the pressing issues:

- Mindset . . . to actually realize these are college students, not high school students.
- Academic librarians must take the initiative and become involved in their college's PSEO high school programs. The college administration and admissions personnel will not likely solicit your help—you must go to them.
- It may be difficult for academic librarians to get access to their LMS sites. LMS administrators may not necessarily be as cooperative when it comes to adding sites to assist off-campus users and individuals not in the college's official registry of employees and students. Academic library staff must collaborate with the LMS administrator and other administrators and IT staff to ensure that access is provided.
- It helps to get the active support of adjunct faculty members at the high school sites. If they collaborate with the academic librarian to put pressure on the college to provide these services, success is more likely to happen.
- Work closely with your admissions staff or the department responsible for issuing student identification (ID) cards and make sure you can come up with a way to get the remote PSEO high school students their barcode number from the library and a student ID or photo ID from the institution.

On the high school side, here are some of the pressing issues:

- Mindset . . . to make these students realize they are college students in these classes, not high school students. The look, feel, and content of the classes must make them feel like a college student.
- Your biggest obstacle is school network filtering. Most technology coordinators are eager to help with this, but identifying problems will take some time to work through. The information you provide (including troubleshooting issues) to technology coordinators is vital to the success of using technology in the classroom at the high school.
- You must work closely with the technology coordinator at the high school in order to make sure your students have access to the learning management system (a shortcut on the desktop is nice), and to any chat or synchronous system you wish to utilize. This means the student must have access to computers on the high school site. Live orientation sessions are useful when you engage the student while they are at a computer.
- Make sure you and your academic library staff are available for these remote students when they need you. They must feel as if they are very much a part of the campus scene.

ON A POSITIVE NOTE

Marketing and promotion of this type of remote service is needed to encourage the administrative support required to continue. Invite school and college administrators to a live class session and let them see firsthand how students are engaged in the class session. Speak to other groups about the use of technology at remote sites and how it makes a difference to these students. Get your vendors involved, too. They like to get the word out about the success of their products, so work with them to show others how successful such an endeavor can be in a time of economic restraint.

IN CONCLUSION

Getting a jump-start on college is the central theme of PSEO high school programs. If students are mature enough and academically prepared, these programs can help them get a head start on their college education. PSEO high school programs offer financial incentives to both parents and the local school system because the programs keep students on the high school site while giving them access to courses in higher education.

The real challenge is to ensure that these locations have unfiltered network access to resources in higher education, especially those provided by the academic library. Once this goal is achieved, your institution will be on its way to providing access to resources needed for teaching and learning in a higher education environment. Academic libraries must make this mission an ongoing goal in order to reach out to these remote students. Collaboration with K-12, school librarians, IT staff, student services staff, and others involved with dual enrollment is absolutely essential to make this goal happen. Our remote PSEO high school students and faculty members must be recognized and adequately served in order to have a successful transition from high school to college.

The use of technology plays a vital role in the collaboration between the academic library and the high school site. There are a variety of options available to make this collaboration happen:

- **Learning management systems:** The LMS system can be cumbersome to set up, but experience in using these programs is an essential part of the college experience.
- **Synchronous learning systems:** Even if it is simple chat, the live connection setup between the academic library and the high school site is an important tool for retention and bridging the gap between the campus and the high school. Instant messaging, video conferencing, and live classroom platforms are great for live learning.
- **Web-based template platforms:** Many academic libraries have access to LibGuides, Campus-Guides, and other web-based template platforms. These guides can cover any type of instruction or assistance and can bypass the LMS on campus.

As enrollment increases nationwide in PSEO high school programs, the academic library must establish a plan to provide library services and support to these students and faculty members. Collaboration with school librarians can help make this possible. Technology is the common factor for both the campus and high school sites. Recognition of this issue and action on the part of the academic library will go a long way to ensure quality academic instruction and academic support at PSEO high school sites.

BIBLIOGRAPHY

Purvis, Sharon. "Enrollment Report." Internal report, Southern State Community College (*SSCC*) *Registrar*, 2011.

ADDITIONAL RESOURCES

National Alliance of Concurrent Enrollment Partnerships (NACEP). http://nacep.org/ (accessed October 29, 2012).

National Resource Center for the First-Year Experience and Students in Transition. http://www .sc.edu/fye/ (accessed October 29, 2012).

Ohio College Access Network. "KnowHow2Go" Columbus, OH: Author, 2009. http://www .knowhow2goohio.org (accessed October 29, 2012).

Owen, Patricia. "A Transition Checklist for High School Seniors." *School Library Monthly* 26, no. 8 (2010): 20–23.

"Preparing 21st Century Ohio Learners for Success: The Role of Information Literacy and Libraries." *Ohio Media Spectrum* 60, no. 1 (2008): 38–44.

"Transitioning to College: Helping You Succeed." http://www.transitioning2college.org/ (accessed October 29, 2012).

U. S. Department of Education. "Helping Students Navigate the Path to College." http://www .edpubs.gov/document/ed005283i.pdf?ck=330 (accessed October 29, 2012).

20

HeLIOS: Hemingway Library Information Online Skills Tutorial

JaNae Kinikin

PURPOSE

The purpose of this article is to describe the collaborative effort between academic and high school librarians in the creation of an information literacy tutorial designed to meet the specific needs of high school students. Librarians at Weber State University (WSU) collaborated with high school librarians to create the Hemingway Library Online Skills (HeLIOS) tutorial (http://helios.weber.edu). This chapter will describe the purpose and goals of this project and the methods used in the development of the tutorial. This will be followed by a discussion of the challenges that occurred in the creation and revision of the tutorial in order to produce a project purposely designed for high school students. This chapter will conclude with an assessment of the success of the information literacy skills tutorial and future plans to improve the tutorial.

INTRODUCTION

Many graduates of U.S. high schools are not prepared for the rigors of college and the workforce. This lack of preparation affects all academic areas, but librarians are specifically concerned about library research skills. In Utah, as in many states, incoming freshmen generally lack the skills to successfully use library resources to complete their assignments. To determine why a deficiency in information literacy skills exists in high school graduates, the faculty at WSU designed and conducted a survey of high school library media specialists in 2005. The results from the survey indicated that limited staffing (one certified librarian and one uncertified library assistant per school or less) at the media center libraries is insufficient to support the student population. To address this concern, the librarians at WSU created an online information literacy skills tutorial designed to be used by teachers, librarians, and students both in the classroom and as an independent learning tool. The goal in creating the tutorial was to help students become more familiar with information literacy and to develop library research skills. This knowledge would greatly ease the transition from high school to college.

LITERATURE REVIEW

A search of the literature on information literacy tutorials shows that the creation of such tutorials is not a new idea (Reece 2005; Yang 2008; Su and Kuo 2010; Donaldson 2000; Phillips and Kearley 2003; Armstrong and Georgas 2006). However, most tutorials are designed to be used by college freshman, not high school students. The majority of existing tutorials are text-based with accompanying graphics. These tutorials, designed to teach general information literacy skills, are normally split into modules that are further organized into short units (Noe and Bishop 2005; Donaldson 2000). Although a modular scheme makes sense for college students who need to know all aspects of the information literacy process, the amount of information covered could overwhelm high school students. With high school students in mind, the WSU team created a tutorial composed of concept lessons to which students could refer on an as-needed basis. Teachers might also assign specific lessons as part of a class curriculum. The WSU team believe that shorter learning objects and just-in-time lessons would be the most efficient and practical method to integrate information literacy into the high school curriculum. The graphic designer of the (HeLIOS) tutorial created the lessons so that they could be paused and continued at a later time. Su and Kuo advocate designing tutorials so that users might stop at any time and start again at their convenience (2010).

Reece, in her article on information literacy tutorials and critical thinking, states that "information literacy instruction should not only be task based. . . . it should also be concept based" (2005, 488). The concept-based approach is critical. It should help students gain a basic understanding of the library and its resources so that they might successfully transition to college. The concept-based approach is also important because different library classification systems are used in high school libraries (Dewey) and college libraries (Library of Congress), but the concept of subject-based organization of books remains the same. In addition to teaching information literacy principles, the HeLIOS tutorial also provides basic, task-based information and "how-to" tips that students can immediately put into practice.

Many existing tutorials are outdated and uninteresting, having been created several years ago. Today's students, especially those in high school, need a tutorial that better reflects various learning styles. Su and Kuo outline the advantages of online tutorials for today's students. Their research focused on college-level tutorials, but their ideas apply equally to high school students and to the HeLIOS tutorial, in particular. Online tutorials need to "engage [students] . . . on their own terms" and offer the opportunity to review the material again and again until it is mastered (Su and Kuo 2010, 320). The HeLIOS tutorial meets these requirements.

Although comic books—and graphic novels—have been used for teaching in other areas, this technique had not been incorporated into the teaching of information literacy skills, except in a very limited manner. For instance, Mike Hall and Matt Upson created a guide for the McPherson College library in a comic book format in 2011 (Zelenski 2011). Vacca suggested that comic books are an effective medium for engaging young readers and that students' interest "increased by leaps and bounds" with the introduction of comic books (1959, 291). Mallia (2007) also advocates the use of comics as a tool for instruction but notes that comics have most often been used as attention grabbers in textbooks. The HeLIOS tutorial uses the graphic novel format to teach information literacy concepts in an engaging format designed to retain the attention of high school students.

BACKGROUND

Weber State University (WSU), located in Ogden, Utah, has an enrollment of over 18,000 students with 2,000 faculty and staff. Thirty-two percent of WSU's students are from Weber County, and 33 percent are from Davis County, the two counties in which the university is located. Overall, 92 percent of the student population comes from the state of Utah. Because the population is predominately local, WSU librarians wanted to create a product that would have an immediate impact within the state. The goal of the project was to develop an information literacy tutorial to prepare students with library research skills essential for college success. They also wanted to give school library media teachers a tool to help reach the large number of students in their individual schools. Working through an information literacy tutorial in high school would give incoming freshman a head start in knowing the research skills required for college-level classes. It would also help prepare them to meet the information literacy requirement at WSU. To meet this requirement, which is unique to WSU, students must successfully complete a face-to-face or online information literacy course or pass an information literacy exam worth one-half credit.

METHODOLOGY

The construction of the tutorial started when researchers invited two media specialists in the Ogden school district who had participated in the 2005 WSU survey to be part of the tutorial design team. An in-house grant application was submitted to WSU requesting the following: (1) payment for two library media teachers and a high school English teacher to design, create, and revise tutorial content; (2) money to hire a graphic designer to take the content and incorporate it into an interactive tutorial; and (3) release time for two WSU librarians to create tutorial content. The grant was funded by WSU in the spring of 2007.

The grant application objectives stated that once they completed the tutorial, students should know how to:

- State an information need (essential question)
- Read a piece of information and paraphrase or summarize the content in their own words (synthesize)
- Search article databases, library catalogs, and the Internet to find resources to meet information needs
- Determine the relevancy of information
- Critically evaluate information
- Understand what plagiarism is
- Determine the audience for a research paper or presentation
- Understand the differences between popular or scholarly sources of information
- Understand and use primary and secondary sources
- Cite information using APA or MLA format

Referencing these objectives, the researchers carefully analyzed the English and library media curriculum at the high school level and Weber State University's information literacy requirement to determine the essential content areas required for high school students at both the secondary and university levels. Additionally, university faculty members were surveyed to determine their opinions on what incoming freshman should know about the library and its resources. Using this information, the researchers created the following objectives which state that students will be able to:

1. Identify plagiarized information and understand that plagiarism is dishonest.
2. Identify the differences between quotation, paraphrase, and summary.
3. Brainstorm potential topics to create a research question.
4. Distinguish between library search tools and web search tools.
5. Recognize that there is a variety of Internet content available and that different sites have different purposes.
6. Critically evaluate a source of information.
7. Give credit to the original creator of the source.
8. Distinguish between primary and secondary sources.
9. Identify keywords from a research question.
10. Use Boolean operators (AND, OR) when searching for information.
11. Locate information using a library catalog.
12. Use call numbers to locate books and other materials in the library.
13. Recognize the types of information found in an article database.
14. Create a citation using MLA format.
15. Understand advanced search techniques, including truncation and the use of quotation marks for phrase searching.
16. Understand that reference books are found online and in the reference area of the library, and are used to find background information or quick facts.
17. Introduced to subject databases for more comprehensive searches in a specific subject area.
18. Students will understand that both books and articles are assigned words to describe their contents. These terms are referred to as subjects.
19. Understand how to use information ethically.
20. Differentiate between scholarly and popular information.

The project leaders assigned team members one or two objectives and asked them to create a storyboard containing text and clip art conveying the information for that objective. Members then presented their storyboards to the team. Comments and suggestions for improvement were given, revisions were made to the storyboards, and they were resubmitted for further review. This process continued until the storyboard was satisfactory to the entire team.

As work progressed on the tutorial, decisions were made, including the color scheme, tutorial navigation, and an acronym for the project. The researchers, being cognizant of their audience, kept the text to a minimum and the vocabulary at a level suitable for the students who would use the tutorial. Screen shots were also used to visually convey many of the concepts discussed in the tutorial. To prevent students from skipping ahead, each page played for a set amount of time. By requiring a set time for each screen, the researchers hoped students would read the information and begin to comprehend the concepts. It was also decided to build the tutorial around a single theme to minimize the amount of information presented in each module. The

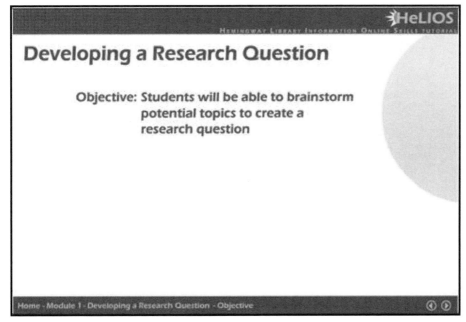

Figure 20.1.
Screen shot from original version of HeLIOS

researchers decided to use tattoos and body modification in examples throughout the tutorial. They felt this topic would catch the attention of high school students. The acronym for the title was selected to recognize the grant provider (the Hemingway family) and to make the tutorial name memorable. HeLIOS in Greek mythology is the personification of the sun, and the sun symbol was used on all of the pages in the original HeLIOS tutorial. The content for the tutorial was completed in July 2008, and all of the materials were submitted to the graphic designer.

Once incorporated into the Flash platform, the tutorial was beta-tested in English classes at two local Ogden, Utah, high schools in the spring of 2009 (see Figure 20.1). Although the tutorial was functional, this beta test revealed that the tutorial had several significant issues, most notably navigation and timing. Additionally, student feedback was unfavorable. Team members were also disappointed with the design because it lacked the interactivity and captivating graphics proposed by the graphic designer, who by then had resigned from the project. The team also discovered that the coding style used would be difficult for another designer to modify and edit.

Even with these setbacks, the team believed that the information in the tutorial was effective in teaching high school students library research skills, as student surveys during the beta test showed that student knowledge of library skills had improved upon completion of the lessons. To continue the project, another grant was written for funds to hire a second graphic designer to develop a more functional version of the tutorial. Two of the original media specialists resigned before the revision of the tutorial was completed. They were replaced by three media specialists who had expressed a willingness to use the tutorial in their schools. The new team revised the tutorial to include more explanatory information, which students had requested in the survey responses after working through the original version. Again, each team member was assigned

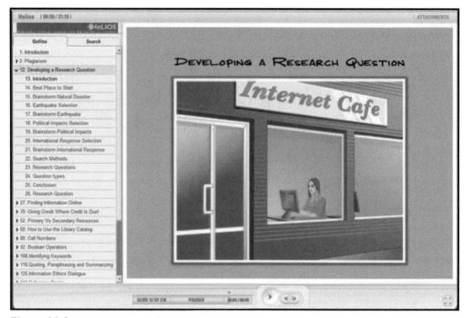

Figure 20.2.
Screen shot from the revised version of HeLIOS, with graphic novel treatment

sections of the tutorial to work on. Once complete, these were given to the graphic designer.

After reviewing other information literacy Internet tutorials, the graphic designer chose to redesign the look of the tutorial by creating it in comic strip format. To this end, he took the information found on several slides and integrated it into a single slide using characters and a script to which high school students could relate (see figure 20.2). This change minimized the number of slides per lesson and resulted in a product that was more engaging to students.

Creating the revised version took more time than was anticipated, but the team concluded that the final product was worth the additional time. This version still has limited interactivity with only quiz questions at the end of each lesson, but the graphic novel aspect should help keep students interested. The sun symbol remains in the header, so those who used the original version will recognize the current tutorial as having similar content.

ASSESSMENT

Sections of the revised HeLIOS version were introduced to high school students in the spring of 2011. The majority of students commented that they liked the graphic novel presentation. The new presentation format along with the introduction of characters that students can relate to should improve attention and comprehension of the material presented in the tutorial and result in an increased lesson completion rate. It is hoped that due to the knowledge gained from the tutorial, teachers will assign specific lessons based on classroom assignments to improve students' awareness of library resources.

All of the lessons in the tutorial were completed in the summer of 2011 and were introduced to students, teachers, and library media specialists in the fall of 2011. To review the information in each lesson, students are required to complete short interactive quizzes that follow each lesson. These questions provide immediate feedback for both correct and incorrect responses and give students immediate insight into their general understanding of the lesson's content. If students feel they need to review the material in the lesson after completing these quizzes, they can do so.

To evaluate the effectiveness of each lesson and student understanding of the concepts covered in each lesson, the tutorial is being assessed using UTIPS (Utah Test Item Pool Service), a statewide testing database to which all educators in the state of Utah have access. Individual lessons will be assigned to students and upon completion of the lessons, students will be directed to the UTIPS assessment database. Future revisions of the HeLIOS tutorial will be based on the results from these assessments.

PROMOTION

To promote the tutorial in the state of Utah, postcards explaining the HeLIOS tutorial were sent to educational media specialists in Utah in September 2011. The tutorial has also been submitted to be included in the PRIMO database, which was created to share instructional materials among librarians. Although the tutorial was specifically designed for high schools in the state of Utah, it can be adapted for use in schools across the country. A proposal to the American Association of School Librarians (AASL) annual conference to present the tutorial to a nationwide audience will be submitted in 2012.

FUTURE PLANS

Teachers and librarians will be surveyed, and the results will be used to improve the design of future versions of the HeLIOS tutorial. Additional assignments and activities may be added to the tutorial to help teachers incorporate the information skills taught in the tutorial into the course curriculum. This strategy is similar to the collaboration that occurred at Kern High School in Bakersfield, California, where librarians at Bakersfield College (BC) worked with high school teachers to create library activities that used library resources to improve the skills of incoming college freshman at BC (Dobie, Guidry, and Hartsell 2010).

Sound will be added to the tutorial to draw student attention and to address multiple learning styles. The inclusion of sound will allow students who are visually impaired to use the tutorial, and it will assist students who have reading difficulties understand the information literacy concepts presented. Students in WSU's communication department will be recruited to provide the voices for the characters. Using student voices will help make the characters come to life.

FUTURE RESEARCH

Training teachers to be literate users of information in teacher education programs is critical. Further research should explore the integration of information literacy concepts into the teacher education program curricula at colleges and universities. Information literate teachers will help create information knowledgeable students. Presently, many teachers do not realize the importance of teaching information literacy skills to students because they were not taught the importance of these skills while completing their own education programs. Learning these skills in high school would ease the transition for students to college-level research and improve the freshman experience.

CONCLUSION

Teaching high school and college students to be information literate library users will remain a challenge. As more and more information is readily available via a quick click from an Internet search engine, creating discerning students of information is critically important and increasingly difficult. Online tutorials used in conjunction with relevant course materials may help overcome this hurdle.

BIBLIOGRAPHY

Armstrong, Annie and Helen Georgas. "Using Interactive Technology to Teach Information Literacy Concepts to Undergraduate Students." *Reference Services Review* 34, no. 4 (2006): 491–7.

Dobie, Dawn, Nancy T. Guidry, and Jan Hartsell. "Navigating to Information Literacy: A Collaboration between California High School and College Librarians." *CSLA Journal* 34, no. 2 (2010): 6–9.

Donaldson, Kelly A. "Library Research Success: Designing an Online Tutorial to Teach Information Literacy Skills to First-Year Students." *Internet and Higher Education* 2 (2000): 237–251.

Mallia, Gorg. "Learning from the Sequence: The Use of Comics in Instruction." *ImageTexT: Interdisciplinary Comics Studies* 3, no. 3 (2007). http://www.english.ufl.edu/imagetext/ archives/v3_3/mallia/ (accessed November 3, 2012).

Noe, Nancy W., and Barbara A. Bishop. "Assessing Auburn University Library's Tiger Information Literacy tutorial (TILT)." *Reference Services Review* 33, no. 2 (2005): 173–187.

Phillips, Lori and Jamie Kearley. "TIP: Tutorial for Information Power and Campus-wide Information Literacy." *Reference Services Review* 31, no. 4 (2003): 351–358.

Reece, Gwendolyn J. "Critical Thinking and Cognitive Transfer: Implications for the Development of Online Information Literacy Tutorials." *Research Strategies* 20, no. 4 (2005): 482–493.

Su, Shiao-Feng, and Jane Kuo. "Design and Development of Web-Based Information Literacy Tutorials." *Journal of Academic Librarianship* 36, no. 4 (2010): 320–328.

Trent, Curtis, and Rachel Kinlaw. "Comic Books: An Effective Teaching Tool." *Journal of Extension* 17 (1979): 18–23.

Vacca, Carlo. "Comic Books as a Teaching Tool." *Hispania* 42, no.2 (1959): 291–292.

Yang, Sharon. "Information Literacy Online Tutorials: An Introduction to Rationale and Technological Tools in Tutorial Creation." *Electronic Library* 27, no. 4 (2009): 684–693.

Zelenski, Judy, ed. "Around the Region-Kansas." *Mountain Plains Library Association (MPLA) Newsletter* 55, no. 6 (August 2011): 16. http://www.mpla.us/documents/ newsletter/ August2011.pdf (accessed November 3, 2012).

21

Pathways for Success: The Evolution of TRAILS and Transitioning to College

Tammy J. Eschedor Voelker, Barbara F. Schloman, and Julie A. Gedeon

TRAILS (TOOL FOR REAL-TIME ASSESSMENT OF INFORMATION LITERACY SKILLS): HTTP://WWW.TRAILS-9.ORG

TRAILS (Tool for Real-Time Assessment of Information Literacy Skills) is a freely available, Web-based tool to measure information literacy competencies in K-12. It is a project of Kent State University (KSU) Libraries and was undertaken as an extension of the libraries' commitment to work with teachers and librarians in area high schools to prepare their students for college.

Federal funding from the Institute of Museum and Library Services and the U.S. Department of Education in 2003 and 2004 created the Institute for Library and Information Literacy Education (ILILE) at Kent State University. The three partners to the grant were the School of Library and Information Science, the College of Education, and University Libraries. Each developed projects that supported the overall ILILE goal "to provide local, regional and national leadership in fostering successful collaboration among K-12 teachers and school library media specialists who are concerned with advancing library and information literacy in the PK-12 school curriculum" (Kent State University 2004).

University Libraries brought a demonstrated commitment to information literacy that was aligned with this ILILE goal. The libraries' active instructional program included focused support for the Kent State University preservice teacher program. Additionally, the libraries had for several decades hosted high school visits and had an interest in formalizing this program. Following the hosting of the Association of Research & College Libraries (ACRL) Immersion Institute in 2000, University Libraries' faculty saw the need for an assessment instrument to measure information literacy competencies in college students. This led to Project SAILS (Standardized Assessment of Information Literacy Skills) and the creation of a tool based on ACRL information literacy standards to measure skills. All of these factors came together with the opportunity presented by ILILE funding to draw upon what had been learned with SAILS development to create an information literacy assessment tool for use in K-12.

From the outset, the TRAILS team established several objectives. To be seen as a credible assessment tool, TRAILS would be standards-based. To ensure accessibility, the tool would need to be freely available on the Internet. As important, usability would require a delivery tool that was intuitive for the school librarian/teacher and responsive in reporting results. Also, the team recognized that it was important that student privacy was assured.

While Kent State librarians felt comfortable with the application of information literacy on a college campus, there was recognition that development of TRAILS would necessitate collaboration with the K-12 community. Ohio is fortunate to have a strong network of school librarians. The project has tapped into their expertise through the Ohio Educational Library Media Associations (OELMA), the state affiliate of the American Association of School Librarians (AASL), and INFOhio, the state information network for K-12. Initial discussions centered on what grade level a TRAILS assessment should address. It was determined that development of an assessment based on ninth-grade standards would be of the most use. The rationale was that a ninth-grade measure could be used to determine the level of student preparation upon entry into high school, as well as subsequently as graduation approached.

Two highly experienced school librarians were brought on board to serve as question development consultants working with the two university librarians who constituted the TRAILS team. Development of the web-based delivery system was contracted to a software engineer. It was determined that the Ohio Academic Content Standards and AASL's *Information Power* would provide the standards foundation for TRAILS. The Ohio standards were seen as representative of state standards across the country. The consultants reviewed all of the Ohio standards, across all subject areas, for any that related to information literacy. These were aligned to *Information Power* standards and then classified into categories.

After several refinements, what emerged were the five TRAILS categories that are used today: (1) develop a topic; (2) identify potential sources; (3) develop, use, and revise search strategies; (4) evaluate sources and information; and (5) recognize how to use information responsibly, ethically, and legally. The consultants next wrote a series of objectives that would address the standards that had been identified. This was followed by writing items that addressed the objectives. A call went out to school librarians working at the ninth-grade level to field test the items. They were asked to have ninth-grade students take a trial assessment comprised of draft items. The objective of this step was to determine if the students understood the items as written and if the items measured what was intended. School librarians shared student feedback on the items. This along with statistical analysis of the results pointed to needed item revisions.

Following revisions, a 30-item assessment was created covering the five TRAILS categories. TRAILS went live in January 2006 and by May of that year had 930 account holders. The results of an annual user survey have since guided enhancements to the delivery system, as well as to the assessments themselves. Based upon requests from the school librarian community to develop assessments for other grade levels, the TRAILS team was successful in obtaining additional grant funding from the Martha Holden Jennings Foundation and the Library Services and Technology Act (LSTA) program. The next grade addressed was sixth in order to provide some assessment measure that would reach into the earlier grades. It went live in 2008. This was followed by development of both third-grade and twelfth-grade assessments, which were launched in the fall of 2010. Potentially, these assessments at the third-, sixth-, ninth-, and twelfth-grade levels provide the opportunity for a school system to follow the development of information literacy skills as a cohort moves through the grades. Assessments available at each grade level include two general assessments covering the five information literacy categories, plus a 10-item assessment for each category.

How TRAILS Works

The school librarian registers for an account at the TRAILS web site (http://www.trails-9.org). After signing in and going to the My Account page, it is possible to create a session for a specific class. Available assessments are available for previewing prior to selection. By choosing the expanded view, the librarian can see for each item what standards are being addressed and what the objective of the item is. The librarian can also request that the system generate a unique code that can be assigned to each student, allowing for the reporting of results by individual student. This is in addition to obtaining a class-level report. Another option is to elect to have the items provided in the same order to all students, rather than using the random default presentation. This makes it possible to read the questions aloud to special needs students or to those for whom English is a second language.

After creating a session, administration details are provided. This includes the session URL and, if the student code option was selected, a listing of unique student codes. When all students have completed the session, the librarian again signs in to his or her account, goes to the My Account page, and closes the open session. Results are immediately available by linked online reports for both the class as a whole and by student code if used. This information is also downloadable as a comma separated values (csv) file. Class review is also possible wherein students can log into the session with their student codes and see which items they missed.

The Use of TRAILS

For many school librarians, TRAILS has provided their first opportunity for an objective measure of student information literacy. They report that having a measure to demonstrate what their students know compared with what is expected at that grade level with regard to information literacy has leveraged more opportunities to work with classroom teachers and their students. It has allowed librarians to make the best use of the time they have with students by being able to target instruction to weak areas. TRAILS gives them data-based results to share with their administration regarding areas of student deficiency and progress. Some librarians report that their use of TRAILS has been included in their school's overall improvement plan and for others in their personal development plan. One librarian reports that use of TRAILS helped her achieve Master Teacher designation (Pandora 2010).

Administration of the assessments is being done in a variety of ways. Many librarians elect to do pre- and post-testing to determine needs and progress. Some use the assessment as a classroom exercise with clickers. Some administer to the entire class cohort as the students enter ninth grade and then again as they prepare to graduate.

Table 21.1.

Performance of U.S. students by grade level who took TRAILS General Assessment 1, 2010–2011

Grade Level	# of Students	Overall %	Percent Correct by TRAILS Information Literacy Categories				
			Develop Topic	Identify Sources	Develop Search Strategy	Evaluate Sources	Use Responsibly
12	2,847	50.33	50.35	52.61	46.49	59.21	42.99
9	18,089	52.19	41.37	59.48	58.73	49.10	52.29
6	22,805	54.01	54.34	66.60	51.75	53.67	43.70
3	11,295	51.84	47.27	47.36	65.73	48.27	50.60

Several school districts have instituted the use of TRAILS district wide to profile student understanding of information literacy and progress. Hinsdale Township (Illinois) High School District 86, the 2012 recipient of the National School Library Program of the Year (NSLPY), uses TRAILS as part of its action research program to evaluate the library curriculum and teaching practices (ALAnews 2012).

Benchmarks

By the fall of 2011, TRAILS had nearly 13,000 registered users representing all 50 states and more than 30 countries. Assessments had been administered in more than 34,000 sessions to over 600,000 students. At the end of each school year, the TRAILS team analyzes student result data by grade level. The analysis indicates whether any of the items are not performing as they should, as well as whether the assessment overall is difficult enough to measure performance. This guides item revision as well as enables the team to establish performance benchmarks for the previous year.

TRAILS-3 and TRAILS-12 went live in the 2010–2011 school year. Use was sufficient that it was possible to establish benchmarks for all four grade assessments. These are based on use of General Assessment 1 by students at the designated grade levels. Table 21.1 shows benchmark performance percentages by TRAILS grade levels. The lower the percentage the lower overall student performance in that skill category. Third and ninth graders were most challenged by develop topic. Sixth and twelfth graders struggled most with the use responsibly category. The TRAILS team encourages use of these measures as only an indicator of areas of strength and weakness.

TRANSITIONING TO COLLEGE: HELPING YOU SUCCEED
HTTP://WWW.TRANSITIONING2COLLEGE.ORG/

Kent State University Libraries have a long tradition of outreach to local high schools. ILILE provided the opportunity and the support for a broader initiative to expose high school students to an academic library. A small group of Ohio academic and high school librarians met in 2005 to discuss ways, other than in-person visits, to achieve such an introduction. An existing web-based project at Bowling Green State University, developed by Colleen Boff, was examined. Called *Pathways to Academic Libraries (P.A.L.)*, the web site offered online instructional videos about the nature of academic libraries and college-level research. The group saw that an expanded version of this web-based model could reach transitioning students regardless of their location or ability to visit a college or university library. The decision was made to create a new web site with updated videos and to include other tools of potential usefulness to both high school seniors and first-year college students.

Funding for the new web site, *Transitioning to College: Helping Students Succeed (T2C)*, was obtained by librarians at Kent State University in 2006 through a minigrant from the Library Services and Technology Act (LSTA) program. Many of the resources on the site are the product of collaborative efforts by academic and school librarians from around the Ohio. The core of the T2C web site is a series of five learning modules. Each learning module includes a video, handouts, guiding lesson plans and activities, as well as links to additional resources to allow for a variety of possible applications. These are non-institution specific, making them relevant to any academic setting. Although all of the videos were filmed at Kent State University's Main Library, no mention is made of the institution or location, and all the scripts, supporting handouts, and web pages are broadly applicable across all higher education institution types. This is also in recognition of the need for resources that are both freely available and broadly applicable for use by school systems that often have budgetary restraints that do not allow for field trips to local colleges for an in-person visit or that are not located conveniently near such institutions.

Although T2C has a strong emphasis on college research expectations and the use of library resources, the site was also envisioned to offer a broader scope of guidance in other areas of college success, such as where to seek help on campus, study tips, tips on how to avoid plagiarism, and a guide to college-related terminology. Throughout the videos, an emphasis is placed on helping students overcome psychological or emotional barriers to using college resources and support services. One of the key goals of the creators was to ensure that students have a positive introduction to academic libraries, and achieving a positive affective response was seen as key to helping students make the best use of academic resources and services. One way that this is approached is by presenting the videos from a student view. The narrative of the videos follows two first-year students and their upper class mentor, who provides tips for success as the freshmen students navigate the new and sometimes confusing environment of a college campus.

KSU Libraries sought feedback on the value and use of the T2C web site via a survey in the fall of 2010. Because this site does not require an account or login, it was difficult for the creators to know who was using the resource and whether it was serving its intended purpose. Therefore, input was sought from librarians by posting a link to a survey on a variety of discussion lists serving both school library media specialists and academic librarians. The brief survey asked five questions:

1. How did you first hear of Transitioning to College?
2. How often (your best estimate) have you used the Transitioning to College website?
3. What do you like best about the Transitioning to College website?
4. In what ways have you used the resources on the Transitioning to College website?
5. How could the Transitioning to College website be improved?

Most respondents learned about the site through information at a professional conference or via a discussion list. The T2C site managers were happy to learn that the website's tools were being equally used in both secondary and postsecondary environments, with students from freshmen in high school to graduate school being mentioned in the survey responses. Praise was given to the usefulness of the video content and the inclusion of sample college syllabi.

Of particular interest were the responses to the final question about how the site could be improved. As the T2C project was marking its fifth anniversary, the KSU Libraries recognized the need to reassess and continue to improve and support the site. A variety of extremely valuable comments were received, including:

- A desire for more samples of college syllabi and writing and research projects
- The inclusion of more diversity among the actors
- A discussion of the difference between Dewey decimal and Library of Congress classifications
- Tips or conversation starters that librarians can use to promote the site to teachers
- The addition of a section specific to state-supported resources in Ohio
- Addition of more recent technologies such as handheld devices
- More options for the formats, online delivery, and downloading of the videos
- The provision of related online quizzes with answer banks
- A section for school counselors
- The general updating of the videos and the desire for additional videos; some of the topics suggested for additional videos included interviews with college professors about what they expect, web site evaluation, paraphrasing and in-text citation, and tips on how to take notes for research

THE FUTURE: ITS OPPORTUNITIES AND CHALLENGES

The present emphasis at the state and federal level to do more to prepare and encourage students to go to college suggests that TRAILS and T2C might have greater overall impact if stronger and more obvious linkages existed between them. School librarians focused on developing information literacy in their students as an important 21st-century skill can benefit from using TRAILS to profile the level of proficiency that students have at a given time. Use of TRAILS-12 in the senior year of high school provides an indicator of student readiness to succeed as an information seeker in college. The resources in T2C can appeal to different aspects of the college preparation experience. By highlighting the expectations for college work, differences between the school and academic library, and some of the "language" and terminology of college, high school students can begin to develop an understanding of the college environment. Because T2C was developed through collaboration between academic and school librarians, its resources try to answer the question "What does the high school student need to know to be prepared for college?"

Current grant funding from the Martha Holden Jennings Foundation will allow the team to develop purposeful connections between the TRAILS and T2C sites and to work on a more common branding between them. Input from the initial survey of T2C users will guide the team in updating the resources and developing plans for the next generation of the site. The team always has an interest in strengthening the assessment items. The current grant is making it possible to develop illustrations to accompany a select number of items in TRAILS-3 to provide visual clues to understanding an item in addition to the written text. These images were successfully field-tested in spring 2012 and then formally added to the third grade assessments in fall 2012. An important initiative led by governors and chief state school officers in 48 states, two territories, and the District of Columbia came to fruition in 2010 with the release of a set of standards for English-language arts and mathematics for K-12. Known as the Common Core State Standards, these "define the knowledge and skills students should have within their K-12 education careers so that they will graduate high school fully prepared for college and careers" (Common Core State Standards 2011). As of May 2012, 45 states had adopted these standards. In response, TRAILS aligned each of its assessment items to the appropriate Common Core State Standards during the summer of 2012.

This is also a period of increasing demands for accountability at all education levels. TRAILS has received a number of requests for reliability/validity measures for the assessments. To address this need, work will be undertaken in the next two years to establish these measures, starting with TRAILS-9 and TRAILS-12. This work will provide an additional layer of assurance as to the usefulness of these assessment tools. This will be in addition to the annual data analysis that is performed.

The greatest challenge for TRAILS and T2C is sustainability going into the future. As freely available products, their ongoing management is largely dependent on institutional support. Grant funding makes enhancements possible. Undeniably, the support from the school librarian community is a key strength.

BIBLIOGRAPHY

ALAnews. "Hinsdale Township High School District 86 Named National School Library Program of the Year." *American Libraries*. May 1, 2012. http://americanlibrariesmagazine. org/news/ala/ hinsdale-township-high-school-district-86-named-national-school-library -program-year (accessed May 8, 2012).

Common Core State Standards Initiative. "Common Core State Standards." Washington, DC: Author, 2011. http://www.corestandards.org/about-the-standards (accessed May 8, 2012).

Kent State University. ILILE: Institute for Library & Information Literacy Education. Kent, OH: Author, 2004. http://www.ilile.org/ (accessed May 7, 2012).

Kent State University Libraries. Project SAILS: Standardized Assessment of Information Literacy Skills. 2012. https://www.projectsails.org/ (accessed May 7, 2012).

Pandora, Cherie P. "Using TRAILS for DATA-Driven Decision-Making." *Ohio Media Spectrum* 62 (Spring 2010): 32–34.

ADDITIONAL READINGS

Burhanna, Kenneth J., Julie A. Gedeon, Mary Lee Jensen, and Barbara F. Schloman. "Reaching Forward: Three High School Outreach Initiatives at Kent State University." In Nancy Courtney, ed., *Academic Library Outreach*, pp. 9–20. Westport, CT: Libraries Unlimited, 2008.

Burhanna, Kenneth J., and Mary Lee Jensen. "Collaborations for Success: High School to College Transitions." *Reference Services Review* 34 (2006): 509–519.

Owen, Patricia L. "Using TRAILS to Assess Student Learning: A Step-by-Step Guide." *Library Media Connection* 28 (May 2010): 36–38.

Schloman, Barbara F., and Julie A. Gedeon. "Creating TRAILS." *Knowledge Quest* 35 (May 2007): 44–47.

22

Libraries and the High School to College Transition: A Selective, Annotated Bibliography

Tammy J. Eschedor Voelker

The following alphabetical list of resources focuses on examples in the library literature of projects, tools, collaborations, and research studies pertaining to the work of librarians serving students transitioning from high school to college. The emphasis of these articles, books, chapters, and web sites is on work aimed at improving students' mastery of information literacy skills to support their success in college and beyond. The geographic focus of this bibliography is North America. Although the literature pertaining to this area of study saw its first escalation in the 1980s, the selective nature of this bibliography necessarily limits the focus to more recent scholarship, particularly to developments in the past 15 years, coinciding with the advent of standardized information literacy objectives at both the secondary and higher education levels and the creation of national collaborative efforts between school and academic librarians (see *Blueprint for Collaboration* later in this chapter). Other resources of potential interest can be found referenced at the end of each chapter of this work and linked from several of the web sites listed later in this chapter.

Adeyemon, Earnestine. "Integrating Digital Literacies into Outreach Services for Underserved Youth Populations." *Reference Librarian* 50, no. 1 (January/March 2009): 85–98.
Adeyemon highlights programs at the Kelvin Smith Library of Case Western Reserve University focused on improving digital and information literacies of undeserved youth and community members. This article describes three outreach programs, one to middle school students, one to community members and one to high school students transitioning to college. A detailed overview of the curriculum, program design and assessment is provided for the middle school program, with additional valuable information on an outreach to local middle school teachers as well. Adeyemon then highlights the four-week immersive learning and work experience culminating in a final media project for high school juniors. The community

outreach projects that are described also include outreach to high school students and provide ideas for partnerships within one's institution for outside outreach.

Allen, Susan M. "Information Literacy, ICT, High School, and College Expectations: A Quantitative Study." *Knowledge Quest* 35, no. 5 (May 2007): 18–24.
Allen shares an extensive project she undertook to assess the information and communication technology (ICT) literacy skills of the students in her school system. Considering college preparation, and after having undergone a review of both the technology and information literacy landscape both in the literature and in her middle and high schools, she describes a process that led to the revision of the curricular approach to ICT in her system. She shares her experience with assessing high school seniors using the pilot tests of the scenario-based Educational Testing Service (ETS) assessment of ICT skills and describes her school's ongoing assessment of recent graduates to self-report how prepared they felt for their college-level work.

Ameika, Martha. "Introducing College Research at the High School Level: A Jump Start on Success." *Voice of Youth Advocates* 31, no. 5 (2008): 408–409.
This work describes a South Carolina high school library media specialist's successful outreach to invite librarians and faculty from local colleges and universities to present sessions on information literacy topics to her high school seniors. The article details the topics covered, from the use of databases to the importance of avoiding plagiarism, as well as the outcomes for her students and school, including notable increased use of research databases, new research requirements by teachers, and the interest from others to expand the program across the district.

American Association of School Librarians (AASL) and Association of College & Research Libraries (ACRL) Task Force on the Educational Role of Librarians. *Blueprint for Collaboration*. Chicago: American Library Association, 2000. http://www.ala.org/acrl/publications/ whitepapers/acrlaaslblueprint.
Referred to throughout the literature, this blueprint for action that was created in 2000 still serves as a call to arms for school and academic library collaboration for information literacy initiatives. This web site recommends a variety of possible collaborative efforts and highlights examples of successful projects, sources of possible funding, and related professional associations.

Bruch, Courtney, and Katherine Frank. "Sustainable Collaborations: Libraries Link Dual-Credit Programs to P-20 Initiatives." *Collaborative Librarianship* 3, no. 2 (2011): 90–97.
Bruch and Frank share a unique approach to collaborative information literacy work. They describe a grant-supported project to integrate information literacy at the curricular level to a pre-existing dual credit program at Colorado State University (CSU). The project was a collaboration between academic librarians, the university writing program director, duel-degree program instructors at area high schools, and library media specialists. The Senior-to-Sophomore (STS) program instructors in the CSU program were invited to participate via a credit-bearing semester-long graduate course that guided the instructors through information literacy standards, lesson plans, assessment techniques, and more. The project reached 19 instructors and more than 170 students who were granted access to university resources for the duration of their work in the STS program. The authors share concerns for sustainability for such programs and tips for implementation focusing on the importance of leadership roles, resource streams, ongoing professional development, and community buy-in.

Burhanna, Kenneth J. "Instructional Outreach to High Schools." *Communications in Information Literacy* 1, no. 2 (2007): 74–88.

Providing a thorough analysis of issues and challenges, Burhanna addresses the question of whether academic libraries should be doing instructional high school outreach. Using as an example the successes and challenges faced by Kent State University Libraries' Informed Transitions program, the author reviews key motivations for high school visits, information on a successful expansion of his local outreach program, and observations about balancing the desire/need for outreach with the demands already facing academic instructional librarians. He outlines five big questions to answer before embarking on a formal outreach program, then provides a set of practical guidelines on how to formalize, pilot, assess, and monitor the success of such a program.

Burhanna, Kenneth J. and Mary Lee Jensen. "Collaborations for Success: High School to College Transitions." *Reference Services Review* 34, no. 4 (2006): 509–519.

The authors provide insight on the origins and development of three high school/academic library collaborations at Kent State University. These include Informed Transitions, a local high school outreach program; Transitioning to College, a free web site with videos and resources for the 12-13 transition; and TRAILS, a free tool for online assessment of information literacy skills for the K-12 environment. Stressing the importance of the collaboration between library media specialists, academic librarians, and preservice teacher educators, the article provides a discussion of lessons learned across all three programs and offers a useful list of tips for practical application of such collaborations for the future. Finally, to encourage further research in this field, the authors discuss the need for ongoing formal assessment of such initiatives.

Burrell, Allison, and Linda Neyer. "Helping High School Students Transition to College-Level Work: Can Collaboration between Librarians Make a Difference?" *Learning & Media* 38, no. 3 (2010): 8–9.

This article provides a brief summary of a survey that asked academic librarians to rank the importance of a list of eight information literacy skills to college success and then to estimate the extent to which they see those skills developed in their college students. Further plans for research to help determine the reasons for the gaps detected by survey respondents are shared.

Cahoy, Ellysa Stern. "Will Your Students Be Ready for College? Connecting K-12 and College Standards for Information Literacy." *Knowledge Quest* 30, no. 4 (March 2002): 12–15.

Cahoy's article takes a close look at both the American Association of School Librarians (AASL) and Association of College & Research Libraries (ACRL) information literacy standards and describes their similarities and uniqueness, all while stressing the importance of building understanding of how they can complement each other and provide continuity for the instructional approaches and collaborative efforts of librarians in both secondary and post-secondary settings. The author provides several valuable tips for implementing change and establishing collaboration.

Carr, Jo Ann. "Crossing the Instructional Divide: Supporting K-20 Information Literacy Initiatives." In Carroll Wetzel Wilkinson and Courtney Bruch, eds., *Transforming Information Literacy Programs: Intersecting Frontiers of Self, Library Culture, and Campus Community*, pp. 153–177. Chicago: Association of College and Research Libraries, 2012.

Carr's chapter sets the context of collaboration across K-20 settings for information literacy needs and instruction. She notes the challenges of establishing continuity across different educational levels that have variant standards and governmental oversight, as well as the needs inherent in secondary education for two tracks of students, college bound and career bound. Of particular note is an insightful section outlining key cultural differences between K-12 and academia that pose obstacles to collaboration. Carr then outlines numerous examples of successful collaborations around the United States and issues a challenge for the future. Key to a new action plan is her call for the creation of an Information Literacy Division in the American Library Association, bringing together librarians from all library types. Many other unique ideas for nationwide, statewide and local collaborative efforts are shared, making this a valuable new addition to the literature.

Carr, Jo Ann, and Ilene F. Rockman. "Information-Literacy Collaboration: A Shared Responsibility." *American Libraries* 34, no. 8 (2003): 52–54.

Carr and Rockman assert the importance of collaboration between K-12 and academic librarians to attain the mutual goal of supporting student success in information literacy. They provide a useful analysis of similarities and differences between the information literacy standards developed independently by AASL and ACRL, and encourage a call for participation in a collaborative effort between AASL and ACRL entitled *Blueprint for Collaboration*. Furthermore, they highlight six successful collaborations across the country, providing examples of a variety of approaches for school and academic librarians to work together.

Collins, Bobbie L. "Integrating Information Literacy Skills into Academic Summer Programs for Precollege Students." *Reference Services Review* 37, no. 2 (2009): 143–154.

Collins provides a detailed explanation of the development of an integrated library research component for a summer debate program for high school students at Wake Forest University. Tracing the evolution of the Z. Smith Reynolds Library's involvement with the program since the early 1980s, Collins provides observations on the unique needs of visiting high school students, approaches to collaboration with the summer program directors and teaching assistants, and specific instructional techniques incorporating changing technologies and resources over time. Collins goes on to show how success with this one program lead to involvement in other highs school summer programs and provides advice on how to get involved with such programs to promote information literacy and the university as a whole.

Cosgrove, John A. "Promoting Higher Education: (Yet) Another Goal of Bibliographic Instruction of High School Students by College Librarians." *College & Undergraduate Libraries* 8, no. 2 (2001): 17–24.

Cosgrove reviews the literature for many reasons posited by scholars to engage to library instructional outreach to high school students. He provides an argument related to the value of such outreach for promoting higher education in general and discusses ways in which academic librarians can take advantage of even the most practical high school visits (those intended to fill the immediate need of an assignment and provide access to resources not otherwise available) to engage students in a broader understanding of the value of higher education. He stresses the potential power of a message that conveys to students the assumption that they can and will succeed in college.

Courtney, Nancy, ed. *Academic Library Outreach: Beyond the Campus Walls*. Westport, CT: Libraries Unlimited, 2009.

Courtney's edited work brings together a variety of outreach initiatives of academic libraries. The first section is of particular interest, providing five chapters with a specific focus on K-12 and information literacy outreach. Best practices and lessons learned are shared across numerous examples of collaborative initiatives within North America, and also internationally, to strengthen students' preparation for university-level research.

Dobie, Dawn, Nancy T. Guidry, and Jan Hartsell. "Navigating to Information Literacy: A Collaboration between California High School and College Librarians." *California School Library Association (CSLA) Journal* 34, no. 2 (Fall 2010): 6–9.

The authors detail a successful ongoing collaboration between high school and college librarians from several schools and institutions in the Bakersfield, California, area. A variety of approaches are shared, including the development of a shared list of desired information literacy skill outcomes and 30 corresponding library activities that could be used within the high school library setting; the provision of presentations to area high school teachers on college research expectations; example college assignments and online activities for skill building; the creation by academic librarians of a toolkit for school librarians to help them promote the importance of a research-related curriculum; and a multipronged approach by teacher-librarians to engage their faculty with information literacy lessons and instruction, including scaffolded approaches and assessment techniques. Finally, the article shares ideas on looking forward to the adoption of Common Core Standards and the continued desire to support the work of teacher-librarians and to promote resources for school libraries.

Ercegovac, Zorana. "Bridging the Knowledge Gap between Secondary and Higher Education." *College & Research Libraries* 64, no. 1 (2003): 75–85.

The author provides an overview and discussion of the dynamics of collaborations for transitioning students on four levels: school librarians and K-12 faculty, academic librarians and college faculty, school and academic librarians, and K-16 institutional partnerships. She builds an argument for the need for increased work in the latter two areas, specifically also the involvement of librarians in K-16 institutional partnerships. She also provides examples of lesson plans for a high school faculty/librarian partnership in the sciences that she argues can also be applied at the college level. The lesson plans are mapped to both the AASL and ACRL information literacy standards, and the article includes a useful appendix outlining parallels between these two sets of standards and their performance indicators.

Ewbank, Ann Dutton, Melissa Guy, Julie Tharp, and Ellen Welty. "Collaboration and Connection: A University Outreach Program for High School Librarians and English Teachers." *Library Media Connection* 30, no. 2 (2011): 28–30.

This article highlights a successful program for outreach and collaboration to area high schools at Arizona State University (ASU). The program was undertaken as a joint project of the university libraries, writing program, and academic success center at ASU. The authors provide a guide to their creation of grant-funded, credit-based, stipend-supported workshops that successfully reached out to over 180 area high school teachers and librarians along the theme of preparing students for success in college research and writing. Tips for successful collaboration are offered from the perspective of school librarians reaching out to academic libraries seeking to establish similar relationships.

Fernekes, William R., and Harlene Z. Rosenberg. "Building a High School Archives Program: A Case Study in School-University Collaboration." *Journal of Archival Organization* 6, no. 3 (2008): 151–168.

Fernekes and Rosenberg's article provides an example of a unique high school/university collaboration, detailing the creation of the Hunterdon Regional Central High School Archives (an institutional history collection) via a collaboration with Rutgers University Special Collections and University Archives. All aspects of the project are discussed, including the creation of the advisory body, the establishment of funding, and the creation of archival standards and processes. Of particular interest to those interested in high school to college transitions are the variety of ways in which high school students were involved throughout the process as well as the current and future anticipated impact on the high school curriculum that this collaboration and archive provide.

Fitzgerald, Mary Ann. "Making the Leap from High School to College." *Knowledge Quest* 32, no. 4 (March 2004): 19–24.
Fitzgerald summarizes and analyzes the results of three revealing research studies concerning information literacy competencies of incoming college students and discusses them in the context of the potential impact on school library media programs. The studies shed light on both student competencies and college faculty expectations, finding that many aspects of information and critical thinking skills are lacking among a majority of entering students. The author breaks down the key challenge areas revealed by the studies and offers an analysis of possible actions for school libraries to improve skills of both college-bound and work-bound students. This includes ideas on recommended changes on the organization of libraries, integration of the information literacy curriculum, increased outreach to parents, collaboration with other librarians, and specific focus on teaching long term habits of mind along with the information literacy curriculum.

Gordon, Carol A. "A Room with a View: Looking at School Library Instruction from a Higher Education Perspective." *Knowledge Quest* 30, no. 4 (March 2002): 16–21.
Gordon assesses the specific skill needs of college-bound high school students based on two analyses. First, she discusses the results of a skill survey of graduate students' information literacy knowledge. The results reveal a great deal about what even the most motivated of students did not learn or retain over their K-16 experience regarding information literacy. Second, she provides of a series of example research assignments from courses across the university curriculum and discusses the skills required by each assignment. Gordon discusses these issues in the context of educational theory to explore pedagogical approaches for librarians wishing to prepare their students for their collegiate work.

Gresham, Keith, and Debra Van Tassel. "Expanding the Learning Community: An Academic Library Outreach Program to High Schools." *Reference Librarian* 32, no. 67 (1999): 161.
Gresham and Van Tassel describe an outreach program created by librarians at the University of Colorado at Boulder. Academic librarians, in partnership with area high school librarians, conducted visits and hands-on workshops related to information literacy. Workshops were tailored to each school's needs, and details are provided for a program at Evergreen High School. The article offers a valuable breakdown of hands-on activities related to high school to college library transitions, the evaluation of information, and how to develop search strategies. The article also touches on issues of managing large groups of students as well as making use of on-site technology combined with remote access to the university's resources to optimize the visits.

Gustavson, Amy, and H. C. Nall. "Freshman Overconfidence and Library Research Skills: A Troubling Relationship?" *College & Undergraduate Libraries* 18, no. 4 (2011): 291–306.
Gustavson and Nall's research has implications for those preparing students for college. The article reports the results of a study of over 300 first-semester freshman and contrasts their confidence levels regarding library research skills versus their actual demonstrated skills. The study found that several categories of students tended to be overconfident about their information literacy skills, including those who had reported higher high school GPAs and those with previous library instruction in either high school or college. Discussion of the implication for library instructional approaches is included and can inform decisions about

how to address overconfidence, break down misconceptions, and build better skills for students transitioning to college.

INFOhio and OhioLINK Special Task Force. "Preparing 21St Century Ohio Learners for Success: The Role of Information Literacy and Libraries." Columbus, OH: INFOhio, 2008. http://www.infohio.org/12-13TransitionWhitePaper200809.pdf.

This report is the result of a joint taskforce of INFOhio and OhioLINK, the statewide consortiums for school libraries and academic libraries respectively in the state of Ohio. It outlines six key goals and numerous action points for the provision of improved statewide information literacy instruction and resource support for college bound students. This executive summary provides an overview of needs and issues a well as outlines a plan for action to survey state initiatives, promote standards, improve resources, and form partnerships throughout the state. The web site further elaborates on these initiatives, provides updates on action points, shares success stories, and offers promotional materials and educational tools for librarians.

Islam, Ramona L., and Lisa Anne Murno. "From Perceptions to Connections: Informing Information Literacy Program Planning in Academic Libraries through Examination of High School Library Media Center Curricula." *College & Research Libraries* 67, no. 6 (2006): 492–514.

This informative study reports the detailed findings of a nationwide survey of school library media specialists aimed at ascertaining the information literacy skills most taught and those most commonly neglected at high schools across the nation. The authors gathered data using a breakdown of information literacy skills categorized into the five core ACRL standards (cross-referenced to the AASL standards). They also gathered information on school library resources and library media specialists'(LMS) perceptions of student attitudes. The research identifies the specific skills most likely to be lacking in incoming college freshmen based on the data as well as the barriers and challenges reported by LMS respondents in achieving desired access to students for instruction. Of particular value is the discussion of approaches to overcoming these perceived gaps in instruction, as well as a discussion of recent grant-supported collaborative initiatives between secondary and postsecondary institutions addressing these challenges.

Jackson, Lydia, and Julia Hansen. "Creating Collaborative Partnerships: Building the Framework." *Reference Services Review* 34, no. 4 (2006): 575–588.

The authors describe an Library Services and Technology Act (LSTA) grant project that seeks to build collaborations across school and academic librarians in Madison County, Illinois. An overview is provided about a survey sent to area school librarians to gather information on school library collections, services, and needs in preparation for a workshop that brought together stakeholders to discuss ways to collaborate for information literacy skill building for college-bound students. Tips are shared concerning best practices for building trust and relationships. Details on the grants objectives and evaluation plan are also shared, along with caveats for lessons learned.

Jesudason, Melba. "Academic Libraries and Outreach Services through Precollege Programs: A Proactive Collaboration." *Reference Services Review* 21, no. 4 (1993): 29.

Representing an early example of a discussion of college transitions in the literature, this article remains relevant as it argues the benefits of collaboration between secondary and postsecondary institutions. Benefits discussed include avoiding duplication of instructional effort, allowing continuity in education, saving resources, building the importance of librarians as team players in recruitment and retention, helping minorities, and the improvement of town/

gown relationships. The author contends that university library outreach programs are needed from the elementary level through high school to help ensure transitions and stresses the importance of administrative support at all levels. The specific example of library instruction integration with precollege programs at the University of Wisconsin is shared. A strong emphasis on the importance of outreach to minority students is present.

Johnson, Anna, and Tracy Pulford-Russell. "Preparing our Students to Succeed." *Oregon Library Association (OLA) Quarterly* 15, no. 4 (Winter 2009): 10–12.
This article stresses the need for articulation agreements related to information literacy to address continuity for K-20 education. Pointing out the prevalence of students who move from high school to community college, to university and back again, the authors argue the need for specific learning outcomes to be mutually developed and shared by educators in these three different settings and introduce efforts that have begun in Oregon to build that continuity. This includes the example of information literacy standards articulated in the Associate of Arts Oregon Transfer Degree. The article also argues the importance of academic librarian leadership in the area of state adopted K-20 information literacy standards and the need for librarians to be at the table for any discussion of articulating and aligning learning standards across K-12 and postsecondary curriculums.

Kent State University. "Transitioning to College: Helping You Succeed." http://www.transitioning2college.org/.
Developed in 2005 as part of a larger grant initiative, this web site provides freely available videos and supporting lesson plans, handouts, and other resources to help guide students in the transition to doing college-level research work. The resource is non-institution specific and can be used in any setting, for both high school and beginning college students.

Kent State University Libraries. "TRAILS: Tool for Real-Time Assessment of Information Literacy Skills." http://www.trails-9.org/.
TRAILS is a freely available information literacy skills assessment tool. It provides assessments based on third-, sixth-, ninth-, and twelfth-grade standards, the latter of which is specifically relevant to those interested in assessing the skills and needs of their transitioning students. National benchmarks are available beginning with the 2010–2011 academic year.

Kunda, Sue. "What's a Second Grader Doing in Special Collections?" *Oregon Library Association (OLA) Quarterly* 13, no. 1 (Spring 2007): 22–25.
Kunda provides a brief description of a variety of academic library outreach projects around the United States for K-12 students. This includes a focus on ideas for the use of special collections materials for all age levels. Of particular note is an overview of Calisphere (http://www.calisphere.universityofcalifornia.edu/), a project of the University of California, California Digital Library (CDL) that provides online access to special collections materials organized by theme and time period, and mapped to the state of California K-12 content standards.

Lee, Janet, Bridget Morris, Beckie Brazell, and Jan Loechell Turner. "Information Literacy Collaboration: A Shared Responsibility." *Colorado Libraries* 33, no. 3 (2007): 5–10.
The authors share a detailed breakdown of a Denver area high school senior English class's visit to a university library. Unique to this collaboration is the inclusion of both the academic librarians and public librarians who team taught the sessions. Taking advantage of the students' ability to access public library licensed resources, the public librarians focused their instruction on database searching, while the academic librarians worked on introducing the

university's print collection. Students were able to obtain library cards and use resources from both institutions. Keys to success for collaboration are shared.

Manuel, Kate. "National History Day: An Opportunity for K-16 Collaboration." *Reference Services Review* 33, no. 4 (2005): 459–486.

Librarians at the New Mexico State University Library engaged in a successful ongoing collaboration with area high school and middle school students in instruction for use of primary resources for National History Day projects. This article is valuable in both its correlation of information literacy elements across standards for history education (NHD and Historical Thinking Standards) and in library education standards (AASL and ACRL) and for its detailed examples of teaching methods used in this outreach. Additionally, revealing research is provided on the impact the library instruction had on the students, revealed through a study of the use of primary resources cited in the bibliographies from student NHD projects. Resources and approaches are offered for libraries considering engaging in such collaboration with local schools.

Martorana, Janet, Sylvia Curtis, and Sherry DeDecker. "Bridging the Gap: Information Literacy Workshops for High School Teachers." *Research Strategies* 18, no. 2 (2001): 113–120.

Taking advantage of a University of California–Santa Barbara (UCSB)–supported grant program for university to K-12 outreach, the authors share their provision of a successful train-the-trainer workshop focused on information literacy for high school teachers. Collaborating with school librarians and high school staff development directors, the UCSB team was able to coordinate stipend-supported workshops for in-service days that covered information literacy standards, lesson plans and activities, and access to resources. Some workshop participants opted to remain in contact with the UCSB project team to allow for ongoing assessment of the impact of the workshops on student success. Valuable tips related to planning and assessment are offered, as is an overview of the workshop's long-term impact on teaching approaches and developing further collaborative opportunities on campus.

Nichols, Janet W., Lothar Spang, and Kristy Padron. "Building a Foundation for Collaboration: K-20 Partnerships in Information Literacy." *Resource Sharing & Information Networks* 18, no. 1 (2005): 5–12.

Demonstrating the long-term impact potential of K-20 collaboration, the authors, librarians at Wayne State University, discuss a series of collaborative information literacy programs built successively over a seven-year period. The series included a variety of programs ranging from single and half-day on-site teacher workshops to week-long immersive workshops, leading to the development of an information literacy course for preservice library media specialists through a local library school. Recommendations include a list of eight suggestions for academic librarians wishing to establish collaborations with K-12 colleagues and other units on campus.

Nix, Donna, Marianne Hageman, and Janice Kragness. "Information Literacy and the Transition from High School to College." *Catholic Library World* 81, no. 4 (2011): 268–281.

The authors conducted a study based on the research of Islam and Murno (see earlier in this chapter) but with a new focus on parochial schools. They share the results of a survey of 15 parochial schools in the upper Midwest and compare and contrast the results with those of the previous study, which focused on public schools. Several differences were found, including variation in the information literacy standards most frequently taught and the perceptions of college readiness. This 2011 study also revealed that the availability of teaching technology in or near the school library was a crucial element to curricular success and that library integration into several key courses was a key success factor in preparing high school students.

The authors further discuss the implications of the research for their college level instruction and include a call for further research in key areas.

Oakleaf, Megan, and Patricia L. Owen. "Closing the 12-13 Gap Together: School and College Librarians Supporting 21st Century Learners." *Teacher Librarian* 37, no. 4 (2010): 52–58.

Reviewing a study of the content of college freshmen syllabi, the authors discuss the application of such findings to the implications of information skill needs of the transitioning student in both the high school and college setting. They further recommend step-by-step tips on how teacher-librarians and college librarians can collaborate to replicate such studies at the local level. Stressing the value of such collaborations on the professional development of all librarians involved, they also include recommendations for sharing study findings with local administrators, teachers, and parents to impact change.

Owen, Patricia. "A Transition Checklist for High School Seniors." *School Library Monthly* 26, no. 8 (2010): 20–23.

Noting the disappointing graduation statistics from higher education and the role that information literacy skills plays in overall student success, Owen addresses in practical terms how school librarians can help ensure their senior students' success at college. She summarizes the information skills needed in five main standards-based categories and then provides a useful checklist to help librarians inventory their students' needed areas of improvement. She further shares her approach to using the list in her own work, including developing activities and lessons for each skill, conducting a survey of outgoing seniors asking them to self-assess their confidence in each area, and revising the library media curriculum based on feedback gathered from the self-assessment.

Pearson, Debra, and Beth McNeil. "From High School Users College Students Grow: Providing Academic Library Research Opportunities to High School Students." *Knowledge Quest* 30, no. 4 (March 2002): 24–28.

Pearson and McNeil provide a history of the high school outreach program at the University of Nebraska Libraries. Growing from a small program for gifted students from four schools in the 1980s to a program reaching 26 schools in the 2000s, the article describes how the program is managed, including circulation policies and processes along with instructional approaches. They also share how the needs of students have changed over this time period. Finally, the authors share details on how students participating in the high school outreach program who attend the university are offered an opportunity to test out of a required information literacy course.

Schein, Christine, Linda Conway, Rebecca Harner, Sue Byerley, and Shelley Harper. "Bridging the Gap: Preparing High School Students for College Level Research." *Colorado Libraries* 36, no. 1 (2011): 1–4.

This article highlights two initiatives in the state of Colorado aimed at improving transitioning students' information literacy skills. The initiatives were inspired by discussions among school and academic librarians at several recent Colorado library conferences. The first is the creation of a credit-bearing information literacy course at one community college, the second a series of credit-bearing train-the-trainer workshops for teachers and librarians offered cooperatively by a university and local library media specialists. Ideas for future developments in the state are also shared.

Seymour, Celene. "Information Technology Assessment: A Foundation for School and Academic Library Collaboration." *Knowledge Quest* 35, no. 5 (May 2007): 32–35.

In hopes of inspiring readers to collaborate for a more systematic approach across K-20 for addressing information literacy needs, Seymour provides an argument for the need for regular assessment, discussing three key assessments currently available, Project SAILS: Standardized Assessment of Information Literacy Skills, Information and Communication Technology (ICT) Literacy Assessment, and Tool for Real-time Assessment of Information Literacy Skills (TRAILS). She argues for further incorporation of ICT skills into what librarians currently teach and provides an outline for how to go about building a coordinated approach for continuity in standards, assessments, and instructional approaches at the local level, stressing the ultimate desire to expand to district and statewide coordination.

Smalley, Topsy N. "College Success: High School Librarians Make the Difference." *Journal of Academic Librarianship* 30, no. 3 (2004): 193–198.
Smalley provides the results of a case study conducted to assess the influence of high school librarians on college students' potential for success in college level work. Examining the outcomes of students in a first-year information literacy course, the study was able to ascertain that students coming from a high school district with library media teachers performed better both at the midway point and in final grades. The author discusses the importance of these results and the need for sustained K-16 continuity for information literacy instruction to build up layers of knowledge and skill for the best success.

Smeraldi, Ann M. "High School to College: Resources for Librarians and Teachers." http://researchguides.csuohio.edu/fytransition_educators (accessed March 8, 2012).
Smeraldi created this research guide at Cleveland State University. The guide is geared toward librarians and teachers who want to help their students to transition to college-level research. It sets the stage with links to information on today's students and 21st-century skills and connects to videos and other resources that outline college-level expectations. Links to online information related to successful collaborations and tips on forming partnerships are provided, as well as recommended readings and links to related organizations.

Zoellner, Kate, and Charlie Potter. "Libraries across the Education Continuum: Relationships between Library Services at the University of Montana and Regional High Schools." *Behavioral & Social Sciences Librarian* 29, no. 3 (July 2010): 184–206.
The authors conducted this study to discover the library resources and instructional programs at area high school systems in hopes of better understanding instructional approaches and reassessing their approach to their local high school outreach program at the University of Montana's Mansfield Library. Using a combination of survey methodology and site visits, the authors provide a snapshot of the staffing, budget, collection development practices, technology resources, instructional programming, perceptions of student preparedness for college research, and students' attitudes toward their libraries at 22 western Montana high schools. The discussion section pinpoints key differences between school and academic libraries as well as the potential impact on instructional approaches in both areas. The authors additionally stress the importance of librarians working together to form continuity for transitions.

Index

About the Editor and Contributors

Toni Anaya is the Multicultural Studies librarian and Assistant Professor at the University of Nebraska–Lincoln in Lincoln, Nebraska, where she works with the Institute of Ethnic Studies. Her current area of research is discovering the role of libraries in the retention of students of color and first-generation college students.

Leslie Barton has worked in libraries all her life, beginning at the age of 18 with the Circulation Department at the University of British Columbia's Main Library and including college libraries, public libraries, and now the library at the high school in her hometown of Armstrong, BC. Returning to university studies at the ripe old age of 39, she received a BA at UBC–Okanagan and went on to graduate school at the University of Alberta–Edmonton to study history, switching after one year to education. She received a teaching certificate in 1996 and promptly began taking school librarianship courses online through University of Alberta's School of Library and Information Studies, completing enough to allow her to work as a school librarian and to appreciate the value of active program promotion, advocacy, and collaboration. Currently, she is a social studies teacher as well as school librarian.

Kenneth J. Burhanna is Associate Professor and Head of Instructional Services at Kent State University Libraries (Kent, Ohio). He has written and spoken extensively on the topic of high school outreach and supporting student transitions, including the article "Instructional Outreach to High Schools: Should You Be Doing It?" in the journal *Communications in Information Literacy*. He helped create the Transitioning to College web site and serves on the Tool for Real-time Assessment of Information Literacy Skills (TRAILS) team at Kent State. He also is coauthor of the award-winning *A Practical Guide to Information Literacy Assessment for Academic Librarians* from Libraries Unlimited. More recently, the Academic Library Association of Ohio recognized him as their 2012 Distance Learning Visionary.

Kathleen Conley is a Reference/Instruction Librarian at Harrisburg Area Community College (HACC), central Pennsylvania's community college. She firmly believes in the community college mission and is dedicated to developing information literate students so that they can become more successful within their communities and careers. Kathleen received her MSLIS from the University of Illinois in 2003.

Paula Nespeca Deal is a consultant for INFOhio, assisting with the Transition Task Force and providing support for INFOhio products and services. She provides workshops and presentations in Ohio on 21st-century learning, Google Apps, and Web 2.0 in the library and classroom. She was library media specialist for 35 years in the North Olmsted City Schools.

Leanne Ellis is a School Library Coordinator for the New York City Department of Education. She is the district administrator for the citywide automation system and provides support services to public and nonpublic school librarians through site consultations, professional development workshops, conferences, and grants.

Robert Farrell is an Assistant Professor in the Library Department at Lehman College, City University of New York, and coordinates the college's information literacy program.

Anthony J. Fonseca is the Head of Serials and Collection Development at Nicholls State University, and is the past president of the Louisiana Chapter of the Association of College and Research Libraries (ACRL). He is the coauthor of the Hooked on Horror (Genreflecting) series, as well as various articles on academic librarianship. His MLIS is from Louisiana State University School of Library and Information Science.

Mitchell J. Fontenot is Information Literacy and Outreach Services Librarian at Louisiana State University. He holds a Masters of Library and Information Science from the University of Texas at Austin. Prior to his current position of eight years, he was a law librarian at the Universities of Nebraska and Colorado for 15 years.

Kim Garwood, MA, is Acting Manager, Writing Services at the University of Guelph. She provides writing instruction in courses across the curriculum at undergraduate and graduate levels.

Julie A. Gedeon, PhD, is Director of Assessment and Accreditation, College of Education, at the University of Akron. She is a founding member of Project SAILS, Standardized Assessment of Information Literacy Skills, an assessment aimed at undergraduate students. As a member of the TRAILS team, Julie analyzes TRAILS data to support item and assessment refinement.

Matthew Harrick is currently Reference and Instruction Librarian at Brooklyn College, where he has worked since 2009. He has been involved in the school's early college programs since 2010 and is now responsible for outreach for all the high school programs at Brooklyn College.

Laurie Hathman, MLS, is the Director of the Greenlease Library at Rockhurst University, a Catholic Jesuit institution in Kansas City, Missouri. She has experience with information literacy instruction with high school seniors in advanced college credit courses and is seeking to enhance students' success as they transition to college.

Rhonda Huisman, MAE, MLIST is an Assistant Librarian at Indiana University Purdue University Indianapolis for the School of Education and the Center for Teaching and Learning. She has over 10 years' experience in education as a librarian, adjunct faculty, and grant activity director. She has published, presented, and taught on information literacy, assessment, instructional technology, first-year seminars, and faculty-librarian relationships. Her current research includes examining library impact on transition to college among urban public high school students. She is the mother of four boys and currently lives in Indianapolis.

Curtis L. Kendrick is University Dean for Libraries and Information Resources at the City University of New York (CUNY). In this capacity, he provides leadership for integrating the libraries within the teaching and research mission of CUNY. Mr. Kendrick has also held library management positions at Harvard University, Columbia University, Stony Brook University, and Oberlin College.

JaNae Kinikin received her Master of Arts degree in Library and Information Science from the University of Iowa in 1999. She has worked as the Science and Engineering Librarian at Weber State University in Ogden, Utah, since 2001, and is actively involved in the Mountain Plains Library Association.

Dale Lackeyram, BSc, MSc, PhD, Science Learning and Curriculum Specialist, has been involved in integrating and embedding academic support skills to enhance curriculum at the University of Guelph for the past 11 years. His interests have focused on developing curricula that embed these skills as intrinsic, identifiable, and assessable curriculum components.

Jillian Brandt Maruskin is a Public Services Librarian at Ohio Wesleyan University. She serves as liaison for the English, Education, and Theatre/Dance departments. Her undergraduate experience at Bowling Green State University's Jerome Library propelled her into librarianship. In her spare time, she raises her daughter, runs, and writes poetry.

Clarke Mathany, BSc, BEd, MEd (candidate) is an Ontario Certified Teacher and the supervisor of students who facilitate group study sessions using the Supplemental Instruction Model in first-year courses at the University of Guelph.

Charlene Maxey-Harris is the Diversity Librarian and Assistant Professor at the University of Nebraska–Lincoln Libraries. Her research areas are developing diversity initiatives and cultural competencies in academic libraries and library instruction for first-generation college students. Maxey-Harris is also a 2011–2012 Association of Research Libraries (ARL) Leadership and Career Development Program Fellow.

Louis E. Mays is a retired professor and librarian from Southern State Community College in Ohio. He employment at Southern State began in 1978. He provided instructional support at all four of the college's campuses located in rural southwest Ohio. He is a frequent user of technology.

Brian L. Mikesell is the Director of the Alumni Library at Bard College at Simon's Rock, a small liberal arts college that admits students after the tenth or eleventh grade. He was previously Associate University Librarian at St. John's University, where he also taught in the Division of Library and Information Science.

Megan Oakleaf is an Assistant Professor in the iSchool at Syracuse University. Her research areas include assessment, evidence-based decision making, information literacy instruction, and reference services. Prior to this position, Oakleaf served as the Librarian for Instruction and Undergraduate Research at North Carolina State University and as a teacher in Ohio's public schools.

Kindra Orr is Director of Development and External Relations for the University Library at Indiana University Purdue University Indianapolis (IUPUI), where she helps her colleagues foster student success through information literacy instruction, one-on-one consultation, and a wide array of resources, including the internationally recognized IUPUI Philanthropy Collections. She attended Northwestern University as an undergraduate and earned an MFA from New York University. She lives in Indianapolis with her husband and two children.

Patricia L. Owen is an Ohio school librarian and Nationally Board Certified Teacher (NBCT). Patti presents on transition-to-college and school librarian evaluation issues at Ohio Educational Library Media Association (OELMA), Academic Library Association of Ohio (ALAO), American Association of School Librarians (AASL), and American Library Association (ALA) conferences. A member of both OhioLINK's Dual Enrollment Task Force and INFOhio's Transition-to-College Task Force, Patti authors articles in *Teacher-Librarian*, Library Media Connection (LMC), School Library Monthly (SLM), and *Ohio Media SPECTRUM*.

Anne Marie Perrault is an Assistant Professor in the Library and Information Studies program, Graduate School of Education at the University at Buffalo, the State University of New York. Her research focuses on understanding the information ecologies that support young adults in transition and the role of multiple literacies in the transition process.

Peggy A. Pritchard, MLIS, Associate Librarian (University of Guelph, Canada), is Editor and Coauthor of *Success Strategies for Women in Science: A Portable Mentor*. A two-time teaching award winner, she collaborates with faculty members as well as writing and learning specialists to embed information literacy, writing, and analytical skills training into the curriculum.

Thomas L. Reinsfelder, MSLS, is an Assistant Librarian for Reference and Instruction at Penn State–Mont Alto, Pennsylvania Sate University and works primarily with first- and second-year students. He was a member of the American Library Association's 2011 class of Emerging Leaders.

Debra Cox Rollins worked for 15 years as a school librarian before becoming Coordinator of Information Literacy Outreach at Louisiana State University (LSU)–Alexandria. She has published, presented, and held leadership positions on a variety of information literacy initiatives through the American Library Association's Library Instruction Roundtable (ALA-LIRT), Association of College & Research Libraries (ACRL), LOUIS: the Louisiana Library Network, and the Louisiana Library Association. She earned an MLIS from LSU Louisiana State University's School of Library and Information Science.

Sherri Savage is a recent 2011 Masters of Library and Information Science graduate from San Jose State University. Her MLIS degree was earned through online courses, which gave her the opportunity to work as an auxiliary circulation clerk at Okanagan College in Kelowna, BC. Sherri comes to the librarian profession with a Bachelor of Education Degree and a Bachelor of Arts Degree, majoring in History at the University of British Columbia in Vancouver, BC. Her interest in teaching and enjoyment of the learning environment at a higher learning institution prompted her to pursue a career at an academic library and involvement in information literacy.

Barbara F. Schloman, PhD, is Professor and Associate Dean for Library Public Services, Kent State University Libraries. She has been involved with TRAILS development from its inception in 2004 and serves as its Project Director.

Kathryn B. Seidel is Reference Librarian and Assistant Professor at Baton Rouge Community College. She has a MS in Library and Information Science from the University of Illinois–Urbana-Champaign. Prior to relocating to Louisiana, she served as Assistant Librarian at the John-F-Kennedy high school library in Berlin, Germany.

Jennifer Sigalet of Okanagan College, British Columbia, is the Vernon Campus Librarian, Chair of the Library's Information Literacy Working Group, and the Institute for Learning and Teaching Fellow for Library Services. Jennifer's interest in information literacy and pedagogy began over 20 years ago as a researcher for a native adult education curriculum development team at Okanagan College. Since then, Jennifer has focused on the integration of information literacy skills and research-based course curricula at Okanagan College from developmental to postsecondary programs. As a result, Jennifer is particularly interested in the continuum of information literacy and the role information literacy can play in easing the transition of students from school to higher education.

Ann Walker Smalley has an MLS from Kent State University. Ann has worked in public service in special libraries as well as a consultant to libraries of all types and to nonprofit organizations. She is the Director of Metronet, a multitype library system that offers training, networking, and technical assistance to school, public, academic, and special librarians.

Ann Marie Smeraldi has focused her career in librarianship on information literacy instruction and the needs of first-year college students as they transition to college. As the First Year Experience Librarian for Cleveland State University, she conducts library orientations and classes for freshmen, and serves as the high school liaison.

Ken W. Stewart, MLS, MA, BA, BBA, is a School Librarian at Blue Valley High School in Stilwell, Kansas. A 20+ year educator, he has taught information literacy skills, English, business, and journalism to students with various behavioral and economic backgrounds. Ken is striving to find new methods to prepare students for post-secondary education.

Barbara K. Stripling is the president of the American Library Association (ALA) for 2013–2014 term. She recently joined the faculty at Syracuse University as an Assistant Professor of Practice. Prior to that, she was Director of Library Services for New York City schools for seven years. She received her Doctorate in Information Management from Syracuse in May 2011, and has written and edited numerous books and articles.

LeAnn Suchy received her MLS from the University of Illinois–Urbana-Champaign in 2006. Since then, she has worked as an Academic Librarian at a liberal arts college and currently as the MILI Program Manager at Metronet.

Teresa Tartaglione is the library media specialist for the Martin Luther King, Jr. Educational Campus in New York City, where she serves 3,000 students in six different high schools and is the current president of the New York City School Librarians Association.

Jill E. Thompson, MEd, is a teacher-librarian with the Greencastle-Antrim School District in Greencastle, Pennsylvania. She currently serves as co-director of the Southern Pennsylvania Information Exchange Source (SPIES) regional group and is an active member of the Pennsylvania School Librarians Association.

Tammy J. Eschedor Voelker is Associate Professor at Kent State University Libraries and since 2000 has served as the Humanities Reference and Instruction Librarian. She is the coordinator of the Libraries' Informed Transitions High School Outreach Program and a member of the team that manages the Transitioning to College web site.

Meghann Suzanne Walk, Library Director and social studies faculty at Bard High School Early College–Manhattan, teaches information literacy, history, and library science. Her professional interests include information literacy and pedagogy, with a focus on applying Bard College's Writing and Thinking practices to information literacy and disciplinary instruction.

Kate Zoellner is the Education, Human Sciences and Psychology Librarian at the Maureen and Mike Mansfield Library of the University of Montana. In addition to her role as a liaison, Kate provides outreach to regional high schools and serves as the library's Assessment Coordinator.